MW01110279

Your
Thrift
Savings
Plan

Michael J. Sullivan

Don Mace and Eric Yoder, *Editors*
Stephen E. Young, *Publisher*

Published by
Federal Employees News Digest, Inc.
1850 Centennial Park Dr., Suite 520
Reston, VA 22091-1517
Telephone (703) 648-9551
FAX (703) 648-0265

Publisher of
Federal Employees Almanac
Federal Employees News Digest
Your Retirement: How to Prepare for It—How to Enjoy It
Your Financial Guide: The Estate and Financial Planner for Federal and Postal Employees
Your Job Rights: The Federal Employees Guide to Appeals and Grievances

ISBN 0-910582-20-3

# FOREWORD

First conceived as a slim volume drawing together all available literature on the tax-deferred retirement plan for federal and postal employees, Your Thrift Savings Plan evolved into much more than that. As the author and our editorial staff and advisers reviewed the previously available material, we quickly discovered that the people who invest in the TSP needed more information and help—much more—in deciding their own approaches to building their retirement nest eggs. This is true whether they are in the CSRS or FERS retirement systems, are just starting their careers, midway through them, nearing retirement or living out their golden years with TSP account balances paying part of the way.

One size definitely does not fit all when it comes to investing in anything, including the TSP's family of funds. We do not recommend any particular strategy for investing. Instead, the book provides points to consider when making your own decisions. Before making any investment decision, always consult first with your financial and tax counselors. Remember, past performance offers no guarantees of future performance.

The highly-regarded Federal Retirement Thrift Investment Board has issued many facts and figures about the $20 billion and growing TSP. Author Mike Sullivan, a consultant to Congress during the design of the TSP system, sifted through them to show what they mean. He also produced additional tables and charts to help illustrate in more detail the various aspects of the plan. And he provides the kinds of insights you'll find nowhere else.

Throughout the book you'll find little symbols in the margins that look like keys. These are "key tips" that are especially important—nuggets of information and wisdom in italic type that bear your special attention.

Our thanks to PC Resources of Reston, Va., for its expert typographical and production work, and to John Coleman, of John Coleman Design, the talented Washington D.C. artist who created our cover. And a well-deserved pat on the back for our energetic and multi-talented staffer Laurie Wyatt and special thanks to Michael C. Mace for his help in the proofing process.

We sincerely hope that this volume will help guide you along the path to a comfortable and secure financial future.

Don Mace & Eric Yoder, Editors

AUTHOR'S NOTE

I had the privilege of consulting to the Congress during the development of the Thrift Savings Plan. That process reinforced my belief that personal savings controlled by individual workers would improve the government's retirement policies.

Your Thrift Savings Plan is not a substitute for official government documents describing your individual retirement savings. It's a guide to your essential TSP decisions, based on my 15 years of government and consulting experience in federal employees' compensation and benefits. You should continue to track new details about how the TSP operates, through your semi-annual account statements and other publications.

This book would not have come to birth without the assistance of many colleagues and friends.

Don Mace and Eric Yoder of Federal Employees News Digest persisted through my best and worst moments. I thank them—and their FEND associates—for their dedication to editorial and production quality. My thanks also to Dennis Snook of the Congressional Research Service for his thoughtful comments on how the TSP fits within overall federal retirement policy; David Schoeder of the National Cooperative Bank for his instruction in financial markets; my brother, David Sullivan—a former postal employee—for his advice on how the book would read, and Cynthia Mache, whose computer expertise and steadfast devotion kept the book on course.

There are some investments that involve money, others than require more vital commitments. I thank my parents—Charles and Helen Sullivan—for making both. It's through them that I found the knowledge and beliefs that made this book possible.

Michael J. Sullivan

◇1 TABLE OF CONTENTS

Overview   ix

Chapter One—Introducing the Thrift Savings Plan   1
   The Role of the TSP for FERS Employees
   The Role of the TSP for CSRS Employees
   TSP Payroll Deductions
   TSP Tax-Deferred Savings
   TSP Investment Funds
   The TSP Loan Program
   Withdrawing Your TSP Account Balance
   Growth of TSP Participation
   How You Participate in the TSP

Chapter Two—Plotting Your Course   7
   The TSP and Your Overall Savings
   A Word about Calculating Returns
   Comparing the TSP and Other Investments
   The Importance of Taxes and Investment Costs
   Some Specific Suggestions
   Five Things to Do

Chapter Three—The TSP for FERS Employees   17
   The TSP and Your FERS Retirement Income
   Advantages of the TSP for FERS Employees
   Agency Contributions for FERS Employees
   Tax-Deferred Retirement Savings
   Matching Contributions and Tax Deferral Equal Long-Term Growth
   Should You Be Investing in the TSP?
   How Much Should You Invest?
   Estimating Your TSP Account and Retirement Income
   TSP Participation of FERS Employees
   Five Things to Do

Chapter Four—The TSP for CSRS Employees   29
   The TSP and Your CSRS Retirement Income
   Advantages of the TSP for CSRS Employees
   Should You Invest in the TSP?
   How Much Should You Invest?
   Estimating Your TSP Account and Retirement Income
   A Word about CSRS Voluntary Contributions
   TSP Participation Among CSRS Employees
   Five Things to Do

Chapter Five—Understanding Your TSP Investment Options   37
   Investment Returns and Compounded Earnings
   Overview of the TSP Investment Funds
   A Review of Important Investment Terms
   The G Fund
      How It Works
      Investment Returns

The C Fund
    How It Works
    How Money Is Invested
    Investment Returns
The F Fund
    How It Works
    Investment Returns
Comparing the G, C and F Funds
How You Allocate Your TSP Investments
A Profile of Actual TSP Investment Allocations
Five Things to Do

Chapter Six—Building Your TSP Investment Strategy   **51**
Essential Elements of an Effective TSP Strategy
TSP Long-Term Strategy
Medium-Term Tactics
Short-Term Operations
Some Possible TSP Investment Strategies
Five Things to Do

Chapter Seven—The TSP Loan Program   **77**
Overview of the TSP Loan Program
Qualifying Expenses
Eligibility and Application Procedures
Calculation of Maximum Loan Amounts
TSP Loan Repayment Terms
What Happens if You Can't Repay Your Loan?
Loan Planning and Your Overall TSP Strategy
Comparing TSP Loans and Other Loan Sources
Five Things to Do

Chapter Eight—Withdrawing Your TSP Account Balance   **87**
Summary of Options for Withdrawing Your Account Balance
Transfers to IRA or Other Qualified Retirement Plan
Receiving Your Balance in a Lump Sum Payment
Receiving Your Balance in a Series of Equal Monthly Payments
Some 'Brilliant' Ideas that May Not Be So Smart
Receiving Your TSP Account as a Lifetime Annuity
Summary of Your Annuity Options
Distribution of Your TSP Account Balance at Death
TSP Withdrawals under a Reduction in Force
A Reminder about Paperwork
Five Things to Do

Chapter Nine—A Review of TSP Essentials   **107**

Appendix 1—TSP Information Directory   **A1-1**
TSP Telephone Numbers
TSP Addresses
TSP Booklets

Appendix 2—Account Tables for FERS Employees   **A2-1**
Estimating How Much Your Current TSP Account Balance Will Grow
Estimating How Much Your Future Contributions Will Add to Your TSP Account

Appendix 3—Account Tables for CSRS Employees   **A3-1**
Estimating How Much Your Current TSP Account Balance Will Grow
Estimating How Much Your Future Contributions Will Add to Your TSP Account

Appendix 4—Estimating Approximate Annuity Payments   **A4-1**

Appendix 5—Important TSP Forms   **A5-1**

◇ LIST OF TABLES & CHARTS

1-1 Agency Contributions to the TSP Accounts of FERS Employees 2
1-2 Growth in TSP Participation, 1987-1993 4
1-3 How New FERS Employees Start Participating in the TSP 4

2-1 Saving and Investing for Future Income 7
2-2 TSP Priorities for Different Employees 8
2-3 Average Annual Returns for Various Investment Categories 9
2-4 Average Annual Returns for Mutual Funds, September 1990 - August 1993 10
2-5 Key Features of Various Investment Opportunities 11
2-6 Value of TSP Contributions Over 30-Year Investment Period 12
2-7 Contributing to the TSP Now vs. Contributing More Later—FERS 12
2-8 Contributing to the TSP Now vs. Contributing More Later—CSRS 13

3-1 Combined Retirement Income for FERS Employees 17
3-2 FERS Benefits at Age 65 with 35 Years of Service 18
3-3 Adding the TSP to FERS Retirement Income 19
3-4 Annual TSP Contributions for FERS Employee Earning $30,000 20
3-5 Tax Savings on Your TSP Contributions 20
3-6 Tax-Deferred Growth of TSP Account Over 30 Years 21
3-7 Two Growth Scenarios for Your TSP Account 25
3-8 Estimated TSP Account Balances Under Two Growth Scenarios 25
3-9 Retirement Income at Various Retirement Ages 26
3-10 TSP Participation Among FERS Employees 26
3-11 TSP Participation by Age, FERS Employees 26
3-12 TSP Participation by Salary, FERS Employees 27
3-13 Percentages of Pay Deferred to TSP by FERS Employees 27

4-1 CSRS Retirement Benefits as a Percentage of High-3 Salary 29
4-2 Examples of Retirement Income Targets for CSRS Employees 30
4-3 Two Growth Scenarios for Your TSP Account 32
4-4 Estimated TSP Account Balances Under Two Growth Scenarios 33
4-5 Retirement Income at Various Retirement Ages 33
4-6 Annual Extra CSRS Annuity from Voluntary Contributions 34
4-7 Growth of TSP Participation—CSRS Employees 35
4-8 Percentage of Pay Invested in TSP by CSRS Employees 35
4-9 TSP Investment Levels, CSRS Employees 35

5-1 Returns on Investment of $3,000 a Year 37
5-2 Ingredients of TSP Account Balance for FERS Employee 37
5-3 Effect of Investment Returns on TSP Account Balance 38
5-4 Ingredients of TSP Account Balance for CSRS Employee 38
5-5 Annual G Fund Rates of Return, 1988-1993 40
5-6 G Fund Monthly Returns, 1988-1993 40
5-7 G Fund Real Rates of Return, 1988-1993 41
5-8 Composition of the Standard & Poor's 500 41

5-9   30 Companies with Highest Stock Values, S&P 500   42

5-10   Monthly Calculation of C Fund Gains or Losses   43

5-11   Annual C Fund Rates of Return, 1988-1993   43

5-12   C Fund Monthly Rates of Return, 1988-1993   43

5-13   C Fund Real Rates of Return, 1988-1993   44

5-14   The LBA Bond Index   45

5-15   Annual F Fund Rates of Return, 1988-1993   45

5-16   F Fund Monthly Rates of Return, 1988-1993   46

5-17   F Fund Real Rates of Return, 1988-1993   46

5-18   Comparison of Monthly Rates of Return, 1988-1993   46

5-19   Comparison of Annual Returns, 1988-1993   47

5-20   Comparisons of Monthly Returns, 1988-1993   47

5-21   Which Fund Did Better or Worse Each Month
         January 1988 - December 1993   47

5-22   Comparison of Real Rates of Return, 1988-1993   48

5-23   Investment Allocation of TSP Payroll Deductions   49

5-24   Reallocation of $50,000 TSP Account Balance   49

5-25   Reallocation of $50,000 TSP Account Balance   49

5-26   Overall Use of G, C and F Funds   50

5-27   Investment of New TSP Contributions   50

5-28   Distribution of TSP Account Balances   50

5-29   Summary of Interfund Transfer Activity   50

6-1   Your TSP Time Line   51

6-2   Future TSP Account Balances in Today's Dollars   53

6-3   Possible Account Growth Scenarios   53

6-4   Translating TSP Account Balance into Lifetime Retirement Income   54

6-5   Summary of Factors Affecting Your TSP Investment Strategy   56

6-6   Monthly Rates of Return for TSP Investment Funds, 1988-1993   56

6-7   Standard & Poor's 500, 1926-1993   57

6-8   Growth of Two TSP Accounts over a 30-Year Investment Period   59

6-9   Example of Shift in TSP Investment Mix, 1988-1993   61

6-10   TSP Account Balance is Lower Than Expected   63

6-11   Sample Semi-Annual Account Statement   67

6-12   Sample Month by Month Account Activity   68

6-13   Some Newspaper TSP Indicators   71

6-14   The Three Major Market Trends in the C Fund   72

6-15   G Fund Movements and C & F Fund Returns   74

7-1   Maximum TSP Loan Amounts   80

7-2   Approximate Loan Payments Every Bi-Weekly Pay Period for Each $1,000 Borrowed   81

7-3   Comparison of TSP Loans and Other Loan Sources   84

8-1   Summary of Eligibility for TSP Account Withdrawal Options   88

8-2   Taking a Lump Sum Compared to Purchasing an Annuity   91

8-3   Using Your TSP Account to Fill a Social Security Gap Before Age 62   94

8-4   Using Equal Payments to Maintain Total Household Income   95

8-5   The Social Security Earnings Test   95

8-6   Retirement Income Inventory for You and Your Spouse   99

8-7   Comparison of TSP Annuity with Level and Increasing Payments   101

8-8   Reduction of Annuity for Cash Refund or 10-Year Certain Features   102

8-9   Amount of Initial Payments For Various Annuity Options   103

OVERVIEW

We've filled *Your Thrift Savings Plan* with all the information you need to understand how the TSP works and how you can use this tax-deferred program effectively. The book starts with a primer on the essential elements of the TSP and how it fits into your overall financial planning. Then it offers step-by-step guides to the major features of the TSP and suggestions to help you build your own personal TSP strategy.

The TSP offers—at every stage of your federal or postal career—a flexible range of options to help you build your own savings, investment and retirement strategies. It's ultimately up to you to decide how the TSP can best serve your financial needs and goals.

So, beyond simply describing how the TSP works, we'll also help you build a framework for thoughtful and successful TSP decision-making. We'll identify the most important choices you'll have to make and what you'll want to consider in developing a TSP strategy that makes sense for you. In particular, we'll focus on:

◇ Understanding the major components of the TSP

◇ Viewing the TSP as part of your retirement planning

◇ Linking the TSP with other savings and investments

◇ Deciding how much to invest in your TSP account

◇ Understanding the TSP investment funds

◇ Monitoring the growth of your TSP account

◇ Fitting the TSP into a total retirement savings portfolio

◇ Using your account as a lifelong source of funds

◇ Withdrawing your TSP account to meet your needs

◇ Knowing your rights, responsibilities and resources

In each chapter we highlight particular stages of your TSP decision-making, focusing on the information you'll need and the choices you'll face during your career and when you retire. Within each chapter you'll be able to review easy-reference summaries and read in more detail about specific topics, suiting your questions and needs at the moment.

In Chapter One we introduce the TSP and its essential components. We'll discuss the general advantages of tax-deferred savings plans and the specific design of the TSP. We'll show how the TSP fits into your overall retirement income and your long-term financial planning. Be sure to review Chapter One to make sure you understand the basic terms and concepts of the TSP even if you consider yourself a TSP expert. It never hurts to review the basics.

We'll then focus more closely on how the TSP can help you accumulate long-term savings and retirement income. Chapter Two lays the groundwork for you to plot a personal TSP strategy. It analyzes how the TSP fits within your lifetime pattern of income, spending and savings. You'll learn some of the key questions and issues you should consider in your TSP decision-making and overall financial planning.

There are important differences in how the TSP operates for employees covered under the Federal Employees Retirement System (FERS) and the older Civil Service Retirement System (CSRS). So we've devoted a separate chapter to each group of employees. Federal or postal employees first hired after 1983 are automatically under FERS. Most other employees are in CSRS, unless they voluntarily elected to transfer to FERS or they were covered under FERS when they returned to the government after a break in service. There have been some cases in which employees thought they were covered under one retirement system, but were actually enrolled in the other. If you have any doubt about your retirement coverage status, check with your personnel office to be sure your records are correct.

If you're a FERS employee, see Chapter Three to review how the TSP plays an integral role in your retirement planning. We'll look at how government matching contributions can supercharge your TSP savings potential. You'll learn how the TSP fits within your overall package of FERS retirement benefits and how your TSP investments can significantly boost your retirement income.

If you're a CSRS employee, Chapter Four looks at the TSP from your perspective. Some CSRS employees end their careers able to retire comfortably on their basic CSRS benefits only. But for many CSRS employees, the

TSP offers an important source of additional retirement income. We'll look at how the TSP works for you and how you might use it to supplement your regular retirement benefits.

Then our attention turns to TSP investment options. Once you've decided to save for the long-term through the TSP, what are your choices for building and protecting the value of your savings over time? When you invest in the TSP, what exactly are you investing in? We'll identify the basic characteristics of the Government Securities Investment Fund (G Fund), the Common Stock Index Investment Fund (C Fund) and the Fixed Income Index Investment Fund (F Fund). Chapter Five describes how the funds work and their track records over time.

The TSP offers three investment options. But how can you decide the best mix of investments to suit you at a given time? In Chapter Six we'll explore how to design a TSP investment strategy that fits your career status, family situation, financial goals and personal preferences. You'll be given pointers on how to define investment objectives, monitor your progress and make adjustments along the way. You'll learn how to blend your TSP account with your other financial resources, how to measure investment risks and returns and how and when to adjust your TSP investment strategies.

Your TSP account can help you with mid-career financial needs in addition to long-term savings for retirement. In Chapter Seven we'll look at the TSP loan program. You can borrow from your TSP account for a variety of major expenses. We'll examine when you can use TSP loans, how much you can borrow, application requirements and repayment rules and how TSP loans compare to other loan sources.

When you leave federal or postal service—at or before retirement—you'll have a wide range of choices about whether and how to withdraw your TSP account balance. In Chapter Eight we'll identify your withdrawal options and the most important choices you'll have to make. Then we'll examine each option—transferring your account to an IRA, lump sum payments, equal monthly payments and lifetime annuities. We'll look at eligibility requirements, tax treatment, survivor benefits and other key considerations for each. Throughout we'll focus on how withdrawal options fit within the framework of your overall retirement income circumstances. A technical note: This book provides TSP annuity estimates based on an 8 percent interest rate. Actual rates will vary.

Your Thrift Savings Plan ends with a summary review of "TSP essentials"—the facts, issues and choices you should know as you build and use your TSP account, during and after your career.

Thoughtful and timely decision-making can significantly improve the growth of your TSP account and the quality of your retirement. *Your Thrift Savings Plan* can help you make the most of the TSP for you and your family.

◇ 1 ◇ INTRODUCING THE THRIFT SAVINGS PLAN

Since 1987 federal and postal employees have been able to take advantage of the Thrift Savings Plan (TSP), an attractive and powerful investment opportunity. As the features of the TSP have become better known, more and more employees have decided to participate in the TSP and benefit from its long-term savings potential.

The TSP was born with the Federal Employees Retirement System Act of 1986. This law established a new retirement program—FERS—for federal and postal employees hired after 1983. Employees already covered under the Civil Service Retirement System—CSRS—had an opportunity to transfer to FERS voluntarily or to remain under CSRS. (Relatively few CSRS employees— about 4 percent of eligibles—took that opportunity, however. There have been calls for reopening the FERS system again to CSRS employees, but so far no legislation to allow this has been introduced.)

Two later chapters explain in detail how the TSP works for FERS employees (Chapter Three) and for CSRS employees (Chapter Four). Be sure to keep in mind your basic retirement plan coverage—FERS or CSRS—as you proceed through the book, although we've been careful to differentiate where needed.

CSRS employees receive government retirement benefits through a single "stand alone" pension based on salary and years of government service. FERS employees build a total retirement package from three separate pieces:

◇ A federal civil service pension based on salary and years of service, but smaller than the "stand alone" CSRS formula;

◇ Coverage under Social Security, like virtually all other American workers, and

◇ Additional retirement savings built up over time by employee and government contributions to the TSP.

Congress intended the TSP to play a key role in the overall retirement package for FERS employees. For CSRS employees the TSP occupies a more modest position, as a supplement to the basic pension benefit. This is a crucial point. As a federal or postal employee you are eligible to participate in the TSP whether you fall under FERS or CSRS. But the role of the TSP in your long-term financial planning will differ depending on whether you are a FERS or CSRS employee.

THE ROLE OF THE TSP FOR FERS EMPLOYEES

If your government retirement coverage is under FERS, the TSP is a major component of your retirement income. It encourages you to set aside some of your current income and invest it toward your retirement. Matching contributions from your agency give you a compelling incentive to save. You should participate in the TSP if at all possible. If you don't, you're passing up an opportunity to receive virtually "free money" from the government. And you could end up with total retirement income below your needs and expectations.

If you expect to stay with the federal government or postal service until retirement, your TSP account will play a critical role in guaranteeing retirement income security for you and your family. If you think you may leave the government to pursue other opportunities, a TSP account can give you greater freedom and flexibility in changing jobs, as well.

If you are a FERS employee, perhaps the most attractive feature of the TSP is the availability of government contributions to your account. As you invest in your TSP account, so does your employing agency. The result is that your contributions are magnified, accelerating the growth of your money. For FERS employees this feature of the TSP makes it superior to most other long-term investment opportunities.

Under current law, every FERS employee automatically has a TSP account and can contribute up to 10 percent of pay each pay period. Your employing agency automatically contributes an amount equal to 1 percent of your pay to your account each pay period, even if you don't invest any of your salary in the TSP.

If you do invest in your TSP account, your employing agency makes additional "matching contributions." Under current rules, for every dollar you invest in the TSP up to 3 percent of your pay, your agency matches your investment dollar for dollar. For every additional dollar you invest from 3 percent to 5 percent of your pay, your agency contributes an additional 50 cents.

The combination of the automatic and matching contributions by your agency dramatically increases the savings potential of your TSP account, as shown in Figure 1-1.

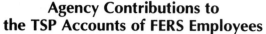

Agency Contributions to the TSP Accounts of FERS Employees

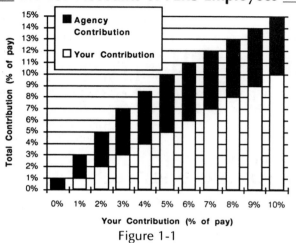

Figure 1-1

For any FERS employee seeking long-term investment growth potential, the TSP is virtually impossible to duplicate. Your agency's contributions to your account ensure that your assets will grow rapidly over time.

Remember that Congress is free to change the FERS matching investment formula at any time.

THE ROLE OF THE TSP FOR CSRS EMPLOYEES

If you are covered under CSRS the TSP can be a valuable supplement to your retirement income. It offers a convenient, relatively simple way to build investments during your career. In particular, for many employees the TSP offers more extensive tax-deferral advantages than an IRA. On the other hand, you may have other investment opportunities or short-term financial needs that you consider more compelling than TSP savings.

There are no government contributions to the TSP accounts of CSRS employees. If you are covered under CSRS your account consists of your voluntary payroll deductions—up to 5 percent of pay—and accumulated investment earnings.

Since the introduction of the TSP, some federal and postal employees have asked why the government doesn't contribute to the accounts of CSRS employees, and why CSRS employees can only invest up to 5 percent of pay rather than the 10 percent ceiling for FERS employees. Here's why: When Congress enacted FERS in 1986, it

sought to make FERS and CSRS generally equivalent overall retirement packages—in terms of benefits for typical workers and total costs to the government. An important element of this balance was enabling FERS workers to use the TSP to bring their retirement package up to the level of CSRS. Federal and postal workers covered under CSRS were then able to choose whether to stay in CSRS with a limited TSP, or transfer to FERS with its combination of a pension, Social Security and a more substantial TSP.

TSP PAYROLL DEDUCTIONS

The TSP is a voluntary plan. You may invest in it or not as you see fit. If you are in FERS you may contribute up to 10 percent of your pay each pay period. If you are in CSRS you may contribute up to 5 percent of your basic pay each pay period. In either case the contribution is always on a pay period basis and is deducted directly from your paycheck.

One virtue of the payroll deduction mechanism is that it simplifies the savings process for you. Once you've made a basic decision about how much you can and want to invest in the TSP, you know that a regular, predictable amount of money will flow into your TSP account. But you do have to make a commitment to this payroll deduction and stick with it. You can't skip pay periods when money's tight and then try to "catch up" by writing a check to the TSP after you've managed to save some cash. If you start to invest in the TSP each pay period and then decide to stop because of a sudden change in circumstances, you'll have to wait six to 11 months before starting to invest again. We'll examine the TSP payroll deduction process in more detail in the final section of this chapter.

TSP TAX-DEFERRED SAVINGS

In addition to taking more money out of our paychecks than we might like and sometimes making our lives miserable on April 15 each year, the federal income tax code also encourages a variety of economic and social objectives. One of these is encouraging workers to save for retirement. Buried inside thousands of tax code pages is section 401(k), originally introduced in 1978, which confers tax-deferred status on certain "qualified" retirement plans. When Congress enacted the FERS legislation in 1986, it gave the TSP the same income tax advantages as comparable 401(k) savings plans in the private sector.

In a nutshell, this means that any money you invest in the TSP is treated as a "pre-tax" investment in your future retirement income. Money you invest in the TSP is directly subtracted from your taxable income. For example, if you make $30,000 a year and invest 5 percent of your pay each pay period in the TSP, only $28,500 of your salary counts as taxable income ($30,000 - $1,500 = $28,500).

Government contributions to your TSP account (FERS only) also are tax-deferred. Likewise the investment earnings on your account, whether you are in CSRS or FERS. Federal income taxes are deferred on your entire TSP account until the point in the future when you receive income from the account. The TSP also enjoys tax-deferred status in most state income tax systems.

The great advantage of the TSP tax deferral is that it allows you to get "more bang for your buck" as you build your account balance. You invest "pre-tax" dollars and accumulate compounded investment earnings over time without paying current-year taxes on those earnings. Both of these tax savings increase your investment potential over time. Throughout the book we'll discuss the tax treatment of your TSP account in more detail, showing you what happens when you invest in the plan, as your account accumulates value over the course of your career, and when you ultimately decide to turn your TSP account into income.

TSP INVESTMENT FUNDS

Chapters Three (FERS employees) and Four (CSRS employees) explain points to consider when deciding whether and how much to invest in the TSP. Then, in Chapter Five, we'll look at how your TSP account grows over time and your TSP investment choices. For the moment let's highlight the basic investment opportunities in the TSP.

After you decide how much you want to invest in the TSP, you choose how you want your account invested. Through your employing agency you tell the Thrift Board how to distribute your account among three different investment funds:

◇ The G Fund—short-term, nonmarketable U.S. Treasury securities that carry an interest rate based on intermediate and long-term Treasury securities;

◇ The F Fund—a fixed income index fund that tracks the performance of the major sectors of the U.S. bond market: U.S. government and corporate bonds and mortgage-backed securities; and

◇ The C Fund—a common stock index fund that tracks the overall performance of the U.S. stock market as measured by the Standard & Poor's 500 stock index.

You may invest entirely in one fund or spread your account among two or three funds. Every six months during the open seasons you can adjust the investment pattern for all new contributions to your TSP account. Also, four times a year at any time during the year you can shift the investment allocation for your total account balance.

In general the G Fund is the safest and most predictable. Its returns shift as interest rates change, but there is no risk of capital loss. The C Fund offers the potential for substantially higher growth, but it's subject to frequent fluctuations in the stock market that involve the risk of

loss. The F Fund occupies a middle ground between the G and C funds—it has potentially higher returns than the G Fund, but with a moderate degree of market fluctuation and risk.

THE TSP LOAN PROGRAM

The TSP is designed for the growth of long-term retirement savings. But it also lets you borrow from your account to meet interim financial needs. Loans may be obtained to help purchase a home, cover medical or education expenses, or in cases of financial hardship. The amount you can borrow increases as your account balance grows, up to a maximum loan of $50,000.

Chapter Seven describes the TSP loan program in detail. It explains situations that qualify for loans, calculation of maximum loan amounts and repayment terms. You'll also learn how to include loan planning within your overall TSP investment strategy.

WITHDRAWING YOUR TSP ACCOUNT BALANCE

The TSP provides a tax-deferred mechanism for building additional retirement income. That is its central purpose. The options you have when you withdraw your TSP account revolve around that key objective.

But you do have a great deal of choice when it comes time to "cash in" your TSP account. In general—whether you leave the government in mid-career or stay until retirement—you can withdraw your account balance as a lump sum, collect a series of payments over a fixed period, or purchase an annuity that will pay you a steady income for the rest of your life (and for the rest of your spouse's life if you elect a survivor benefit option).

You also may choose to transfer your TSP account to an Individual Retirement Account (IRA). Or you may leave your TSP balance in place and withdraw your savings later. If you decide to do this you cannot continue making new contributions after you leave the government, but you can continue managing your money among the three TSP investment funds.

As with building an investment strategy, there is no one best way to make use of your account when you leave the government. The TSP offers different options to meet different individual and family circumstances.

GROWTH OF TSP PARTICIPATION

We've highlighted some of the features that make the TSP an attractive investment vehicle for federal and postal workers. Perhaps the most powerful testimony to the TSP's advantages is the dramatic rise in employee participation since the plan's inception in 1987, as shown in Figure 1-2.

Growth in TSP Participation 1987-1993
(Numbers in Thousands)

TSP Account Category	1987	1993
FERS Agency 1% Contribution Only	400	330
FERS Employees Making Contributions	163	864
CSRS Employees	297	615
Inactive Accounts (no contributions)	10	217
Total TSP Accounts	860	2,026

Figure 1-2

The number of TSP accounts has more than doubled since 1987, now exceeding two million. There are about 1.5 million employees regularly contributing to their TSP accounts every pay period. Participation has grown steadily among FERS and CSRS employees, and many former employees have decided to leave their TSP accounts in place for continued investment.

The total value of TSP accounts is more than $20 billion, and climbing, comparable to the largest mutual individual mutual funds. The average TSP account balance is about $10,000, and will grow substantially as future contributions and earnings compound over time.

HOW YOU PARTICIPATE IN THE TSP

Every year there are two TSP "open seasons" in which employees can start investing in the TSP, raise or lower their payroll deductions, or stop investing. One open season runs from May 15 through July 31. The second runs from November 15 through January 31. The same schedule applies to both FERS and CSRS employees.

To start contributing to the TSP you should first obtain an Election Form (TSP-1) from your agency personnel office. The Election Form allows you to designate a TSP payroll deduction based on a percentage of your basic pay or a fixed dollar amount.

There is an important difference between the two ⊙TIP choices. *If you designate a percentage of pay deduction, the dollar amount you contribute to the TSP each pay period will automatically increase when your pay increases.* For example, if you are currently earning $1,000 per pay period and designate a 5 percent of pay TSP deduction, your TSP deductions will be $50 every pay period. If your pay increases to $1,060 per pay period, your TSP deduction will automatically adjust to $53 every pay peri-

od. Similarly, if you change job locations and fall under a different locality pay schedule, your TSP contributions automatically increase or decrease to reflect your new pay.

On the other hand, if you designate a fixed dollar TSP deduction of $50 per pay period, that deduction will remain the same—regardless of pay increases—until you file a new Form TSP-1 in a subsequent open season.

If you are already investing in the TSP and decide you want to adjust your payroll deduction level—up or down—you also file a Form TSP-1 during an open season. The new deduction level you designate will replace your previous level, and—if you're in FERS—your agency matching contributions will adjust accordingly.

You do not have to file a new Form TSP-1 every open season if you wish to continue your existing TSP deduction level, whether it's a percentage of pay or a fixed dollar amount. Your current deduction level will continue in effect until any future open season in which you file a new Form TSP-1.

Whether you are starting TSP deductions or are adjusting your deduction level, you must file your Form TSP-1 with your agency personnel office during an open season. New and adjusted deduction levels take effect during the first full pay period in either January or July, depending on which open season you're in. If you hand in your form during January or July, your designation will go into effect no later than the next pay period that begins after your agency receives your election form.

There is a waiting period before newly hired FERS employees can begin investing in the TSP. These employees can start to invest in the TSP as of the second open season after beginning to work under FERS. See Figure 1-3.

How New FERS Employees Start Participating in the TSP

If You Start Under FERS	You Can Elect to Make TSP Deductions	Your Agency's 1% Contribution Starts
January-June	The following November 15 - January 31	The first full pay period in January
July-December	The following May 15 - July 31	The first full pay period in July

Figure 1-3

Your contributions and your agency's matching contributions also start the first full pay period in January or July, as long as you file your Form TSP-1 in time—by the end of December or the end of June, depending on the open season.

Once you start investing in the TSP, you always have the option of stopping your payroll deductions at any time. You do this by filing a new Form TSP-1 and designating a zero TSP deduction. Keep in mind what happens if you stop your TSP contributions. If you stop during an open season, you can start again at the next open season. But if you stop between open seasons, you must wait for the second open season before you can resume TSP deductions. This provision is in the law to discourage employees from constant starts and stops and to prevent an excessive administrative burden (and expense) for the Thrift Board and employing agencies.

Whenever you file a Form TSP-1 your agency will send you a Confirmation of Election. Review this document carefully to make sure it reflects your wishes. If there is any discrepancy contact your agency personnel office immediately.

You can only contribute to the TSP when you are employed in a pay status. If you are temporarily in a non-pay status, your deductions stop until you return to a pay status. Employees who retire or separate from federal or postal service cannot continue to make TSP contributions. But they can leave their TSP accounts in place and continue to allocate them among the three TSP investment funds. Re-employed annuitants can make TSP contributions, based on their basic pay of record. Retirees may not add to their TSP accounts after retirement unless they are rehired. Nor may retirees start TSP accounts.

You cannot make retroactive contributions to make up for earlier periods when you could not or did not invest in the TSP. This is very important to understand. If you enter into an extended non-pay status, or you decide not to contribute for a while, you cannot make up the difference by writing a check to the TSP when you return to work or your budget looks brighter. Retroactive contributions have only been allowed in certain exceptional cases in which an employee's retirement coverage was incorrectly recorded.

If you are a rehired employee you can begin or resume TSP contributions during the first regularly scheduled open season, assuming you were eligible to participate in the TSP during your previous period of federal or postal service. If you were not eligible to participate in the TSP during your previous service, you must wait until the second open season before beginning to participate.

If you are a rehired CSRS employees who transfers to FERS you will receive the automatic 1 percent of pay agency contribution immediately. You have 30 days from the date of rehire to file Form TSP-1 to start payroll deductions and agency matching contributions. If the 30-day period lapses you must wait until the next open season to file your election form.

◇2◇ PLOTTING YOUR COURSE

Let's establish a basic framework for understanding how you can use the TSP effectively as a key element in your lifetime financial planning. Making the TSP work for you does not have to be complicated or time-consuming. But it does require you to think about your career and retirement expectations and to plan a TSP strategy that will help ensure adequate retirement income for you and your family.

THE TSP AND YOUR OVERALL SAVINGS

The steadily growing participation in the TSP reflects the plan's appeal as a long-term savings mechanism. But it's important to realize that—like any other investment opportunity—the TSP is well suited to help you meet some financial goals, but less well suited to others. Consider where and how the TSP fits in your overall finances.

Start by thinking about financial transactions in terms of four major categories—income, consumption, savings and investment. Our finances constantly revolve around how we allot money to these categories, now and in the future. During our working years we earn income through employment and other sources. We generally allocate that income to two categories. First, we spend some of our income on current consumption—food, shelter, transportation and so on. If we can, we set aside the remainder as current savings—the income we have left after paying for our purchases.

The distinction between current consumption and current savings is not always clear and simple. Some things we consume today also have savings and investment value for the future. For example, when we buy a car we spend money, but that consumption may enhance our ability to earn income now and in the future. Current consumption of education may significantly increase our future earnings. And a home may provide both current shelter and a long-term asset with growth potential. In general, though, as we earn income during our working years we are constantly choosing between current and future uses of that income. The current income we set aside for future use represents our savings. Investments are things we buy with our savings to protect or increase the value of our savings over time.

The TSP provides a structure for setting aside current income (payroll deductions) as current savings (your TSP account). It enables you to purchase investments (allocations to the G, F and C funds) that accumulate value until you turn them into future income (withdrawal of your account balance).

But the TSP is only one of many savings and investment opportunities available to you. To understand the role of the TSP more thoroughly, we need to examine savings and investment choices more closely. Figure 2-1 shows a range of savings goals, each reflecting a different point in your financial future. Each savings goal suggests certain factors that may affect the investments you might choose.

Saving and Investing for Future Income

Saving for Short-Term Income ("Emergency Fund")

What You're Saving For:	Sudden expenses, such as medical bills/home repair needs
	Unexpected drop in income, such as job loss or reduced hours
Investment Features:	Liquid—ready access to money Stable—money has to be there Interest—keep up with inflation
Possible Investments:	Checking and savings accounts Money market certificates Short-term certificates of deposit

Saving for Medium-Term Income ("Buffer Fund")

What You're Saving For:	Planned expenses, such as college, home, luxury item Reserve fund to adapt to short term or long-term needs
Investment Features:	Growth—build value over time Convertible—can "sell" if needed Flexible—respond to changing markets/goals
Possible Investments:	Mutual funds Individual stocks/bonds Real estate TSP

Saving for Long-Term Income ("Retirement and Estate Fund")

What You're Saving For:	Adequate income during retirement for you and your family
	Estate value for your heirs
Investment Features:	Growth—build value over time
	Tax-Deferred—to enhance growth
	Risk Control—to protect gains
Possible Investments:	TSP
	IRAs
	Mutual funds or selected stocks/bonds

Figure 2-1

This summary of your possible savings goals is by no means exhaustive. But it can help you understand the TSP as a part of your overall savings and compare it to other investment opportunities. In Chapters Three (FERS) and Four (CSRS) we'll examine your TSP savings potential in detail. This will help you understand the role the TSP can play as part of your long-term, retirement-focused savings.

Overall, when you're thinking about your TSP participation, you probably fall into one of three major employee categories, each with its own particular issues and decisions to face. (See Figure 2-2)

TSP Priorities for Different Employees

FERS Employees Not Getting Maximum Government Contributions

Priority:	Start getting maximum matching contributions as soon as possible
Why?	To increase account growth and obtain full value on your savings.
How?	Cut back on current expenses
	Increase current income
	Reduce other investments
See:	Chapter 3 for how matching contributions increase your savings potential
	Chapter 5 to understand your TSP investment options
	Chapter 6 to plan a TSP investment strategy

FERS Employees Getting Maximum Government Contributions

Priority:	Balance TSP Savings and Other Investments
Why?	To meet your total financial needs effectively
How?	Estimate your TSP and FERS benefits
	Consider retirement and interim needs
	Look at the features of competing investments

See:	Chapter 2 to compare the TSP to other investment opportunities
	Chapter 3 to understand tax-deferred savings and retirement income
	Chapter 6 to build a TSP strategy that fulfills your financial goals
	Chapter 7 to understand the TSP loan program

CSRS Employees

Priority:	Balance TSP Savings and Other Investments
Why?	To meet your total financial needs effectively
How?	Measure your basic CSRS benefits
	Define your additional retirement needs
	Look at the features of competing investments
See:	Chapter 2 to compare the TSP to other investment opportunites
	Chapter 4 to understand the TSP as a pension supplement
	Chapter 6 to build a TSP strategy as part of your total finances
	Chapter 7 to understand the TSP loan program

Figure 2-2

These suggestions will help you get started in using the TSP to your best advantage. They focus on the long-term growth of your TSP account and how your TSP account might serve as part of your overall savings portfolio. Don't miss Chapter Eight. It will help you get a clear understanding of what you'll be able to do with your TSP account balance when you leave federal or postal service.

COMPARING THE TSP AND OTHER INVESTMENTS

You have to be careful when you attempt to compare one investment to another. Always start by thinking about your savings goals and what you're trying to achieve. In particular, consider how long you expect to hold the investment and when you may need to convert it to cash.

If you are considering investment of substantial sums, professional advice is usually worthwhile. You may start by obtaining information from investment brokers. But you should also seek guidance from a neutral party who profits by providing sound advice, not by selling any particular investment.

Figure 2-3 provides a comparison of average returns during the 1970s, 1980s and the beginning of the 1990s. The comparison covers categories of investment that might be well suited for short-term, medium-term and long-term savings goals.

A WORD ABOUT CALCULATING RETURNS

Throughout the book and in the appendices we will present estimates of your TSP account growth based on varying investment returns.

When we refer to the annual return for the TSP funds we mean the total gain—or loss—over the entire 12 months, including the effect of monthly compounding. For example, a 7 percent annual return means that $100 in your account on January 1 gains 7 percent ($7) over the course of the year. A year later the original $100 is $107.

This concept of annual returns corresponds to the reported returns for the three TSP investment funds on the Thrift Savings Plan's Fact Sheets. For example, the TSP's 1993 annual returns were 10.13 percent for the C Fund, 9.52 percent for the F Fund and 6.14 percent for the G Fund. These figures include the compounding of the earnings for each of the 12 months during 1993.

Estimates of how your account might grow in the future reflect the account projections presented on page 12 of the Thrift Savings Plan Information Booklet. In those projections, the rates of return—4, 7 and 10 percent—are annualized rates before adding the effects of monthly compounding. For example, the 4 percent rate of return is translated into monthly earnings of 0.33 percent which, when compounded over 12 months, produce a total annual return of 4.07 percent. The 7 percent rate of return corresponds to monthly earnings of 0.58 percent and a total annual return of 7.23 percent. The 10 percent rate corresponds to monthly earnings of 0.83 percent and a total annual return of 10.47 percent.

When we use the term annual real return, we mean the actual total return for the year, less the reduction in purchasing power due to inflation during that year. For example, if the total annual return in a year was 7 percent, then $100 at the beginning of the year grew to $107 by the end of the year. However, if there was 3 percent inflation during the year, then by the end of the year it takes $103 to maintain the value of the original $100. The real gain during the year was not $7, but $4 ($107 minus $103), reflecting a real return of 4 percent (7 percentage points minus 3 percentage points).

Average Annual Returns for Various Investments

	1970s	1980s	1990s
Treasury Bills	6.3%	8.9%	5.9%
3-Month CDs	10.0%	10.5%	6.5%
S & P 500	5.9%	17.5%	10.6%
Small Company Stocks	11.5%	15.8%	14.1%
Long-Term Government Bonds	5.5%	12.6%	12.8%
20-Yr. Corporate Bonds	6.2%	13.0%	12.2%
International Stocks	10.1%	22.8%	0.3%
Residential Real Estate	12.9%	11.5%	5.0%
INFLATION	7.4%	5.1%	4.2%

Figure 2-3

How do these broad investment categories compare to the returns to date from the TSP's three investment funds? During the six years 1988-1993, the C Fund, tracking the S&P 500, averaged annual growth of 14.1 percent. The F Fund, tracking the major U.S. bond market sectors, earned a 9.6 percent annual return. The G Fund, reflecting intermediate and long-term interest rates, had 8 percent annual earnings.

Of course, a much wider range of investment opportunities is available to you outside the TSP. You can tap into a wide range of investment markets through any of several thousand mutual funds. Mutual funds generally offer the advantages of carefully structured and monitored portfolios without the time and expense of managing your own account.

Mutual funds—on a taxable basis for maximum flexibility, or on a tax-deferred basis through an IRA for long-term growth—may deserve your attention as a complement to your TSP investments. Be sure to shop carefully and obtain all the guidance you need before investing substantial sums.

CSRS employees—and FERS employees already investing 5 percent of pay in the TSP—may want to consider carefully the merits of additional TSP investments compared to investments in mutual funds or—if available—a spouse's 401(k) plan. If you steer your mutual fund investments through an IRA, you can enhance your long-term gains through tax deferral of your investment earnings. However, keep in mind that steering your mutual fund investments through an IRA or 401(k) plan reduces the mutual fund's liquidity—your ability to get access to your funds if you need them in the interim.

Figure 2-4 shows the average annual returns for various categories of mutual funds from September 1990 through August 1993. The first column shows the actual average return. The second column shows the average return after adjusting for sales loads, fund fees and taxes on the fund's gains. The average annual returns for the three TSP investment options over the same period are included for comparison purposes.

The returns shown in Figure 2-4 occurred during a period of strong stock and bond market performance. The future returns of individual mutual funds or categories of funds are uncertain.

Average Annual Returns for Mutual Funds
September 1990 - August 1993

Fund Category	Average Annual Return	After Loads, Fees and Taxes
Aggressive Growth	21.1%	18.3%
Growth	17.6%	14.8%
Growth and Income	15.7%	13.0%
Equity-Income	16.6%	13.9%
Small Company	23.0%	20.9%
International	6.9%	5.1%
Global	10.7%	8.1%
Balanced	15.1%	12.1%
Convertible Bonds	17.9%	14.9%
Corporate-Junk	18.6%	13.6%
World	10.6%	7.0%
Corporate-General	13.1%	9.9%
Government-General	11.2%	8.1%
Government-Mortgage	11.0%	7.7%
Government-Treasury	14.8%	12.3%
Municipal	11.0%	9.9%
TSP C FUND		16.5%
TSP F FUND		12.8%
TSP G FUND		7.5%

Figure 2-4

We've shown the returns of mutual funds before and after loads, fees and taxes for an important reason. When comparing investment opportunities, be sure to take into account all the factors that will affect the investment's growth and income potential.

THE IMPORTANCE OF TAXES AND INVESTMENT COSTS

Take particular note of two factors. First, make sure you understand what the terms currently taxed, tax-deferred, and tax-exempt mean. A currently taxed investment, such as a mutual fund not administered through an IRA, will provide you with higher liquidity—ready access to your assets if needed. But the taxes will reduce the long-term compounded growth of the investment relative to a similar tax-deferred investment. Tax-deferred investments—such as TSP funds or mutual funds administered through an IRA—can provide higher long-term growth, but with very limited access to your assets in the interim. When considering tax-exempt investments—such as municipal bonds—remember to factor in your tax savings when you evaluate and compare returns and potential growth. For example, if you are in a 28 percent tax bracket, a municipal bond paying 4 percent interest provides a return equal to a taxable bond earning 5.6 percent. If you are in a higher tax bracket, the effect of the tax savings is even greater. It's not a good idea to include municipal bonds or any other tax-exempt investments in an IRA because you would be wasting the tax-deferred advantage of the IRA.

Second, when you're examining an investment prospectus or listening to an investment broker's sales pitch, be sure to pay close attention to the costs involved in making your investment. Insist on a specific description of all charges and examples of how they would affect the value of your assets. In particular, the growth of the mutual fund industry has brought with it a diverse array of distribution networks and wide variations in how funds finance their marketing, sales and management costs. Don't let all the terms—front-end loads, back-end loads, 12(b)-1 fees—confuse you. Take the time to understand what charges you'll pay and when you'll pay them. Figure out how those charges will work in your personal situation, taking into account how much you'll be investing and for how long. This will help you understand how sales loads, redemption fees and other costs compare and which might best suit your investment plans. Above all, don't let an obsession with costs distract you from the essential task of identifying well-managed funds that fit your investment objectives.

In general, as millions of new individual investors have poured billions of dollars into mutual funds and IRAs, the financial services market has become more competitive, offering lower investment costs. Nevertheless, private investment commissions, fees and loads are still higher—and often much higher—than the management fees and administrative expenses of TSP investing. Currently, annual TSP administrative expenses cost you in the range of 0.1 to 0.15 percent—that is, $1 to $1.50 for every $1,000 in your account. By comparison, the "expense ratio" of mutual funds averages about 1.25 percent—$12.50 per $1,000. Remember this when you're trying to decide whether to make additional investments in the TSP or pursue outside investment opportunities. The TSP isn't automatically a better place to put your money, just because its investment expenses are lower. But it does mean that another opportunity would have to earn slightly higher returns to make up for its larger costs.

Tax status and investment costs are just two of the factors you should weigh when deciding where to put your money. Figure 2-5 compares nine major investment categories according to five considerations:

◇ Current Income—the ability of the investment to provide you with income on an ongoing basis;

◇ Real Capital Growth—whether and to what extent the investment can increase the value of your assets over time, over and above inflation;

◇ Safety of Assets—whether your investment is protected from or subject to the possibility of losses;

◇ Liquidity—the degree to which you can draw on or sell off your assets for current income or to move them to another investment; and

◇ Tax Treatment—how the income and gains from your investment are taxed.

Remember that, with the exception of real estate and certain types of highly speculative investments, *you can invest in a wide range of financial instruments through an*

Key Features of Various Investment Opportunities

Investment Category	Current Income	Real Capital Growth	Safety of Assets	Liquidity	Tax Treatment
Savings and Checking Accounts	Yes, but very low interest	None	Fully or partially insured	Access to funds at any time	Interest taxed
Certificate of Deposit	At end of CD term; rates vary by length	Potential for small growth if reinvested	Fully or partially insured	Penalty if withdrawn before term	Interest taxed
Money Market Mutual Funds	Yes, based on short-term rates	Zero or low real asset growth	Very safe	Can withdraw at any time	Interest taxed
Municipal Bonds	Yes, rates vary	Bond's sale price can fluctuate	Generally safe, some chance of default	Can sell at any time	Tax exempt
Corporate Bonds	Yes, rates vary	Bond's sale price can fluctuate	Generally safe, some chance of default	Can sell at any time	Interest taxed
Common Stocks	Some pay dividends	Potential for high long-term growth	Subject to short-term movements and loss	Can sell at any time	Dividends taxed; tax on capital gain/ loss when sold
Mutual Funds	Yes, interest and/or dividends	Varies with type of fund's investments	Fluctuations and potential for loss, varies by type of fund	Can sell at any time	Dividends and gains taxed; taxes deferred if you buy fund through an IRA
Real Estate	Yes, if rental property	Varies widely	Market conditions may result in sale at a loss	Low—some access through home equity loans	Rental income taxed; capital gain/loss may be taxed at sale; mortgage payments deductible
Thrift Savings Plan	No	C Fund— high growth potential; F and G funds— moderate growth	C Fund— frequent short-term fluctuations; F Fund— some losses due to market conditions; G Fund—no risk of loss	Low—some access through loans	Taxes deferred; account balance taxed when withdrawn

Figure 2-5

IRA and gain tax advantages (while losing liquidity). Compared to the TSP, an IRA has—for many employees— less substantial tax advantages. If you are single, your IRA contributions are not tax-deductible if you earn more than $35,000, and they're only partially deductible if you earn $25,000-$35,000. If you're married, your IRA contributions are not deductible if your joint income is $50,000 or more, and they're only partially deductible if your joint income is $40,000-$50,000. In contrast, all your TSP contributions are tax-deductible, regardless of your income.

Nonetheless, if long-term, tax-deferred growth is your key financial goal, consider supplementing your TSP account with additional investments in an IRA and/or a spouse's 401(k) plan, if available. If you want to combine long-term growth with flexibility and liquidity in the interim, mutual funds held outside an IRA may be the best place to start. Current taxation of income and capital gains will reduce your long-term growth potential somewhat, but you may be able to achieve substantial growth and a balanced portfolio through a selection of several well-managed funds.

If you are a CSRS employee, or a FERS employee putting more than 5 percent of pay in the TSP, look closely at how your TSP investments compare to other opportunities. If you are a FERS employee investing less than 5 percent of pay, any additional savings you can lock up for the long run probably should go first toward raising your TSP contributions to the 5 percent level and getting the maximum government contribution to your account.

SOME SPECIFIC SUGGESTIONS

Let's focus on some basic concepts and considerations you might want to keep in mind as you build and adapt your TSP strategies. Throughout the book we'll elaborate on these essential points in more detail.

> **Suggestion #1:** Contribute as Much as You Can as Early as You Can

Even with a modest 4 percent annual rate of return on TSP investments, a FERS employee making $30,000 and contributing 5 percent of pay to the TSP will build an account of about $174,000 over a 30-year period. At age 65 that account would translate into a lifetime retirement income of $15,000 a year, including inflation protection and survivor benefits. Even waiting only five years before starting to contribute can significantly reduce your long-term savings potential. In our example, the final TSP account would be about $131,000 instead of $174,000. The long-term loss would be $43,000, compared to a short-term cost of $7,500 in the five extra years of contributions. Annual retirement income at age 65 would drop from $15,000 to $11,000.

Could you "catch up" for the five years by contributing more later on? Yes. But *you would have to contribute almost 8.5 percent of pay for 25 years to equal 30 years of 5 percent of pay contributions.* And because your extra contributions above 5 percent aren't matched by your agency, you would end up paying a high price to catch up. What would have cost you $7,500 in the first five years instead ends up costing you $26,250 over the next 25 years—an extra $1,050 (3.5 percent of pay) a year for 25 years.

And remember, this example is based on a conservative 4 percent annual investment return. With higher investment returns the cost of delaying your investments becomes even greater. That's how compound

interest works. The dollar you contribute now will generate substantially more long-term savings than the dollar you contribute even a few years down the road.

Figure 2-6 shows how contributions accumulate value over 30 years. Even with a modest 4 percent annual real rate of return, the effects of compounded earnings are striking.

Value of TSP Contributions over 30-Year Investment Period

4% Annual Real Rate of Return

$1 You Contribute	Invested For	Is Worth This at End of 30-Year Period		
		Matched 100%	Matched 50%	Unmatched
Year 1	30 years	$6.63	$4.97	$3.31
Year 6	25 years	$5.43	$4.07	$2.71
Year 11	20 years	$4.45	$3.33	$2.22
Year 16	15 years	$3.64	$2.73	$1.82
Year 21	10 years	$2.98	$2.24	$1.49
Year 26	5 years	$2.44	$1.83	$1.22

Figure 2-6

Higher rates of return would yield even more dramatic growth. For example, $1 invested for 30 years at a 7 percent real annual return would generate $7.61 at the end of the period. If that $1 was fully matched, it would generate a 30-year value of $15.22.

Contributing to the TSP Now vs. Contributing More Later

FERS Employee Earning $30,000, 4% Annual Real Return

Contributes 5% of Pay For:	10 Years	20 Years	30 Years
Total Employee Contributions	$15,000	$30,000	$45,000
Final Account Balance	$36,900	$91,800	$173,700
Employee's Money	41%	33%	26%
Agency Money and Earnings	59%	67%	74%

Contributes 10% of Pay For:	7 Years	15 Years	23 Years
Total Employee Contributions	$21,000	$45,000	$9,000
Final Account Balance	$36,341	$92,400	$169,569
Employee's Money	58%	49%	41%
Agency Money and Earnings	42%	51%	59%

Figure 2-7

The price of delaying your contributions is especially steep if you're a FERS employee, because you permanently forfeit the compounded value of agency matching contributions. If you don't obtain maximum matching contributions early in your career, you'll pay a price if you try to "catch up" with unmatched dollars later on. For example, every fully-matched dollar you contribute in Year 1 is worth almost three times as much as every unmatched dollar you contribute 10 years later.

The longer you wait to begin contributions, the more compounded growth you forfeit and the more costly it becomes to catch up later. You can catch up by contributing more later in your career, but in the process you pay a higher cost for your final account balance. This is true for both FERS and CSRS employees, as shown in Figures 2-7 and 2-8.

Figure 2-7 shows a FERS employee earning $30,000 a year and contributing 5 percent of pay to the TSP over periods ranging from 10 to 40 years. It also shows what the effect would be if the employee tried to achieve the same final account balance by contributing 10 percent of pay later on.

By beginning 5 percent of pay contributions immediately, a FERS employee can obtain all of the potential agency matching contributions and the compounded earnings on those agency contributions. If you view your TSP account as a long-term investment that you buy through your contributions, your early contributions significantly reduce the cost of your investment.

Contributing to the TSP Now vs. Contributing More Later

CSRS Employee Earning $40,000, 4% Annual Real Return

Contributes 3% of Pay For:	10 Years	20 Years	30 Years
Total Employee Contributions	$12,000	$24,000	$36,000
Final Account Balance	$14,800	$36,800	$69,600
Employee's Money	81%	65%	52%
Investment Earnings	19%	35%	48%
Contributes 5% of Pay For:	**6 Years**	**14 Years**	**22 Years**
Total Employee Contributions	$12,000	$28,000	$44,000
Final Account Balance	$13,697	$37,301	$70,453
Employee's Money	88%	75%	62%
Investment Earnings	12%	25%	38%

Figure 2-8

The same principle holds true for CSRS employees, even without agency matching contributions. By contributing now you gain tax-deferred and compounded value over time. The result is a better buy on your total TSP investment.

Figure 2-8 shows the different results realized by a CSRS employee contributing 3 percent of pay now, compared to waiting and trying to catch up by investing 5 percent of pay later on.

Whether you're a FERS or a CSRS employee, the sooner you begin contributing the more long-term value you'll obtain. By delaying, you limit the growth potential of your savings and get less value for your money. But even starting late is better than not starting at all. Investing in the TSP carries significant tax and interest benefits, even for those who can invest only for a short time. The TSP's tax deferral and—under FERS—matching contributions can make a difference even for short-term investors.

➤ **Suggestion #2**: Build, Maintain and Refine Your Understanding of How Your TSP Account Connects to Your Long-term Financial Goals

There is a basic and understandable satisfaction with the very act of saving—you know you've got more "stashed away" than you had yesterday and the account balance is bigger every time you check. But where is your account headed and what will its real value be when you need it?

If you're a new, relatively young employee you may think of your TSP account as too small to focus on. But you'll pay closer attention to it when the account balance becomes more substantial and retirement becomes something to start thinking about.

Or you may be an older, longer-term employee who falls into an opposite trap. You already have $50,000 in your TSP account and you see the possibility of a $150,000 balance by the time you retire. Everything's great!

What's the problem with these two attitudes? If you don't take the time to focus on your TSP expectations and goals, you may be in for a rude awakening.

When you're younger, you have a good opportunity to **TIP** *be more aggressive and experimental in your investment choices—you have more time to work with, and the dollar amount at risk is lower than it will be later on.* Settling into a very conservative TSP portfolio may be easy and safe, but it may cost you a substantial amount of compounded earnings potential over the long haul.

When you're older, your TSP account balance may be a considerable sum, perhaps the largest cash reserve you've ever accumulated. But large numbers can be deceiving. A TSP account of $150,000 may be worth less than you suspect when you calculate your retirement income. For example, if you retire at age 65 and use your $150,000 TSP account to purchase an annuity, your annuity payment will be about $1,000-$1,200 a month, depending on what type of annuity you select. That's a nice monthly check. But it may be smaller than what you expect a $150,000 account would buy.

The lesson is simple. The more you know and the sooner you know it, the better off you'll be in making sure the TSP works to your maximum advantage. Paying attention to your TSP options from your first open season to the day you leave government service—and beyond—will help make your retirement more comfortable.

Planning can also help you avoid "over-saving." The notion of saving too much may sound silly, but think about it. Of course, the worst long-term outcome would be to enter retirement without adequate income and savings. But the opposite can happen, and it may not be your best lifetime financial strategy. You could reach retirement with more than enough retirement income. In general, no problem. But if your abundant retirement savings came at the expense of painful financial choices or lost opportunities along the way, that could be a bittersweet outcome.

Careful TSP planning can help you avoid reaching retirement without a truly secure income. It can also help avoid looking back in your golden years and thinking, "If only I'd known I could have afforded that after all."

➤ **Suggestion #3:** When You Estimate Your TSP Account Growth, Use Conservative Assumptions about Investment Returns

You always have control over your TSP contribution level and your mix of TSP investments. You cannot, however, control the returns that investment mix will generate. By planning your contributions in terms of a conservative investment expectation, you protect yourself against uncertain economic conditions. If your investments outperform your expectations you'll have a higher account balance and more freedom to adjust your investments.

Begin by using a 4 percent annual real (after inflation) rate of return as your primary reference point when you are assessing your TSP contribution level. This baseline will give you a projected account growth based on a relatively safe investment strategy and modest salary increases. You will then free yourself to try higher-risk—and potentially higher return—investment strategies if you choose. If your actual returns exceed your expectations, so much the better.

On the other hand, if you base your account planning on a more optimistic investment assumption, actual returns may lag behind your expectations. This will present you with three choices, none of which are particularly attractive. First, you may choose to increase your contribution level. These higher contributions will have a shorter compounding period and, as a result, lower long-term earnings potential. Second, you may choose to engage in a higher-risk investment strategy to catch up. Because you were too optimistic before, you now decide to be even more optimistic. Third, if you're unable to raise your contributions or realize higher investment returns,

you'll be forced to scale down your long-term TSP goals.

➤ **Suggestion #4:** Plan Your Investment Decisions on a Solid Base of Knowledge, Rather than Reacting to Pieces of Information

One of the most common and costly mistakes some investors make is overreacting to bits of potentially misleading information. Beware of the rumor or "hot tip"—"I heard the stock market's going to go through the roof next month!" Well, maybe it will and maybe it won't.

When you're making your TSP investment decisions be careful about what information you use and how you use it. Many hot tips turn out to be baseless rumors. And don't forget that in many cases today's hot tip has already been "discounted" by the market—talk of stock values going up next month may have already shown up in stock values going up this month as investors buy to get in on the rumored run-up.

Beyond tips and rumors, even real and accurate information can be misleading and costly if you interpret it incorrectly. For example, during the 72-month period from January 1988 through December 1993 the C Fund had a sustained period of strong performance. The total compounded growth of the C Fund over these six years was 120.1 percent. Over the entire six years, the C Fund grew at an annual compounded rate of 14.1 percent and a monthly compounded rate of 1.1 percent. But the C Fund generated this total growth through a series of widely fluctuating monthly returns. In 27 of the 72 months the C Fund had negative returns and in 32 months the G Fund outperformed the C Fund. When it comes to the stock market, strong years include weak months. Strong months include weak days. And even strong days include shaky hours.

As you go about building, adjusting and using a TSP investment strategy, act at your discretion, react at your peril. If you overreact to short-term fluctuations you may significantly reduce your TSP investment gains.

➤ **Suggestion #5:** Tailor Your Use of the TSP to Your Goals and Circumstances

When thinking about how much to contribute to the TSP, consider your current situation and goals. Don't let someone else tell you what you "should" contribute to the TSP. Here are some basic guidelines you may want to keep in mind:

◇ *Higher contribution levels help give you greater* **TIP** *career flexibility. If you might leave federal or postal service before retirement, a larger TSP account will be a cushion that can give you more freedom of choice.* The more retirement equity you have in your TSP account, the more you loosen the "golden handcuffs" of a government pension. You'll have more freedom in deciding where to work and when to retire. The TSP can help you protect your long-term retirement income and give you greater leeway in considering other opportunities.

◇ If you're married, look at your TSP account in terms of combined career plans and retirement incomes.

The sooner you fit your TSP contributions into a total picture of combined retirement income, the more comfort and flexibility you and your spouse will enjoy. How much retirement income will your spouse be entitled to, and when? Does your spouse have a savings plan with employer matching contributions? If you're a CSRS employee, make sure to take advantage of the matching contributions in your spouse's plan before you contribute unmatched dollars to the TSP. If you're a FERS employee, make sure both you and your spouse obtain maximum matching contributions before either one of you contributes additional unmatched dollars to your plans. Be sure to pay attention to the investment opportunities and withdrawal rules of both plans.

◇ *If you are hoping to retire at a relatively young age, your TSP account may play an especially important role in the period before you can receive other savings and benefits.* For example, Social Security benefits are not payable until age 62. You cannot collect from an Individual Retirement Account without penalty until age 59½.

◇ Think about your overall savings tendencies. If you are generally able to save on your own, compare the relative advantages of directing "extra" savings to the TSP or to other savings vehicles. But if you find it difficult to save, using TSP payroll deductions to force yourself to save may be important. Be realistic.

◇ Look at your TSP contributions in terms of your total savings portfolio. Remember the long-term, deferred focus of the TSP. Balance this focus against your expected need for more readily available funds at various stages of your career.

These are just a few examples of the personal factors you might think about in framing a general TSP strategy. The essential point is that the TSP is a tool for you to use to your best advantage. When you're thinking about how much to contribute to the TSP, don't assume there's one right answer.

5 THINGS TO DO

1. Take a current reality check about your guaranteed retirement income, including your government annuity, savings and any other sources of income you might have. Examine how the TSP can best supplement them.

2. Look at your current income and how you allocate it between consumption and savings. How well does your actual savings correspond to your realistic savings needs? Compare the benefits of your current "luxury" spending versus more income and security in later years.

3. Check when the next TSP open season will occur. It will be from May 15 through July 31, or from November 15 through January 31. Begin to plan now for using that opportunity to help meet your retirement income and savings needs. Remember the extra benefits of getting an early start.

4. Think about all your financial goals and how you expect to achieve them. How much can you achieve with a well-planned savings and investment strategy? What do you have to do to get there? How can the TSP help?

5. Relax. We all have pressures—financial and otherwise—that we have to cope with as we chart our course. Effective financial planning is important, and successful use of the TSP can help you a great deal. But your financial world is not likely to turn upside down tomorrow. You don't have to make every decision right now. Take the time to consider your goals and your opportunities, then act.

⟨3⟩ THE TSP FOR FERS EMPLOYEES

Throughout your federal or postal career you have the opportunity to begin investing tax-deferred dollars in the TSP. If you're already participating in the TSP, you regularly have the chance to assess the current status of your TSP account and your overall financial circumstances, and increase—within limits—or reduce your investment levels.

This chapter will help you consider two fundamental questions. Should you be investing in the TSP? And if so, how much should you invest? As we'll see, the answers depend on your short-term and long-term financial goals. There's no one answer for everyone. You should make your own decisions from an informed and realistic viewpoint.

THE TSP AND YOUR FERS RETIREMENT INCOME

It's easy for FERS employees to underestimate the importance of the TSP as a key component of long-term retirement planning. Whether you are expecting to remain with the government for a full career or leave government service for other employment, the TSP is a main building block for your financial security in retirement. Figure 3-1 lists the essential building blocks of your total retirement income.

Combined Retirement Income for FERS Employees

Civil Service (FERS) Pension

+

Social Security

+

TSP Account

+

Other Pensions (if any)

+

Other Financial Assets

Figure 3-1

If you stay in government and retire on a FERS pension, your TSP account will play a critical role in supplementing the basic benefits provided through the FERS pension and Social Security. A well-planned TSP strategy will in many cases be vital in ensuring that you end up meeting your retirement income expectations.

If you leave the government for another job, you can take your TSP account with you and continue building up tax-deferred savings through an IRA or another employer-sponsored savings plan. Or you can choose to leave your money in the TSP and let it continue accruing investment earnings, and then withdraw it later on. If you have a varied career with several employers, then the TSP and similar plans become all the more important. You may not stay with any one employer long enough to obtain substantial guaranteed retirement benefits. Tax-deferred savings in a personal account can constitute a large share of your retirement income under the increasingly common "mixed career" scenario. But you will realize that potential only if you take advantage of the favorable savings opportunities offered by the TSP and similar programs.

Failing to appreciate the importance of the TSP is not unusual among younger government workers in the early stages of their careers. Only about half of all FERS employees age 20-29 invest their own money in the TSP and obtain the advantage of agency matching contributions. Older FERS employees are much more likely to participate—about four out of every five FERS workers above age 50 invest in the TSP.

If you're a younger FERS employee, retirement may be a distant and secondary target. And you may not have a great deal of money to spare for investing in the TSP. You may not pay much attention to your retirement status and rights until much later in your federal or postal career. As far as your basic FERS pension and Social Security benefits are concerned, this is not a serious problem. You will keep accruing pension and Social Security credits while you work, whether you're paying close attention to the process or not. And you'll at least automatically receive a 1 percent of pay contribution to your TSP account from your employing agency. But if you overlook your larger TSP investment opportunities for any significant length of time, you will permanently forfeit most of your savings potential for that period. You may be able to "catch up" to some extent with large TSP payroll deductions later in your career. But you would have given up government matching contributions during the interim, plus all the compounded and tax-deferred investment earnings your TSP account would have generated during that period.

Your government annuity and Social Security are "defined benefits" and will accrue automatically, based on your time in federal and/or postal service and your salary progression. But what you develop through the TSP—beyond the 1 percent automatic agency contribution—is entirely up to you.

To get a clearer picture of the idea of a "total retirement income package," let's look at an example of a long-term FERS employee. Imagine you're a FERS employee who starts working for the government at age 30 and plans to retire at age 65 with 35 years of FERS service. For each year you work under FERS, the basic pension formula will credit you with 1.1 percent of your "high-three average salary"—the average salary for your highest three consecutive years of earnings. This usually is the average salary for your final three years with the government.

In this example you would receive a basic FERS pension equal to 38.5 percent of your high-three average salary—1.1 percent per year times 35 years. Note that the 1.1 percent annual FERS credit only applies if you retire at age 62 or later with at least 20 years of service. If you retire before age 62 or with less than 20 years of service, the FERS pension pays you 1 percent for each of your years in FERS.

Social Security also will credit you for all 35 years of your FERS service, based on all your earnings each year up to the "maximum taxable wage base." This maximum is the highest earnings on which you pay Social Security taxes each year; all earnings up to that level are counted when computing benefits. The maximum wage base is adjusted each year—in 1994, $60,600.

Social Security tracks your earnings for all your employment (federal and non-federal), adjusts each year's earnings for inflation during your career, and then calculates a benefit based on your average career earnings. The Social Security formula is weighted to provide—as a proportion of career earnings—higher benefits to workers who had lower-paying jobs during their careers.

Remember that in our example the FERS basic annuity will pay you 38.5 percent of your high-three salary for 35 years of service, regardless of how high or low that high-three salary is. Social Security will pay a varying benefit—in percentage terms—depending on your average salary level over your entire career.

Let's look at how your Social Security benefit would vary, depending on whether you had lower, average or higher salary levels over the course of your career. Start with the combination of FERS and Social Security benefits at age 65, based on current law, as shown in Figure 3-2.

FERS Benefits at Age 65 with 35 Years of Service

Annual Retirement Income
FERS Basic Pension Plus Social Security

"High-3" Salary	$30,000	$45,000	$60,000
FERS Basic Pension	$11,550	$17,325	$23,100
Social Security	$11,400	$12,600	$14,400
Total Retirement Income	$22,950	$29,925	$37,500
As Percentage Of High-3	76.5%	66.5%	62.5%

Figure 3-2

The combination of the FERS basic pension and Social Security provides substantial retirement benefits for a full federal or postal career. But these two components alone may not be enough to meet your retirement expectations and goals.

This brings us to the TSP as the third component of your federal retirement income package. Everyone, of course, has a personal retirement income goal that depends on a wide range of circumstances and preferences. But let's say that your central goal is the most common one—to generally maintain the overall standard of living you enjoyed just before retirement.

There are different estimates of how much retirement income is necessary to maintain a pre-retirement standard of living. One commonly cited benchmark is that your retirement income should be at least 80 percent of your pre-retirement income—reflecting reductions in work-related expenses such as transportation, food and clothing and potentially lower taxes. Note that this 80 percent target is only a general benchmark. It assumes that you can maintain essentially the same standard of living at a slightly lower income level during your retirement years. Your own retirement target may be higher—or lower—than 80 percent. Think of the 80 percent figure as a minimum goal for planning purposes. Reaching 80 percent replacement of your pre-retirement salary will probably ensure that you can retire at a reasonable level of financial comfort. But it may not guarantee you the retirement standard of living that you desire. As you plan for your retirement during your working years, try to bring your personal target into sharper focus. The sooner you begin to think about specific goals, the more likely you'll achieve those goals. And the TSP probably will play a key role in fulfilling your retirement income expectations.

The importance of the TSP in reaching this minimum 80 percent target varies depending on your career earnings. As we'll see in Chapter Eight, when you leave the government you'll have a wide range of options for turning your TSP account balance into immediate or future income. For now, let's assume that you want to translate your TSP account into monthly payments that will supplement your FERS pension and Social Security checks.

In this case, you would use your TSP account at age 65 to buy an "annuity"—a steady stream of monthly payments that you'll receive for the rest of your life. To reach your goal of total retirement income equal to 80 percent of your pre-retirement earnings, you'd have to meet an "income target" from your TSP account as shown in Figure 3-3.

Adding the TSP to FERS Retirement Income

Annual Retirement Income

**FERS Basic Pension Plus Social Security
Plus TSP Annuity Based on 8% Increase**

"High-3" Salary	$30,000	$45,000	$60,000
Retirement Goal	$24,000	$36,000	$48,000
FERS + Social Security	$22,950	$29,925	$37,500
Annual TSP Annuity Needed	$1,050	$6,075	$10,500
TSP Account Needed	$12,000	$70,000	$115,000

Figure 3-3

The TSP gives you an opportunity to meet your retirement income target under all three salary examples. At lower salary levels a relatively modest TSP account would provide the small supplement needed to reach the 80 percent total income target. If you are able to make more substantial contributions to the TSP, you'll be able to exceed your target. If you enjoy higher salary levels during your career, you'll need to build up a larger TSP account to meet the total retirement target, because Social Security benefits are weighted toward lower-income workers. Of course, because of your higher salary, you'll probably be in a better position to make larger TSP payroll deductions and achieve your goal.

We've started with this example to give you a better idea of how the TSP fits into your total retirement package. The exact amount you'll need to put in the TSP to meet your goal will depend on how soon you start investing, how your earnings change during your career, how much interest your TSP investments earn and whether you increase or decrease your payroll deductions at various times. We'll examine these factors in more detail later in this chapter.

ADVANTAGES OF THE TSP FOR FERS EMPLOYEES

In considering the first two questions you'll face in your TSP planning—Should I be investing? And if so,

how much should I invest?—we've started by discussing the role of the TSP as part of your total retirement income planning. Now let's look more closely at why the TSP is —for FERS employees—probably superior to all other available vehicles for accumulating savings and retirement income.

There are two primary advantages of the TSP for FERS employees—agency contributions to your account and the tax-deferred accumulation of your account balance over time. Taken together, they make the FERS TSP a powerful engine for generating investment income. There are other attractive features of the FERS TSP—the convenience of payroll deductions, diversified investment choices, a flexible range of options for "cashing out" your account when you leave the government and mid-career access to your account through the TSP loan program. But comparable features also are available in other investment vehicles.

As a FERS employee, when you think about the TSP, focus on its two essential advantages—matching contributions and tax deferral. These two features make the TSP virtually a must investment, and you should build your long-term financial strategies with the TSP as a cornerstone.

AGENCY CONTRIBUTIONS FOR FERS EMPLOYEES

When you begin working for the government as a FERS employee, you will automatically have a TSP account in your name at the second "open season" after you begin working. (If you're a brand-new FERS employee, check out Figure 1-3 to see how this works.) After the waiting period, your employing agency will automatically begin contributing an amount equal to 1 percent of your basic pay each pay period to a TSP account that has been set up for you. Your basic pay is your regular salary or wages not including overtime or special pay differentials. This automatic 1 percent contribution will be made every pay period until you leave government service, except for any period(s) you are in a non-pay status, such as leave without pay.

For example, if you earn $1,000 a pay period, your agency would automatically contribute $10 to your TSP account every pay period. If your pay goes up, your agency will automatically increase its contribution accordingly. You will receive this automatic 1 percent contribution as long as you are in a pay status under FERS, whether or not you invest your own money in the TSP.

You can obtain significant additional contributions from your agency when you invest your own money into your TSP account. Your agency will "match" any money you invest in your TSP account up to investments of 5 percent of pay. When you invest any amount up to 3 percent of your pay through regular payroll deductions to your account, your agency will match your investment dollar-for-dollar each pay period. For example, if you invest 3 percent of pay, you will receive a total agency contribution of 4 percent of pay—the 1 percent automatic contribution plus a 3 percent agency match. Any TSP investments you make between 3 percent and 5 percent of pay will be matched by your agency at a rate of 50 cents on the dollar. For example, if you invest 5 percent of your pay, your agency will make a total agency contribution of 5 percent of pay—the 1 percent automatic contribution, plus 3 percent to match (dollar-for-dollar) your first 3 percent invested, plus 1 percent to match (50 cents on the dollar) your next 2 percent invested.

You may extend your own TSP payroll deductions up to (in most cases, excluding top-salaried employees) 10 percent of your pay, but there are no additional agency contributions after your deductions exceed 5 percent of pay.

Remember that the matching formula is subject to change by Congress. Proposals to make the benefit less generous regularly circulate on Capitol Hill.

Figure 3-4 shows how the availability of agency contributions can significantly increase the amount flowing into your TSP account.

Annual TSP Contributions for FERS Employee Earning $30,000

Employee Contributes		Agency Contributions		Total Contributions
		Matching	Automatic	
0%	$0	$0	$300	$300
1%	$300	$300	$300	$900
2%	$600	$600	$300	$1,500
3%	$900	$900	$300	$2,100
4%	$1,200	$1,050	$300	$2,550
5%	$1,500	$1,200	$300	$3,000
6%	$1,800	$1,200	$300	$3,300
7%	$2,100	$1,200	$300	$3,600
8%	$2,400	$1,200	$300	$3,900
9%	$2,700	$1,200	$300	$4,200
10%	$3,000	$1,200	$300	$4,500

Figure 3-4

 One overwhelming advantage of the TSP for FERS employees is the opportunity to "leverage" additional investments from your agency by investing a small portion of your pay on a regular basis. A FERS employee who contributes 5 percent of pay into a TSP account each pay period actually realizes an investment twice that size due to the automatic and matching contributions from the employing agency. This "leveraging" of agency money, plus compounded investment earnings from up to three types of TSP investment funds, plus the tax-deferred accumulation of all investments and earnings, combine to make the TSP program a unique opportunity for FERS employees.

TAX-DEFERRED RETIREMENT SAVINGS

The second primary advantage of the TSP for FERS employees is that your entire account balance accumulates on a tax-deferred basis—your payroll deductions, your agency's automatic and matching contributions and all compounded investment earnings over time. The term "tax-deferred" means you pay taxes on your savings when you withdraw the money. You don't avoid paying taxes on your TSP account. But the deferral of taxes makes saving money a little easier on your budget and helps your account grow at a faster rate. It also means you'll be paying taxes on the money at a time—in retirement—that you'll probably be in a lower tax bracket.

Here's how tax deferral works and how it adds to the value of your TSP account. First, when you designate a portion of your pay for investment in the TSP each pay period, that investment is not included in your federal taxable income. It is also excluded from taxable income for most state income taxes. For tax year 1993, New Jersey and Pennsylvania were the only states that did not exclude investments in the TSP and similar plans when calculating taxable income. Sometimes this current tax-year exclusion is referred to as the investment of "pre-tax" dollars. In the year the investments are made, you achieve a current year tax savings on every dollar you invest in the TSP. Figure 3-5 shows the tax savings for an employee earning $30,000 a year. To simplify, other taxes and deductions are ignored. There would be additional state income tax savings in most states.

Tax Savings on Your TSP Contributions

$30,000 Annual Earnings, 5% of Pay Contribution, 28% Tax Rate

	TSP Investment Tax-Deferred	Other Investment No Tax Deferral
Annual Basic Pay	$30,000	$30,000
Amount Invested	$1,500	$1,500
Net Taxable Income	$28,500	$30,000
TSP Current Tax Savings = $420 ($1,500 at 28% tax rate)		

Figure 3-5

Higher salaries, investment levels or tax rates would yield even greater current tax savings from the "pre-tax" status of TSP payroll deductions. For example, an employee earning $50,000 a year and investing 10 percent of pay in the TSP, with a 33 percent tax rate, would save $1,650 in federal taxes. That employee effectively would be paying only $3,350 to make a $5,000 investment in the TSP. (And the matching agency contributions would bring the total investment for the year to $10,000—of which only a third came from the employee's own pocket.)

The second key aspect of TSP tax deferral is that your

agency's automatic 1 percent of pay contribution and matching contributions to your account are not subject to income tax until you collect your account balance. In effect, you receive a salary supplement from your agency, invest that money in the TSP and don't pay taxes on that extra salary until you use it as retirement income.

Third, and very important, all earnings on your investments and your agency's contributions accumulate over the life of your TSP account on a tax-deferred basis. The effects of compound interest over time, especially when coupled with agency contributions, can turn this ongoing deferral of investment income into a powerful advantage for the TSP over currently taxed investment opportunities.

For example, if you invest in a commercial mutual fund and the fund sells some of its stocks at a gain, you pay taxes on your share of the fund's gain—capital gains tax if the fund held the asset for more than a year, ordinary income tax if the asset was held for less than a year. You can defer the taxes on your earnings if your mutual funds are invested through an IRA. Remember, however, there is a $2,000 annual limit on IRA contributions and, depending on your income, the IRA contributions themselves may not be deductible. Also, there are no matching contributions to an IRA.

Over extended investment periods, the effects of the tax deferral can substantially increase the long-term growth of your investments. For example, if two investments—one tax-deferred, the other currently taxed—earn a 7 percent annual return, at the end of 30 years the tax-deferred investment can be 50 percent or more larger than the currently taxed investment. When comparing tax-deferred and currently taxed investments, take into account the range of potential returns, the ultimate growth potential over the long-term and the liquidity of the investment in the interim.

You may decide that certain currently taxed investments suit your investment goals better than additional investments in the TSP. Be sure, however, that you build your total portfolio on complete information and an understanding of how tax-deferral adds to long-term growth, and take into account the value of the agency matching contributions.

Note that the TSP and similar plans provide a tax deferral, not an exemption from taxes altogether. Again, you will pay taxes on your TSP account when you receive it as retirement income. But when you pay taxes on your TSP income, you will still realize a substantial gain from the long-term effects of the tax deferral.

The important advantages of tax deferral are your ability to use "pre-tax dollars" to make your current investments less expensive, and the more rapid accumulation of investment earnings over time. There is a third potential advantage—that ultimately, in retirement, you may end up paying taxes on your TSP income at a lower tax rate. But this is by no means a certainty. Your tax rates may not necessarily decline as you move from work to retirement. The difference between your working and retirement incomes may not be that great, or tax rates in general may be higher when you retire. It's impossible to forecast tax code changes years or decades down the road. Focus on the known and direct effects of tax deferral—current savings and future growth—as you consider your desired TSP contribution levels.

MATCHING CONTRIBUTIONS AND TAX DEFERRAL EQUAL LONG-TERM GROWTH

The power of the TSP as a savings vehicle becomes clearer when we look at the combined effects of matching contributions and tax deferral working together over the life of your TSP account. Let's look again at our employee earning $30,000 a year, investing 5 percent of pay in the TSP over a 30-year period and earning a 7 percent annual rate of return on TSP investments.

Figure 3-6 shows the flow of new investments into the TSP account, the accumulation of investment earnings, the account balance at the end of each year, and the amount of taxes deferred assuming a 28 percent tax rate. The example is based on a constant $30,000 salary over a 30-year period. As you project your TSP account growth it's important to keep in mind its "real value" in today's dollars. So we've stripped away the future effects of inflation and pay raises by assuming that the two will be equal and offset each other (although judging from past caps on pay raises this may not be a safe assumption).

What about job promotions above and beyond cost-of-living increases? Yes, they will add to the future growth of your TSP account. But career patterns vary widely. Some employees will achieve only modest salary growth, in real terms, beyond their current levels. Others will receive a few promotions fairly quickly and then "top out" at a certain grade. Others will enjoy numerous promotions over an extended time. In Chapter Five we'll show you how to update your TSP account projections when you receive pay increases and how to estimate the effects of possible future promotions.

Tax-Deferred Growth of TSP Account Over 30 Years

$30,000 Salary, 5% of Pay TSP Deduction, 7% Investment Earnings, 28% Tax Rate

Year	Annual Investment Earnings	Taxes Deferred	Account Balance
5	$1,082	$816	$17,908
10	$2,725	$1,145	$43,023
15	$5,029	$1,606	$78,248
20	$8,261	$2,252	$127,652
25	$12,794	$3,159	$196,944
30	$19,152	$4,430	$294,131
30-Year Total	**$204,131**	**$58,843**	**$294,131**

Figure 3-6

In this example, the employee accumulates a 30-year ending balance of $294,131. Over that period the total value of all deferred taxes—on employee and agency contributions and on compounded investment earnings—is $58,843, 20 percent of the ending account balance. The employee pays those taxes as the account balance is received as income during retirement. But during the employee's career, the tax deferral greatly accelerates the growth of the account's value.

By comparison, an equivalent 30-year, $1,500 per year investment in an IRA or other tax-deferred investment would have an ending balance of $147,066, reflecting the absence of agency contributions. To make up for the TSP agency contributions, an IRA would have to realize consistently higher earnings—about 11 percent annually instead of 7 percent—to generate the TSP ending balance.

An equivalent investment in a non-deferred investment vehicle would have a 30-year ending balance of $99,584. A non-deferred investment without agency contributions would have to realize investment earnings of about 12 percent over the full 30-year period to match the TSP account's performance.

Two other aspects of this example deserve attention. Notice that over the 30-year investment period much of the total ending account balance is realized in the later years. The total ending balance in our example was $294,131. More than half of the total accrued in the last nine years of the 30-year period, and about one-third accrued in the final five years. The continual compounding of investment earnings means that lengthening your TSP investment period by even a few years can dramatically boost your ultimate account balance.

And, it means that the amount of money you're able to put into your TSP account early in your federal or postal career will play a large role in determining the size of your account at the end of your career. In our example, $22,161—7.5 percent—of the final balance of $294,131 was the product of compounded earnings on the original first-year investment.

This sequence of examples illustrates how the combined features of the TSP offer a compelling opportunity for devoting current dollars to an important future objective—retirement income security. In Chapter Five we'll look at your TSP investment options and the range of potential investment earnings you're likely to realize on your TSP account over time. In Chapter Six we'll talk about how to design and carry out a personal TSP strategy. And in Chapter Eight we'll look at what your choices are at the end of your federal or postal career, when you decide to "collect" your TSP account balance and translate it into retirement income.

SHOULD YOU BE INVESTING IN THE TSP? _____

The power of agency contributions and tax-deferred savings growth make the FERS TSP an overwhelmingly attractive opportunity. As a long-term savings mechanism it's difficult, if not impossible, to match. Over the mid-term the ability to obtain loans from your account balance protects against fears that your money will be completely "locked up" when you need it to meet important interim needs. And from a short-term perspective every dollar invested sooner rather than later prevents you from missing potential matching contributions and enjoys a longer period of compounded investment earnings.

So, rather than "should you be investing" in the FERS TSP, the more fruitful question to ask is "under what circumstances should you not be?" The simple answer, of course, is that you absolutely, positively cannot afford to because of pressing short-term financial constraints. The money just isn't there as you squeak by from paycheck to paycheck. If you feel a tight cash flow prevents you from investing in the TSP, it's worth taking the time to look at your financial situation with a cold, calculating eye. You might find possibilities that you didn't realize were there. In conducting this "financial review" you should be looking at two goals, in the following order:

◇ If at all possible, restructure your individual or family budget to "free up" as much of your paycheck as possible for TSP investments. Remember that up to 3 percent of pay, every dollar you find and save is really two dollars saved because of agency matching contributions. And percentages four and five of your salary that you save in the TSP are matched 50 cents on the dollar. In effect, you're forcing the government to give you a pay raise.

◇ If, after thorough review, you can't find room to save in your current budget, then turn your attention to coming up with a plan that will cut your expenses, increase your income or restructure your debts so that you can begin investing in the TSP as soon as possible.

Try to identify any "marginal" expenses that you can do without. For example, cutting back on the costs of dining out, delaying a new car purchase, scaling back vacation plans or refinancing loans are potentially useful places to start. Almost all of us can find some "soft" spots in our budgets if we search hard enough. Given what the TSP can do for you and your family over time, it's well worth looking.

If opportunities to cut spending just aren't there, you might want to consider the other side of the ledger—income. Even a modest part-time job commitment might be enough to tip the balance, take some pressure off your cash flow and enable you to begin investing in the long-term value of the TSP.

But if you simply cannot free up money for TSP payroll deductions right now, then turn your sights to the future. Look at your expenses and income again, but take a slightly longer view. Try to develop a specific plan that reduces expenses, increases income or chips away at your debts over a defined period with a realistic target. If you don't address the situation aggressively, you run the risk that circumstances will not change for the better anytime soon. And as months pass into years the lost savings potential of the TSP will grow larger and larger. Remember that every dollar of agency matching money is a dollar—plus future, tax-deferred earnings on that dollar—that you'll never be able to reclaim.

Don't simply say: "Well, we'll be able to afford the TSP when I get my raise next year." By the time your raise comes through prices will be up and there will be a hundred new places to spend your money. *If you can't invest today, plan today to invest tomorrow.*

If you are married, be sure to go through this planning exercise with your spouse and look at your joint resources and expenses. In particular, take a close look at your choices if your spouse also has a long-term savings plan at his or her job. Some employer-sponsored savings plans are superior to the TSP, but many are not. If you and your spouse have two different savings plans available but limited funds to invest right now, take a close look at where your available funds should go. Focus on the TSP matching formula and any matching formula in your spouse's plan. Remember, your 1 percent automatic contribution is locked in—compare the matching formula above and beyond the automatic 1 percent. In the TSP you can get an additional 3 percent agency match by investing only 3 percent of pay because the initial matching rate is dollar-for-dollar. And you can obtain 4 percent in additional matching funds by investing 5 percent of your pay.

There may be some very specific situations in which putting off investing in the TSP is the logical thing to do. In general these would be situations in which there is a clearly better use of your money for a defined purpose and time period. For example, you may be spending your last dime on current education that will increase your earnings potential within a reasonable timeframe. By all means look for another way to finance your schooling. But if none is available, your potential gains may outweigh the TSP in the short-term. Or you may need to retain as much income and readily available savings for a specific short-term requirement, such as a down payment on a house. Here too the immediate financial goal may warrant a slight delay in TSP investment. Remember, though, to set a specific target for when you'll be able to begin participating in the TSP. Then do what you need to do to meet that target.

A final caution. If it takes you some time—and more than a little effort and sacrifice—before you start investing in the TSP, try to anticipate and avoid any situations that would force you to stop your payroll deductions once they're underway. For example, if you strain to get your TSP contributions up to 5 percent of pay, try to build up an "emergency fund" of ready cash. You don't want a short-term event—such as a car repair bill or the need to replace furniture—to disrupt your long-term TSP strategy. Once you stop your TSP contributions, it may take you quite a while to resume them again. Try to plot and sustain a steady course.

If you are unable to make TSP contributions, your potential gains from the program will be very limited. If you receive only the 1 percent of pay automatic agency contribution, and realize 7 percent real annual returns on your TSP investments, it will take about 30 years to build up savings equal to one year's salary. If you only realize a 4 percent real rate of return, it would take you about 40 years to build up one year's salary.

HOW MUCH SHOULD YOU INVEST? _____

The availability of agency matching contributions determines the best level of investment for most FERS employees. Because these matching contributions give you the opportunity to "leverage" your payroll deductions to obtain additional savings growth from the government, a TSP investment level of at least 5 percent of pay is advantageous for all FERS employees, with only two exceptions:

◇ You should not jump to a 5 percent of pay TSP investment unless you are confident that you'll be able to manage this payroll deduction comfortably every pay period. There's little point in pushing aggressively to a 5 percent savings rate if it's going to lead to undue strain and force you to reduce or discontinue your TSP investments. If you are not comfortable initially with a 5 percent payroll deduction, make every effort to attain at least a 3 percent deduction, matched dollar-for-dollar by your agency.

◇ A 5 percent of pay TSP deduction may not be advisable if you have important short-term financial needs. For example, you may need to finance a new home or pay medical bills or tuition fees, and your TSP account isn't large enough yet to serve as a significant loan source. You may want to invest less than 5 percent of pay in the TSP until that specific financial hurdle has been overcome. Calculate carefully and explore any possibilities for reducing expenses or increasing income. Invest 5 percent of pay in the TSP if you can, but invest less if you must.

The more difficult question for many FERS employees will be whether it is worthwhile to extend TSP investments beyond 5 percent of pay. Remember, agency matching contributions reach their maximum when you invest 5 percent of pay. Anything you invest between 5 percent and 10 percent of pay will not generate any further agency contributions. But because of the tax-deferred status of the TSP it may be advantageous to invest as much as you can in the TSP.

Once you've reached the 5 percent of pay level and guaranteed maximum matching contributions, take a careful look at your overall financial picture before you rush beyond 5 percent of pay. You may wish to invest that extra money in an IRA with its greater range of investment choices—especially if you qualify for full tax deductibility of your IRA contributions. Take advantage of matching contributions in a spouse's 401(k) plan, if available—or your spouse's TSP, if he or she also happens to be a FERS federal or postal employee. Or you may want to keep your extra money in more liquid investments.

In particular, think about your complete financial needs and the full range of investments that might help you meet them. Look at the adequacy of your short-term "emergency fund" and your possible need for a medium-term "buffer fund."

Eventually you'll enjoy the added flexibility of access to your TSP account for certain loan purposes. But the loan program will not offer a substantial "buffer fund" until you've invested in the TSP for several years. If your medium-term needs are likely to arise before you're eligible for a substantial TSP loan, then other, more liquid investments might be advisable. For example, mutual funds may provide good medium-term growth potential with the assurance that you can sell some of your shares if you need to.

As you're considering whether or how much to extend your TSP contributions beyond 5 percent of pay, review several specific factors:

◇ Check to see if your total finances are balanced among short-term, medium-term and long-term goals. See Chapter One for a model framework linking savings goals and investment vehicles.

◇ Compare the features of the TSP with other investment opportunities. See Chapter Two for a comparison of the TSP with other investments in terms of returns, investment control, tax treatment and liquidity. Then turn to Chapter Five for more details on the three TSP investment funds.

◇ Project your TSP account growth and your resulting loan eligibility. Chapter Seven covers how the TSP loan program works. If your medium-term needs involve expenses that qualify for TSP loans, build up your TSP account to make sure you reach your loan targets.

As you progress through your federal or postal career, your long-term employment plans and retirement expectations should become increasingly focused. In the early years of your career your main TSP objective should be rapid build-up of your account to obtain the benefits of a long compounding period. As the years pass and your TSP account grows, you'll be able to gauge more closely whether that growth is above or below your retirement income goals.

There is one specific instance in which you should not invest 10 percent of pay in the TSP. Your maximum allowable contribution to the TSP is 10 percent of your pay or an annually adjusted IRS limit, whichever is less. If you are a very highly-paid employee you may be subject to the IRS limit ($9,240 in 1994).

If your 1994 salary is above $92,400 and you invest 10 percent of pay in the TSP every pay period, you would hit the IRS limit at some point late in the year. The TSP would have to stop accepting your contributions to the TSP for the remainder of the year. As a result, you would not obtain maximum matching contributions from your agency. Set your salary deduction so that you will be eligible to invest—and get matching contributions—all year.

ESTIMATING YOUR TSP ACCOUNT AND RETIREMENT INCOME

The size of your account balance at the end of your FERS career will depend on a wide range of variables—your current salary and future pay increases, how your TSP investments perform, whether you periodically increase or reduce your contributions, your age when you withdraw your TSP account, and so on. But it is possible to draw a general picture of your TSP growth potential and what it means in terms of your annual retirement income.

It's important that you have at least a general notion of your expectations as you participate in the TSP. That will enable you to monitor your account growth, measure whether you're progressing in line with your long-term target and give you a basis for considering possible adjustments to your TSP strategy.

We'll discuss your TSP strategy in more detail in Chapter Six. For now, let's get a general fix on how the TSP might work for FERS employees at different ages and salary levels.

If you're in the TSP for a relatively brief period—five or 10 years—the size of your final account balance will depend primarily on the amount of your contributions and resulting agency contributions. Earnings on your investments will add to your TSP account, but differences in investment earnings will not be as important as the basic level of money flowing into your account.

If you're in the TSP for a longer period, two factors will greatly affect your final account balance. First, how your TSP investments perform may dramatically raise or lower the compounded growth of your account over time. Second, over a longer career, the pattern of your future promotions and pay increases will affect your contribution levels.

To give you a basic picture of your TSP potential, we've developed two scenarios for the growth of your account. Both are based on "real dollars"—dollars with today's purchasing power. In other words, we've eliminated the effects of future inflation on your account growth, and looked instead at what your account will be relative to what a dollar is worth today.

In the case of investment earnings, that means looking at the "real return" on your TSP investments over and above inflation. For example, if your TSP investments provide 7 percent earnings over the course of a year, but there was 3 percent price inflation that year, the real gain on your investments was 4 percent. Similarly, your future salary increases will consist partly of adjustments to roughly keep up with the cost of living. You may also receive grade or step increases that raise your salary in real terms, above inflation.

Figures 3-7 and 3-8 depict the potential growth of your account under two scenarios. Both sets of figures include agency contributions of 5 percent, under the current matching formula. Remember that this formula is subject to change.

Two Growth Scenarios
for Your TSP Account

Conservative:
4 Percent Real Account Growth Each Year

In this scenario, your account grows by 4 percent per year above the inflation rate. This represents a conservative outlook in which your TSP investments earn a modest real rate of return and you receive grade or step increases every few years that enable your salary to grow a bit above the cost of living.

Growth Potential:
7 Percent Real Account Growth Each Year

In this scenario, your account grows by 7 percent per year above the inflation rate. This could occur through various combinations of investment performance and salary increases. It is a realistic potential growth level in light of historical investment returns, even without extensive grade or step promotions.

Figure 3-7

Figure 3-8 shows your approximate final account balance if you consistently contribute 5 percent of pay to the TSP. It includes a range of salary levels and number of years in the TSP. You can approximate your own circumstances by comparing the figures from two sections. For example, if your salary is $25,000, your approximate TSP balance would be about halfway between the amounts for the $20,000 and $30,000 salary levels.

Estimated TSP Account Balances
Under Two Growth Scenarios

For Employee Contributing 5% of Pay to the TSP

$20,000 Salary	Conservative 4% Real Growth/ Year	Growth Potential 7% Real Growth/ Year
5 Years	$11,000	$12,000
10 Years	$25,000	$29,000
15 Years	$41,000	$53,000
20 Years	$61,000	$87,000
25 Years	$86,000	$136,000
30 Years	$116,000	$205,000
35 Years	$153,000	$302,000
40 Years	$198,000	$440,000

$30,000 Salary	Conservative 4% Real Growth/ Year	Growth Potential 7% Real Growth/ Year
5 Years	$16,000	$18,000
10 Years	$37,000	$44,000
15 Years	$61,000	$80,000
20 Years	$91,000	$130,000
25 Years	$129,000	$204,000
30 Years	$174,000	$308,000
35 Years	$229,000	$453,000
40 Years	$297,000	$660,000

$40,000 Salary	Conservative 4% Real Growth/ Year	Growth Potential 7% Real Growth/ Year
5 Years	$22,000	$24,000
10 Years	$50,000	$58,000
15 Years	$82,000	$106,000
20 Years	$122,000	$174,000
25 Years	$172,000	$272,000
30 Years	$232,000	$410,000
35 Years	$306,000	$604,000
40 Years	$396,000	$880,000

$50,000 Salary	Conservative 4% Real Growth/ Year	Growth Potential 7% Real Growth/ Year
5 Years	$28,000	$30,000
10 Years	$63,000	$73,000
15 Years	$103,000	$133,000
20 Years	$153,000	$218,000
25 Years	$215,000	$340,000
30 Years	$290,000	$513,000
35 Years	$383,000	$755,000
40 Years	$495,000	$1,100,000

Figure 3-8

These figures give you a preliminary read on your likely range of potential account growth. Appendix 2 provides a more detailed set of tables for computing your expected account balance under various circumstances.

What do these projected account balances mean in terms of additional retirement income? That again depends on several factors, including your age when your retire, how you withdraw your TSP account and translate it into income, interest and investment conditions when you retire, whether you spend some of your account balance to buy survivor protection and so on.

But let's go ahead with a simplified picture to give some points of reference as you think about your TSP participation. The following table shows approximate retirement incomes based on an account balance of $100,000. The amounts are based on a "single life annuity"—lifetime income from when you buy the annuity until you die—with annual annuity increases of 3 percent to keep up with inflation after you retire.

Retirement Income at Various Retirement Ages

Account Balance $100,000, Buying Single Life Annuity at 8% Interest with 3% COLA

Payments Begin At	Annual Income	Monthly Income
Age 55	$7,600	$635
Age 60	$8,400	$700
Age 62	$8,800	$730
Age 65	$9,500	$790
Age 70	$11,000	$915

Figure 3-9

You can use Figures 3-8 and 3-9 to get a "quick read" on your projected TSP account and the additional retirement income it could provide. Take the range of your expected outcomes from Figure 3-8 and then refer to Figure 3-9 to see what that account might buy you in retirement. For example, if you project an account balance of $250,000, multiply the amounts in Figure 3-9 by 2.5 (that is, $250,000 divided by $100,000). Don't worry about a precise calculation. But establish a basic reference point as you consider your TSP participation and your retirement income expectations.

We've used examples based on a 5 percent of pay contribution to the TSP. You can use the worksheets in Appendix 2 to develop estimates based on other contribution levels.

TSP PARTICIPATION OF FERS EMPLOYEES

The history of employee participation in the TSP reflects the necessity and popularity of the plan as a retirement savings mechanism. The percentage of FERS employees investing in the TSP through payroll deductions has increased steadily since the plan's inception in 1987.

There are about 1.2 million federal and postal employees covered under FERS. Of these, about 70 percent invest in the TSP through payroll deductions and the other 30 percent only receive automatic 1 percent of pay contributions from their employing agencies.

Figure 3-10 shows the steady growth in TSP participation among FERS employees since 1987.

Since 1987 the total number of federal and postal employees covered under FERS has roughly doubled, from under 600,000 to about 1.2 million. As employees covered under CSRS retire or separate from government service, they are replaced by new FERS employees. Over time FERS coverage will be the clearly dominate retirement system of the federal and postal work force.

But while the FERS work force was doubling, the number of FERS employees investing their own money in the TSP grew more than fivefold—from 163,000 in 1987 to 831,000 in 1993. The percentage of all FERS employees investing in the TSP increased from 29 percent in 1987 to 70 percent in 1993, climbing steadily over the entire period.

TSP Participation Among FERS Employees

(Numbers in Thousands)

Year	Total FERS Employees	Contributing Own Money No.	%	Not Contributing (Agency 1% Only) No.	%
1988	651	291	44.7%	360	55.3%
1989	807	390	48.3%	417	51.7%
1990	932	503	53.9%	429	46.1%
1991	1,027	609	59.3%	418	40.7%
1992	1,137	738	64.9%	399	35.1%
1993	1,188	831	70.0%	357	30.0%

Figure 3-10

In part, the growth in participation reflects the fact that the FERS work force as a whole is becoming older and working in higher grade and pay levels. In general, the older and higher-paid you are the more likely you are to invest in the TSP. As you age you're more likely to focus on retirement planning, and as your pay increases you'll likely find it easier to set aside some current income for retirement savings.

Figure 3-11 shows how age affects TSP participation among FERS employees.

TSP Participation by Age, FERS Employees

Age Group	Contributing to the TSP	Average % of Pay Deferred Contributors	All Employees
20-29	52%	4.3%	2.2%
30-39	63%	5.1%	3.2%
40-49	68%	5.7%	3.9%
50-59	77%	6.8%	5.2%
60-69	81%	7.4%	6.0%
70 +	72%	7.7%	5.5%
All FERS Employees	63%	5.4%	3.4%

Figure 3-11

The likelihood of investing in the TSP increases steadily as FERS employees become older. Likewise, older FERS employees are more likely to extend their TSP payroll deductions beyond 5 percent of pay. Many younger employees focus on reaching the 5 percent of pay level to obtain maximum agency matching contributions, but are less likely to make additional, unmatched investments.

Figure 3-12 shows a similar pattern of TSP participation at different salary levels.

TSP Participation by Salary, FERS Employees

Salary ($1,000s)	Contributing to the TSP	Average % of Pay Deferred	
		Contributors	All Employees
10-19	42%	4.3%	1.8%
20-29	61%	5.2%	3.2%
30-39	78%	5.8%	4.5%
40-49	86%	6.2%	5.3%
50-59	90%	6.7%	6.0%
60-69	87%	7.1%	6.2%
70 +	88%	7.5%	6.6%
All FERS Employees	**63%**	**5.4%**	**3.4%**

Figure 3-12

Higher-paid FERS employees are more likely to invest in the TSP and to invest larger percentages of pay. Lower-paid workers are less likely to participate, but many of those who do manage to invest in the TSP are able to reach the 5 percent of pay level to obtain maximum agency matching funds.

It is likely that these general patterns will continue in the future. This is unfortunate in that younger workers are in a position to benefit substantially from the TSP by having a longer period of compounded investment earnings. The longer they wait before participating in the TSP, the more they are sacrificing the advantages of a long compounding period and the benefits of agency matching contributions.

Likewise, it's understandable that lower-paid workers find it more difficult to "free up" money for investment in the TSP. But the best way for a lower-paid worker to take advantage of the TSP is to get as close to a 5 percent of pay (fully matched) payroll deduction as early in a career as possible. Even small early-year investments can yield significant long-term results.

The evidence suggests that the basic question faced by FERS employees is whether or not to invest in the TSP at all. Almost two-thirds of those who do decide to participate in the TSP reach the 5 percent of pay deduction level that results in maximum agency matching funds.

Among FERS employees who invest at all in the TSP, 83 percent reach the 3 percent of pay level which agencies match dollar-for-dollar, and 64 percent reach the 5 percent of pay level needed to obtain maximum matching funds. Of those who choose to make TSP deductions over 5 percent of pay, most jump all the way up to the maximum 10 percent of pay deduction.

TSP Deferrals by FERS Employees

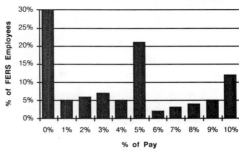

Figure 3-13

Overall, TSP participation rates have been steadily increasing. Among the FERS employees who first became eligible to invest in the TSP in July 1988, the participation rate increased from 24.6 percent in 1988 to 42.2 percent in 1989, 54.3 percent in 1990 and 63.5 percent in 1991. This suggests that newly hired FERS employees go through a phase in which they gradually become more aware of the TSP and figure out how to incorporate TSP investments into their finances.

5 THINGS TO DO

1. If you are contributing less than 3 percent of pay to the TSP, review your entire budget carefully to find a way to reach a 3 percent payroll deduction as quickly as possible. Passing up 100 percent matching contributions now will substantially reduce your compounded earnings and your potential final account balance.

2. If you're currently contributing 3 percent or 4 percent of pay, push ahead to a 5 percent deduction at your first opportunity. Even though the matching rate declines from 100 percent to 50 percent on these contributions, that still provides a nearly unbeatable return on your investment.

3. Estimate your final account balance using a conservative assumption about future growth. Start with a 4 percent annual growth rate as your benchmark. Then you might want to use higher growth assumptions to start understanding investment returns and their potential impact on your TSP account.

4. Break down your estimate to see what your account balance will look like at various stages of your career. This will give you a sense of your "walk away" value if you decide to change your career plans. It may also give you an idea of how much you'll be able to borrow from your TSP account at various points.

5. Think about your estimated account balance as retirement income. It's easy to look at a $250,000 or $500,000 projected account balance and fall prey to the deception of large numbers. Take the time to translate the big number into its actual value as a source of income after you retire.

◈4◈ THE TSP FOR CSRS EMPLOYEES

The TSP for employees under CSRS differs from the FERS TSP in two major ways. First, there are no agency contributions to the accounts of CSRS participants. Second, CSRS employees may invest only up to 5 percent of basic pay through payroll deductions, rather than the 10 percent of pay maximum for FERS employees. There are also a few other administrative differences concerning spousal notification and other matters.

The two major differences highlight the essential distinction between the roles of the TSP for FERS and CSRS employees. For FERS employees the TSP is an essential part of the total retirement package. For CSRS employees the TSP is a supplement to the retirement benefits provided through the basic CSRS pension formula. Congress clearly and intentionally incorporated this distinction in the design of the TSP.

When the FERS legislation took effect in 1987, virtually all federal and postal workers who began employment in 1984 or later were automatically covered under FERS and its TSP provisions. Employees already covered under CSRS at that time were given an opportunity to choose between remaining under CSRS or transferring to FERS coverage. The overwhelming majority of CSRS employees decided to remain under CSRS.

CSRS employees with lengthy federal or postal careers enjoy substantial retirement benefits from the basic CSRS pension. But many have decided to use the TSP as an additional source of retirement income. As of September 1993, more than 600,000 CSRS employees were investing in the TSP to enhance their long-term savings potential.

THE TSP AND YOUR CSRS RETIREMENT INCOME _____

CSRS employees enjoy the security and predictability of a "defined benefit" pension formula based on years of service and salary level. CSRS employees therefore are able to project with a high degree of accuracy the benefits they will receive at their expected retirement date.

CSRS annuities pay a fixed percentage of "high-three" average salary—the average salary for the highest three consecutive years of earnings. The percentage paid as a pension is a simple calculation based on years of federal and/or postal service.

Figure 4-1 shows the basic structure of CSRS retirement benefits. Under normal retirement rules, you become eligible to retire at designated ages if you have a certain amount of service.

CSRS Retirement Benefits as ____ a Percentage of High-3 Salary ____

Years of Service	You Can Retire at	CSRS Benefit as % of High-3
5	Age 62	7.50%
10	Age 62	16.25%
15	Age 62	26.25%
20	Age 60	36.25%
25	Age 60	46.25%
30	Age 55	56.25%
35	Age 55	66.25%
40		76.25%

Figure 4-1

Under this benefit formula CSRS employees with varying career patterns are able to build substantial retirement income exclusively or primarily through federal or postal employment. For example, employees who retire at age 55 with 30 years of service—the earliest "normal" retirement age for most employees—receive a defined CSRS benefit equal to 56.25 percent of high-three salary. They may also enjoy additional retirement income—other pensions or Social Security—from work before or after their government careers.

CSRS employees with still longer federal or postal careers—for example, those retiring at age 62 with 35 years of service or at age 65 with 40 years of service, receive even higher levels of guaranteed retirement income. They may require relatively little in additional benefits or savings to achieve and maintain financial security after retirement.

In this context the "restricted" TSP for CSRS employees offers a chance to build additional retirement savings. For those who remain with the government to retirement, TSP account balances can be translated directly into retirement income. For those in the middle of their careers, the TSP may offer some career flexibility by providing a pool of retirement savings that will keep its value whether they remain with the government or not.

Let's suppose that your retirement income goal is to "replace" 80 percent of your pre-retirement income. This 80 percent figure is a commonly used benchmark of a minimum, adequate retirement income. The reasoning behind the 80 percent figure is that when you retire you'll no longer have to pay certain work-related expenses, such as transportation, food and clothing costs. You may also face somewhat lower income taxes due to age-based exemptions. You can maintain your pre-retirement standard of living with slightly less income, the reasoning goes.

There's no need to fix the 80 percent target in concrete. As you approach retirement you should measure your minimum income requirements carefully anyway. You may have major expenses such as medical bills, a high mortgage payment or college costs for your children. You might also want to consider your expected retirement activities—for example, recreation, education or travel—and how they might affect your retirement income needs. Think of the 80 percent as a minimum benchmark and build from there as you plan your retirement finances.

Figure 4-2 shows your CSRS retirement income with varying years of service. It then shows how much additional retirement income you would need to reach the 80 percent replacement benchmark. In these examples, we've added 4.5 months of extra retirement credit for unused sick leave, equal to 0.75 percent of your high-three average salary (this is available to CSRS employees only).

Examples of Retirement Income Targets for CSRS Employees

| | Years of Credited CSRS Service | | | | |
	20	25	30	35	40
Retirement Goal as % of High-3	80%	80%	80%	80%	80%
CSRS Pension as % of High-3	37%	47%	57%	67%	77%
Needed from Other Sources	43%	33%	23%	13%	3%

Figure 4-2

As you plan for your retirement under CSRS, think carefully about your expected retirement age and your guaranteed retirement benefits. If you have Social Security coverage from work outside the government, contact the Social Security Administration to obtain an estimate of your projected benefits. Your federal annuity might offset some or all of your Social Security benefit. The calculation of your Social Security benefits may involve the "windfall benefit" and/or "government pension offset" provisions. Information about these provisions and your projected Social Security benefits is available through the Social Security Administration.

Once you have an approximate estimate of your CSRS and Social Security benefits (if any), you can assess the value of the TSP from a more informed perspective. If your known retirement benefits are not as substantial as you'd like them to be, the TSP's tax-deferred savings opportunity can be an important supplement to your long-term savings. The sooner you evaluate your situation, the more you'll be able to take advantage of the TSP's compounded investment earnings.

ADVANTAGES OF THE TSP FOR CSRS EMPLOYEES

The critical point for CSRS employees thinking about the TSP is to approach your decision-making from a thoughtful perspective. Yes, the TSP for CSRS employees is limited in two key respects compared to its FERS counterpart—there are no agency contributions to your account and your maximum investment level is 5 percent of pay.

But all the other advantages of the TSP are available to CSRS employees—convenient payroll deductions, investment diversity, flexible options when you "cash-out" your account and access to loans for important financial needs during your career. Add to these the major advantage of having your TSP investments and compounded earnings accumulate on a tax-deferred basis, and you still have a plan that compares favorably with many other outside investment opportunities.

Even without agency contributions to your account, the 🔑 *impact of tax deferral on your current cash flow and future account growth is still considerable.* For example, if you invest $2,000 in the TSP, and you have a 28% tax rate, you effectively reduce the cost of your investment by $560, making the TSP investment more affordable. Over time, as this initial investment grows in value, the deferral of taxes on investment earnings adds substantially to the long-term value of the initial investment.

The tax-deferred status of the TSP can combine with compounded investment earnings to generate substantial account growth over long investment periods. You will ultimately pay taxes on the account balance when it is received as income—at retirement, when you may be in a lower tax bracket. Along the way tax deferral greatly enhances the compounded growth of the account by giving you a larger accumulation of investment earnings to compound each year.

Tax deferral does not mean you avoid paying taxes on the growth of your TSP investments. But by paying the tax after the investment period rather than during the investment period, you realize a significant long-term gain.

If you are a CSRS employee in the latter stages of your federal or postal career, it is important to be realistic about the savings potential of the TSP. Even with consistently good investment performance, there are limits to how big an account you'll be able to build up over five or 10 years. Nonetheless, you still have the opportunity to build a supplement to your retirement income or a pool of capital that may serve other financial goals.

If you are a younger CSRS employee, the TSP demands your careful consideration. First, your longer time until retirement gives you a more substantial savings opportunity. Second, if your long-term career plans include the possibility of leaving government service for other employment, the TSP can help you build an adequate total retirement package. TSP savings can enhance your income security and your career flexibility.

Wherever you are in your career, the TSP deserves your consideration as a potentially useful savings option. But decisions about whether and how much to invest are less clear for CSRS employees than they are for FERS employees.

For example, many IRAs offer advantages similar to the CSRS TSP. If you're already comfortably settled into a regular pattern of contributions to an IRA with satisfactory investment performance, and you don't have additional money to devote to the TSP, you may decide to maintain your current course.

But remember that you may not get as large a tax deferral advantage through an IRA. Depending on your income level, you may only be able to defer taxes on investment earnings in an IRA, compared to the full deferral of taxes on contributions and investment earnings under the TSP. Also, the TSP's loan program may be valuable to you. You cannot make any temporary withdrawals from an IRA before age 59 1/2 without paying tax on the withdrawal plus a 10 percent penalty.

You may attach great value to "liquidity"—the ability to gain unrestricted access to your funds on short notice—and conclude that this feature of a money market account, mutual fund or other investment is better for you than the TSP. If you expect to be a long-service CSRS employee with a substantial guaranteed retirement benefit, your short-term emergency fund and your medium-term buffer fund may be higher savings priorities than additional retirement income. If so, other investments may suit your financial goals better than the TSP.

Weigh these considerations carefully, focusing directly on the issue of retirement income. Remember, different investments are best suited to meet different objectives. If you have income to invest for the long run, the TSP offers an attractive way to accumulate deferred income. If the question is how best to allot a more limited supply of funds, you must measure which investment vehicles best fit your financial priorities.

SHOULD YOU INVEST IN THE TSP?

Under the limited supplemental TSP for CSRS employees the decision about whether to invest can be more complicated and a closer call than for FERS employees. There may be alternative uses for your investable income that better suit your situation and goals.

But it's not a "flip a coin" question. There are serious questions you should consider in weighing the TSP against other investment opportunities. Start with a careful assessment of your current career situation, future career plans and retirement income expectations. In particular, you may begin with the following questions and considerations:

◇ Do you expect to remain in federal/postal employment straight through to retirement?

◇ When will you be eligible to retire? Do you plan to work beyond first eligibility to a later retirement date?

◇ What will your CSRS benefits be at your expected retirement date? Will that be an adequate retirement income by itself, or do you need to be building a supplemental source of retirement income? If you are married, remember to consider your spouse's retirement coverage when thinking about your expected retirement income.

◇ If you're unsure about the adequacy of your projected retirement income, you should isolate retirement income as a specific financial objective. The tax-deferred status of the TSP and IRAs make them advantageous for long-term savings purposes. Your focus on supplemental retirement income may tilt your investment priorities toward one or both of these savings vehicles.

◇ If you're not concerned about a retirement income shortfall, you're freer to compare the TSP to other investment opportunities, looking at variables such as profitability, risk, liquidity and short-term versus long-term growth potential.

◇ If you're not planning to stay with the government until retirement—or you want to keep your options open—your retirement planning becomes all the more important. You may leave federal/postal employment eligible for a deferred CSRS pension, but that annuity will lose some of its purchasing power to inflation by the time you begin receiving it. And depending on your age, you may not have much time to build up another pension with your new employer. *The TSP may become a very important retirement supplement for you. When you separate from government service you'll be able to take your TSP account with you by transferring it to an IRA or another TSP-like savings plan.*

If developing supplemental retirement income is high on your financial priority list, you should focus on it as soon as possible. A thoughtful decision now may help you avoid a more fearful decision down the road, when you have much less time to reorient your retirement income planning.

Start with conservative assumptions about your TSP retirement account growth. If you prudently begin planning to supplement your retirement income through the TSP, and then end up at retirement with more money than you expected—well, worse things have happened.

If additional retirement income is a priority, then the TSP, an IRA or a spouse's 401(k) program, if available, probably represent the best investment opportunities—alone or in combination. If you conclude that retirement income is not a high priority for your savings planning, you may turn your attention to other investments that offer more ready access to your funds.

For example, your retirement income projections may be reassuring and you might be more concerned about current financial needs or saving for a boat, a vacation home, or financing your own business. In this case, more flexible investments with competitive growth potential may be more appealing than the retirement-oriented features of the TSP.

HOW MUCH SHOULD YOU INVEST?

The pattern of actual TSP deductions among CSRS employees is clear and revealing. Of those participating in the TSP, more than 70 percent are investing at the maximum level of 5 percent of pay. The remainder are distributed fairly evenly across the range of 1 percent to 4 percent investment levels. Undoubtedly many CSRS participants would invest more than 5 percent of pay in the TSP if allowed to do so.

Another pattern also is informative: Older and higher-paid employees tend to invest more. Older employees are more likely to be thinking of retirement than younger workers. Higher-paid employees are more likely to have the disposable income to afford maximum TSP investment levels.

If you can afford to, it makes sense to accelerate your TSP account growth as early as possible in your potential compounding period. Be as aggressive as you can at first, then scale back later on if you need to address other financial goals. This is preferable to investing at low levels in early years and then trying to catch up later. However, be sure to invest at a level you can afford. You don't want to make the maximum contribution only to have to stop investing altogether after discovering you can't live on your remaining income. Once you stop investing in the TSP, it can be many months before you can start again.

Quite obviously, your current financial circumstances will in large measure determine the level of TSP contributions you can afford. The primary focus of your contribution strategy is how important additional retirement income is compared to other financial goals.

ESTIMATING YOUR TSP ACCOUNT AND RETIREMENT INCOME

The exact amount of your account balance at the end of your career will depend on a wide range of variables—your current salary and future pay increases, how your TSP investments perform, whether you periodically increase or reduce your contributions, your age when you withdraw your TSP account and so on. But it's possible to draw a general picture of your TSP growth potential and what it means in terms of your annual retirement income. And it's important that you have at least a general notion of your expectations as you participate in the TSP. That will enable you to monitor your account growth, measure whether you're progressing in line with your long-term target and give you a basis for considering possible adjustments to your TSP strategy.

If you're in the TSP for only a brief period of time—five or 10 years—your final account balance will depend primarily on the amount of your contributions and resulting agency contributions. Earnings on your investments will add to your TSP account, but differences in investment earnings will not be as important as the basic level of money flowing into your account.

However, if you're in the TSP for longer periods, then two factors will have a major impact on your ultimate account balances. First, how your TSP investments perform may dramatically affect the compounded growth of your account over time. Second, over a longer career, the pattern of your future promotions and pay increases will affect your contribution levels.

Two Growth Scenarios for Your TSP Account

**Conservative Baseline:
4 Percent Real Account Growth Each Year**

In this scenario, your account grows by 4 percent per year above the inflation rate. This represents a conservative outlook in which your TSP investments earn a modest real rate of return and you receive grade or step increases every few years that enable your salary to grow a bit above the cost of living .

**Realistic Growth Potential:
7 Percent Real Account Growth Each Year**

In this scenario, your account grows by 7 percent per year above inflation. This could occur through various combinations of investment performance and salary increases. It is a realistic potential growth level in light of historical investment returns, even without extensive grade or step promotions.

Figure 4-3

To give you a basic picture of your TSP potential, we've developed two scenarios for the growth of your account. Both are based on "real dollars"—dollars with today's purchasing power. In other words, we've eliminated the effects of future inflation (by assuming that your basic salary growth will match it, although past caps on pay raises have allowed inflation to surge ahead of civil service pay raises), and looked instead at what your account will be relative to what a dollar is worth today.

In the case of investment earnings, that means looking at the "real return" on your TSP investments, over and above inflation. For example, if your TSP investments provide 7 percent earnings over a year, but there is 3 percent price inflation that year, the real gain on your investments was 4 percent.

Similarly, you may also receive future grade or step salary increases that raise your salary in real terms, over and above simply keeping up with the cost of living.

Figure 4-4 shows your approximate final account balance if you consistently contribute 5 percent of pay to the TSP. It includes a range of salary levels and number of years in the TSP. You can estimate your own circumstances by comparing the figures from two sections. For example, if your salary is $25,000, your approximate TSP balance would be about halfway between the amounts for the $20,000 and $30,000 salary levels.

Estimated TSP Account Balances Under Two Growth Scenarios For Employee Contributing 5% of Pay to the TSP

$20,000 Salary	Conservative 4% Real Growth/ Year	Growth Potential 7% Real Growth/ Year
5 Years	$6,000	$6,000
10 Years	$12,000	$15,000
15 Years	$21,000	$27,000
20 Years	$31,000	$44,000
25 Years	$43,000	$68,000
30 Years	$58,000	$102,000
35 Years	$76,000	$151,000
40 Years	$99,000	$220,000

$30,000 Salary	Conservative 4% Real Growth/ Year	Growth Potential 7% Real Growth/ Year
5 Years	$8,000	$9,000
10 Years	$18,000	$22,000
15 Years	$30,000	$40,000
20 Years	$45,000	$65,000
25 Years	$64,000	$102,000
30 Years	$87,000	$154,000
35 Years	$114,000	$227,000
40 Years	$148,000	$330,000

$40,000 Salary	Conservative 4% Real Growth/ Year	Growth Potential 7% Real Growth/ Year
5 Years	$11,000	$12,000
10 Years	$25,000	$29,000
15 Years	$41,000	$53,000
20 Years	$61,000	$87,000
25 Years	$86,000	$136,000
30 Years	$116,000	$205,000
35 Years	$153,000	$302,000
40 Years	$198,000	$440,000

$50,000 Salary	Conservative 4% Real Growth/ Year	Growth Potential 7% Real Growth/ Year
5 Years	$14,000	$15,000
10 Years	$31,000	$37,000
15 Years	$51,000	$67,000
20 Years	$76,000	$109,000
25 Years	$107,000	$170,000
30 Years	$145,000	$257,000
35 Years	$191,000	$378,000
40 Years	$247,000	$550,000

Figure 4-4

These figures give you a preliminary read on your likely range of potential account growth. Appendix 3 provides a more detailed set of tables for computing your expected account balance under various circumstances.

What do these projected account balances mean in terms of additional retirement income? That again depends on several factors, including your age when you retire, exactly how you withdraw your TSP account and translate it into income, interest, tax and investment conditions when you retire, whether you spend some of your account balance to buy survivor protection and so on.

But let's go ahead with a simplified picture to give some points of reference as you think about your TSP participation. The following table shows approximate retirement incomes based on an account balance of $100,000. The amounts are based on a "single life annuity"—lifetime income from when you buy the annuity until you die—with annual annuity increases of 3 percent to keep up with inflation after you retire.

Retirement Income at Various Retirement Ages

Account Balance $100,000, Single Life Annuity at 8% Interest with 3% COLA

Payments Begin At	Annual Income	Monthly Income
Age 55	$7,600	$635
Age 60	$8,400	$700
Age 62	$8,800	$730
Age 65	$9,500	$790
Age 70	$11,000	$915

Figure 4-5

You can use Figures 4-4 and 4-5 to get a "quick read" on your projected TSP account and the additional retirement income it could provide. Take the range of your expected outcomes from Figure 4-4 and then refer to Figure 4-5 to see what that account might buy you in retirement. Don't get obsessed with a precise calculation. There are many variables that will affect the evolution of your account over time. But these tables will give you a basic reference point as you consider your TSP participation.

A WORD ABOUT
CSRS VOLUNTARY CONTRIBUTIONS

CSRS employees—and employees retiring and awaiting final OPM adjudication of their CSRS benefits—are eligible to make additional voluntary contributions to their retirement. Unlike the TSP, voluntary contributions do not have to be made through regular payroll deductions. Instead, you can voluntarily contribute any amount (in multiples of $25) whenever you can afford it. The maximum you are allowed to contribute is 10 percent of your total career salary while under CSRS. There is no comparable voluntary program for FERS employees.

A voluntary contribution account accrues earnings at specified annual interest rates, and is partially tax-advantaged. Unlike the TSP, your voluntary contributions are not tax-deferred. A voluntary contribution of $1,000 costs you $1,000 because it comes out of already taxed salary. In contrast, $1,000 you put in the TSP costs less than $1,000 because of the TSP tax deduction. For example, if your tax rate is 28 percent, your $1,000 in TSP contributions has a net current cost of $720—$1,000 minus $280 in reduced taxes.

But the earnings on your voluntary contributions are tax-deferred. You don't pay taxes on the investment earnings until you withdraw your account. You may receive your voluntary contributions account as a cash refund or as additional annuity payments on top of your regular CSRS benefits.

An advantage of voluntary contributions is that you can take the money out before you retire. But taxes must be paid on the accumulated interest. And if you take out the money, you must withdraw the full amount and you cannot make such contributions again.

If you set up a voluntary contribution account and use it to receive extra annuity payments when you retire, the amount you receive is based on a fixed formula. If you retire at age 55, you will receive an extra annual annuity of $7 for every $100 in your account. The annuity amount per $100 increases by $0.20 for every year you are above age 55 at retirement—for example, at age 60 you would receive $8 for every $100 in your account.

Figure 4-6 offers examples of additional CSRS annuity payments from a voluntary contribution account at various ages. For purposes of comparison with purchasing a TSP annuity, we've based the examples on an account of $10,000, a tenth of the amount used in Figure 4-5.

_____ Annual Extra CSRS Annuity from Voluntary Contributions _____
Based on $10,000 Account

If You Retire at	Additional Annual CSRS Annuity of
Age 55	$700
Age 60	$800
Age 62	$840
Age 65	$900
Age 70	$1,000

Figure 4-6

You may decide to use voluntary contributions as an additional source of long-term savings growth. You have the option of receiving the accumulated savings as a lump sum payment. Interest paid on voluntary accounts is adjusted annually. It was 6.25 percent in 1994.

TSP PARTICIPATION AMONG CSRS EMPLOYEES

Participation by CSRS employees in the TSP has grown steadily since 1987. In June 1987 there were about 297,000 CSRS employees investing in the TSP. By September 1993 the number of CSRS participants had more than doubled, rising to about 615,000. These numbers are striking in light of the fact that the overall population of CSRS employees is constantly declining, as some of them leave government service and positions are filled by newly hired FERS employees.

Growth of TSP Participation, CSRS Employees

September of:	CSRS Employees Investing in the TSP
1987	372,000
1988	388,000
1989	423,000
1990	461,000
1991	515,000
1992	588,000
1993	615,000

Figure 4-7

Overall, CSRS employees who do invest in the TSP overwhelmingly opt for the maximum allowable 5 percent of pay investment. Almost 70 percent choose that maximum, with the remainder spread evenly across investment levels from 1 percent to 4 percent of pay. The average TSP investment for CSRS employees is 4.2 percent of pay. The average and the distribution across different rates have not varied significantly since 1988.

Percentage of Pay Invested in TSP by CSRS Employees

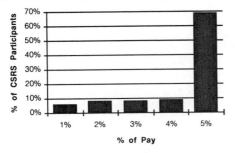

Figure 4-8

The patterns of TSP participation among CSRS employees are generally similar to those among FERS employees. Older and high-paid employees are more likely to invest in the TSP and to invest higher percentages of pay than their younger and lower-paid colleagues, as shown in Figure 4-9.

TSP Investment Levels, CSRS Employees

Age Group	Average % of Pay Invested	Salary ($1,000s)	Average % of Pay Invested
20-29	3.5%	10-19	3.7%
30-39	3.9%	20-29	4.0%
40-49	4.2%	30-39	4.2%
50-59	4.6%	40-49	4.3%
60-69	4.6%	50-59	4.4%
70 +	4.7%	60-69	4.5%
		70 +	4.6%

Figure 4-9

CSRS employees tend to invest more in the TSP as they get older and as their salaries increase. As you age, saving for retirement becomes a more important financial goal. And as your salary increases, you may find it easier to set aside a larger share of your current income for retirement. But even among the younger age groups and the lower salary levels, more than half of the CSRS employees investing in the TSP do so at the maximum 5 percent of pay level.

5 THINGS TO DO

1. Estimate your final account balance using a conservative assumption about future growth. First use a 4 percent annual growth rate as your benchmark. Then you might want to use more optimistic growth assumptions to start understanding investment returns and their potential impact on your TSP account.

2. You may want to break down your estimate to see what your account balance will look like at various stages of your career. This will give you a sense of your "walk away" value if you decide to change your career plans (Chapter Eight describes how you may withdraw your money, and the consequences, when you leave government service). An estimate may also give you an idea of how much you'll be able to borrow from your TSP account at various points (see Chapter Seven for more details on the TSP loan program).

3. Think about your estimated account balance as retirement income. It's easy to look at a $100,000 or $200,000 projected account balance and fall prey to the deception of large numbers. Take the time to translate the big number into its actual value as a source of income after you retire.

4. Think about your career plans. If you're planning to stay in federal or postal service until retirement, look

closely at when you'll become eligible for retirement and what your TSP account will provide you as a supplement at that time. If what you see doesn't look like a comfortable retirement foundation, push ahead a few years to see how the increases in your CSRS and TSP income affect your anticipated retirement decision.

5. Compare your anticipated TSP account growth with other investment opportunities. Is the amount of long-term savings and retirement income from the TSP worth it, or are you better off concentrating on more liquid savings? If you need the extra retirement income, the TSP's tax-deferred status is probably a good bet. But if your retirement income is secure without the TSP, you may want to balance TSP investments against other opportunities that may give you more flexibility.

⟨5⟩ UNDERSTANDING YOUR TSP INVESTMENT OPTIONS

This chapter focuses on how your TSP account accumulates value over time. We'll start by examining how investments grow, then turn to the three TSP investment funds. The goals will be to highlight the key differences among the three funds and to identify the major factors you should consider in designing your personal TSP investment strategy.

We'll also look at some of the important mechanics of the TSP investment process. These include the management of the three funds, how you go about allocating your TSP contributions among the three funds, how to shift your investment allocations and how the Thrift Savings Board credits investment earnings to your account.

Undoubtedly one of the most important sections of the chapter will be the discussion of the earnings performance of the TSP funds in past years. We'll look closely at these patterns to give you a solid background for making your own investment choices. Always remember, though, that past patterns of investment performance offer no guarantees of how any of the TSP funds will perform in the future.

INVESTMENT RETURNS AND COMPOUNDED EARNINGS

Before looking at each of the three TSP funds, let's consider how important your TSP investment earnings are to the long-term growth of your account. Consider an employee investing $3,000

a year in the TSP—either a CSRS employee investing only his or her own money (it would take a minimum $60,000 salary to do this since the investment limit for CSRS employees is 5 percent of pay), or a FERS employee getting a combination of personal investment plus agency contributions. Figure 5-1 shows three different long-term investment outcomes—earnings of 4, 7 and 10 percent per year. How big a difference will this make in the employee's ending account?

Over a 10-year investment period, the difference between earning 4 percent and earning 10 percent is $14,400, increasing the ending balance by about 39 percent. Over 20 years the difference is almost $100,000, and the account earning 10 percent is more than double the account earning 4 percent. Over 30 years the total difference is nearly $400,000 and the highest-earning account is more than three times the size of the lowest-earning account.

Let's look closely at a 20-year account earning a 10 percent average return from the perspective of both FERS and CSRS employees. Figure 5-2 breaks down the ingredients of this ending account balance for a FERS employee who accomplished a $3,000 annual investment by investing 5 percent of a $30,000 salary and getting the full 5 percent agency contribution.

Returns on Investment of $3,000 a Year

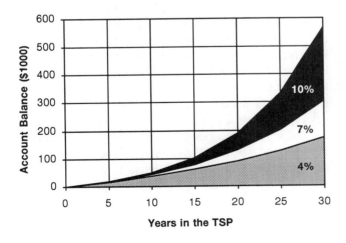

Figure 5-1

Ingredients of TSP Account Balance for FERS Employee

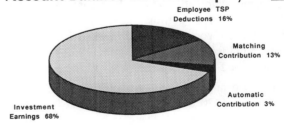

Total Account Balance $190,200

Figure 5-2

This example illustrates the overwhelming power of compounded investment earnings when they accumulate steadily over a long holding period. Note that only 16 percent of the employee's final account balance came out of his or her own pocket—two-thirds came from investment earnings and the rest from agency contributions. Even at lower rates of investment return, the earnings share of the final account balance is considerable. At a 7 percent annual rate of return, investment earnings would account for about 54 percent of the total value of $130,500. At a 4 percent annual earnings rate, about 35 percent of the $91,800 value would be attributable to investment earnings.

Figures 5-3 and 5-4 show the comparable growth in account balances for a CSRS employee with the same profile—$30,000 salary, TSP payroll deductions of 5 percent of pay and annual investment earnings of 4 percent, 7 percent and 10 percent.

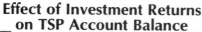

Effect of Investment Returns on TSP Account Balance

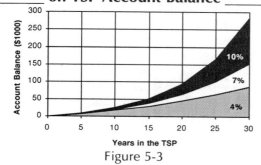

Figure 5-3

Ingredients of TSP Account Balance for CSRS Employee

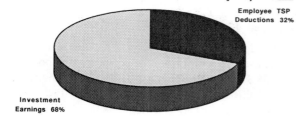

Employee TSP Deductions 32%

Investment Earnings 68%

Total Account Balance $95,100

Figure 5-4

Note the difference between the FERS employee getting agency automatic and matching contributions and the CSRS employee getting no agency share—almost $100,000 in favor of the FERS worker. But even for the CSRS employee, investment earnings still make up two-thirds of the final account balance.

It's also important to note that the direct tax savings each year—$420 at a 28 percent tax rate—total $8,400 over the 20-year period. The employee's $30,000 in TSP payroll deductions actually cost about $21,600 when tax savings are considered. These tax savings are a "discount" for the employee as he or she "buys" the total value of the

account over the 20-year period. Some of this savings will be paid back to the government as income taxes when the employee receives income from the final account balance. But the taxes will be only a fraction of the "value-added" resulting from the tax savings over the 20-year period.

As these examples show vividly, the performance of your TSP investments over time will significantly affect the ultimate value of your TSP account. The longer you participate in the TSP, the more dramatic the influence of differences in investment performance. So let's turn to the TSP investment options available to you, first with an overview and then with detailed looks at each of the three investment funds.

OVERVIEW OF THE TSP INVESTMENT FUNDS

Whether in FERS or CSRS, you are free to allocate your TSP investments as you see fit among three different investment funds. You may invest your entire account in any one of the funds or diversify your investments by spreading them among two or three funds.

The three TSP investment options are:

◇ The G Fund—Government Securities Investment Fund

◇ The C Fund—Common Stock Index Investment Fund

◇ The F Fund—Fixed Income Index Investment Fund

These funds track the overall performance of U.S. financial markets. Each fund is a "broad-based" investment vehicle designed to reflect the average performance and value of a particular segment of the financial market, not a single investment or a handful of investments within that market segment.

The G Fund reflects the average of interest rates payable on all U.S. Treasury securities with maturities of four years or longer. The C Fund tracks the overall performance of the U.S. stock market, not just a limited portfolio of a few major companies. The F Fund reflects the interest and market value of major government and corporate notes and bonds and mortgage-backed securities. Each fund offers you a chance to gain investment earnings based on broad growth trends within major financial markets. The C Fund and F Fund are diversified portfolios spread across numerous specific investments. This diversification gives you added protection against the effects of any single security, stock or bond performing poorly during a particular period. The G Fund is a special issue security that reflects the composite interest rate of intermediate and long-term Treasury securities.

The three TSP funds reflect "passive" rather than "active" investment strategies. The Federal Retirement Thrift Investment Board (Thrift Savings Board) administers the three funds. Later sections will describe in more detail how the Board operates each of the three funds. The essential point to understand is that the Board does not "pick and choose" investments from month to month or year to year. Instead, the TSP funds are maintained and updated to make sure that they reflect broad performance trends as closely as possible.

The use of passive, indexed investment funds gives you the opportunity to concentrate on assessing, selecting and benefiting from broad-based growth in these market sectors.

You don't have to suffer the time, expense and risk of trying to pick individual investments in hopes that they'll "outperform" the market as a whole. If you're the type of investor who likes to pick and choose individual stocks and bonds or mutual funds that target particular investments, you'll have to do that somewhere else than the TSP.

But even under the TSP's investment approach you still face an important range of choices. The three TSP funds reflect the characteristics and earnings patterns of these markets. You're in a position to choose the mix of market features and future expectations that you feel best fits your investment goals.

A REVIEW OF IMPORTANT INVESTMENT TERMS

As you look more closely at each of the three TSP investment funds, there are some basic concepts that you should keep in mind.

The term rate of return describes the total growth—or decline—in the value of the TSP funds, including all income, reinvestment of income and capital gains or losses over a specified period. Remember that the rate of return includes the full growth or decline in an investment's value.

For G Fund securities, the rate of return reflects an average interest rate payable at a specific time. The C Fund rate of return is the change in the total value of all stocks in the fund, including changes in the prices of the stocks and the reinvestment of all dividends. The F Fund rate of return reflects the change in the market value of a wide mix of intermediate and long-term notes and bonds, plus the reinvestment of the interest paid on those bonds.

The term real rate of return describes the rate of return minus the underlying rate of inflation. For example, if in a given year an investment fund has an 8 percent annual rate of return, while the Consumer Price Index—the most common inflation measure—increases 5 percent in that year, we would say that the real rate of return was 3 percent (8 percentage points less 5 percentage points). This concept helps you focus on how much the growth of your investment account reflects a real, or actual increase in value and purchasing power over time.

Another key concept at the heart of most investment discussions and decisions is the tradeoff between return and risk. Generally speaking, investments offering the potential for higher rates of return also pose a higher degree of risk. This tradeoff between return and risk is a central consideration in your TSP investment options.

The two most important elements of investment risk are *credit risk* and *market risk*.

Credit risk is the chance that a borrower will default on a scheduled payment of principal or interest, thereby diminishing or erasing the value of the debt instrument held by the creditor. Credit risk is primarily associated with corporate bonds and is not a significant factor in the operation of the TSP investment funds. The G Fund's Treasury securities are backed by the full faith and credit of the U.S. government. If the government defaulted on its securities we'd all have much bigger problems to worry about than the value of our TSP investments. The F Fund includes a mix of government and corporate bonds, but the corporate bonds are high-quality instruments with low probabilities of default. And again the broad-based nature of the TSP funds protects you. In the unlikely event of default on a particular corporate bond, the effect on the overall value of the F Fund would be small.

Market risk is the factor that really matters when we talk about the risks associated with the three TSP investment funds. Market risk is the degree of fluctuation in the value of an investment over time. The larger and more frequent the ups and downs, the riskier the investment. Its value at any future points is less predictable and may involve actual losses.

In the case of stocks in the C Fund, market risk reflects stock price fluctuations due to broad economic conditions or changes—real or perceived—in companies' performance and profitability. Market risk in the F Fund arises primarily from the relationship between the value of intermediate and long-term bonds and the short-term interest rate patterns and expectations that affect the selling prices of those bonds. We'll look at this relationship when we focus in more detail on the operation of the F Fund. There is no market risk associated with the G Fund as the term is traditionally used, because the G Fund maintains the selling value of its securities. However, the interest rates payable on Treasury securities do shift over time. The mix of securities in the G Fund ensures that changes in the average G Fund interest rate are gradual.

What makes market risk important for TSP investors is the extent to which it generates fluctuations—up or down—in the value of the three investment funds. This movement in investment values over time is often referred to as the volatility of an investment. The more the value of an investment fluctuates, the greater is the volatility of that investment.

THE G FUND

The G Fund is the Government Securities Investment Fund. All G Fund investments are in short-term, non-marketable U.S. Treasury securities specially issued to the TSP. The actual G Fund rate of return is set once a month by the U.S. Treasury and all G Fund investments earn interest at that rate for the month.

How the G Fund Works

The G Fund interest rate is defined by law to equal the average of the interest rates on all Treasury marketable securities outstanding with four or more years to maturity. The Treasury calculates the rate from the closing market "bid" prices on the last day of the month for about 100 different Treasury securities.

Because the calculation of the G Fund rate takes into account the total value of outstanding securities, it is weighted toward longer-term securities with higher outstanding values. Typically the G Fund rate of return reflects the earnings of Treasury securities with an average maturity of about 14 years. But the exact average maturity of G Fund investments will vary over time, as investors adjust their government security purchases.

This process gives G Fund investments the benefits of longer-term securities and their generally higher yields, but purchased on a short-term basis through the Treasury's special issue to the TSP. So, higher long-term interest rates are realized without the risk of waiting for the securities to reach maturity and possibly facing losses of value during that waiting period.

The Thrift Savings Board invests employee and agency contributions allocated to the G Fund as soon as the contributions are credited to participant accounts. The Treasury maintains these daily investments on a "book entry" basis—there are no trading costs in the transactions between the TSP and the Treasury.

G Fund Investment Returns

The actual G Fund rate of return is the statutory rate less TSP administrative expenses. In 1993 these expenses reduced the return by 0.12 percent, or $1.20 for every $1,000 of G Fund account balance.

Annual G Fund Rates of Return, 1988-1993

1988	8.81%
1989	8.81%
1990	8.90%
1991	8.15%
1992	7.23%
1993	6.14%
Total Return, 1988-1993	**58.70%**
Annual Compounded Return	**8.00%**

Figure 5-5

Figure 5-5 shows the annual rates of return for the G Fund for the years 1988-1993. Over the entire six-year period the G Fund had a total return of 58.7 percent. That is, $1 invested in January 1988 would have a value of $1.59 at the end of 1993. This growth was equal to an average annual return of 8 percent for the entire period.

The G Fund has provided a fairly steady rate of return. There is some movement in the rate of return over time, but the variation from one year to the next is small.

Except when dramatic economic events deliver a sudden shock to financial conditions in general—and inflation expectations in particular—you can expect the G Fund's rate of return to shift fairly gradually from one year to the next. At any point, how the G Fund is performing gives a good indication of how it is likely to do in the near future. The G Fund reflects a blend of intermediate and long-term interest rates, which generally move up and down gradually.

This pattern of gradual change holds true when we look at G Fund rates of return on a monthly basis. During the 72 months from January 1988 through December 1993 the average monthly rate of return was 0.64 percent. The highest monthly rate during this period was 0.78 percent, and 0.45 percent was the lowest monthly rate. The average change in the monthly rate of return from one month to the next was 0.03 percent—again, what the G Fund is doing now provides a strong indicator of the likely range of movement rates in the near-term future.

__ G Fund Monthly Returns, 1988-1993 __

	1988	1989	1990	1991	1992	1993
Jan.	0.69%	0.76%	0.68%	0.69%	0.57%	0.58%
Feb.	0.62%	0.67%	0.64%	0.62%	0.56%	0.49%
Mar.	0.66%	0.78%	0.72%	0.68%	0.62%	0.52%
Apr.	0.68%	0.75%	0.71%	0.66%	0.62%	0.51%
May	0.71%	0.76%	0.76%	0.68%	0.64%	0.51%
June	0.72%	0.70%	0.71%	0.66%	0.60%	0.51%
July	0.72%	0.69%	0.72%	0.69%	0.60%	0.49%
Aug.	0.76%	0.66%	0.72%	0.69%	0.57%	0.49%
Sept.	0.76%	0.68%	0.73%	0.64%	0.54%	0.45%
Oct.	0.75%	0.71%	0.76%	0.62%	0.55%	0.47%
Nov.	0.68%	0.65%	0.70%	0.61%	0.56%	0.45%
Dec.	0.74%	0.67%	0.70%	0.62%	0.58%	0.49%
Year	**8.81%**	**8.81%**	**8.90%**	**8.15%**	**7.23%**	**6.14%**

Figure 5-6

This pattern of gradual change is one of the G Fund's most attractive features for many TSP investors. *At any point, you may not know whether the G Fund rate of return is likely to increase or decline. But you can be fairly confident that any change in either direction will be gradual,* and you can have a reasonably accurate picture of the general range in which the G Fund rate will fall in the near future.

The tradeoff for this predictability and safety is that the G Fund does not offer an opportunity for dramatic gains in the value of your TSP account. It does provide you with an opportunity to enjoy steady growth in the real value of your assets, over and above the underlying rate of inflation.

In fact, over the past decade, G Fund related securities have performed quite strongly in real terms. Figure 5-7 shows the real rate of return for the G Fund from 1988-1993, the actual rate of return less the underlying inflation rate in each year.

G Fund Real Rates of Return, 1988-1993

Year	G Fund Return	Inflation	G Fund Real Return
1988	8.8%	4.1%	4.7%
1989	8.8%	4.8%	4.0%
1990	8.9%	5.4%	3.5%
1991	8.2%	4.2%	4.0%
1992	7.2%	3.0%	4.2%
1993	6.1%	2.7%	3.4%
Total 1988-1993	58.7%	26.7%	26.3%
Annual Compounded	8.0%	4.0%	4.0%

Figure 5-7

If the G Fund had been operating in the early 1980s, real rates of return would have been even stronger during that period. During those years inflation rates began declining, but the memory of the high inflation levels of the late 1970s was still fresh. Investments comparable to the G Fund enjoyed 8-9 percent real rates of return during the early 1980s. As the 1980s proceeded and inflation ran at relatively low levels, the real rate of return for G Fund investments moved downward to a 3-4 percent range. But even at this level of real return the G Fund constitutes a very attractive combination—modest but steady growth in real asset values with virtually no risk of potentially costly short-term market fluctuations.

We remind you that there is no assurance that future G Fund rates of return will resemble the rates shown in the preceding tables. If you invest some of your TSP account in the G Fund, you should monitor G Fund performance and determine whether that performance continues to suit your TSP account objectives and retirement income goals. In Chapter Five we'll give you some tips about how to monitor your TSP account and your investment returns.

As you begin to participate in the TSP, or as you reassess your TSP investment strategy along the way, you should keep in mind the essential characteristics of the G Fund:

◇ The G Fund provides a steady rate of growth with very gradual shifts in earnings from month to month and year to year.

◇ The G Fund offers protection against sudden short-term losses, giving you a safe investment option when

caution is appropriate—such as right before you retire or apply for a TSP loan.

◇ The G Fund gives you a "bottom-line" benchmark that you can use to project your minimum expected account balance based on a conservative investment strategy.

◇ The G Fund provides a "safe haven" in short-term periods of economic crisis or market uncertainty—such as periods of very high inflation or global developments that make the financial markets even more volatile than normal.

THE C FUND

The C Fund is the Common Stock Index Investment Fund. As with the G Fund, the C Fund has its investment objective and structure defined by law. The C Fund must reflect the overall performance of the U.S. common stock market, and it must do so by investing in a stock "index" fund.

A stock index fund is a collection of stock holdings expressly designed to provide an accurate picture of the overall performance of the stock market. Rather than trying to pick individual stock "winners," C Fund participants invest in an array of stocks that are considered representative of overall stock market performance.

How the C Fund Works

In complying with the legal requirement to build the C Fund around an established stock index, the Thrift Savings Board decided to use the Standard & Poor's 500 (S&P 500) stock index as the C Fund's reference point. This index includes the common stocks of 500 companies traded in U.S. stock markets, for the most part on the New York Stock Exchange.

While the S&P 500 occasionally drops companies from the index—usually due to mergers and acquisitions or Chapter 11 bankruptcy proceedings—and adds replacements, the composition is fairly consistent. The S&P 500 encompasses the distribution of companies shown in Figure 5-8.

Composition of the Standard & Poor's 500

Industrial Companies	400
Utilities	40
Financial Companies	40
Transportation Companies	20

Figure 5-8

The total value of the S&P 500—the combined value of the 500 companies based on price per share times the number of outstanding shares—make up about 70 percent of the total value of all companies on all U.S. stock markets.

The specific investment portfolio of the S&P 500 at any time depends on the roster of companies and their current market values relative to one another. For example, Company X has 20,000 outstanding shares currently valued at $30 per share, for a total market value of $600,000. Company Y has 10,000 outstanding shares that currently sell at $20 a share, for a total value of $200,000. Company X has a total market value three times that of Company Y. Company X's performance will count three times as much as Company Y's in determining the overall performance of the index. Over time the value ratios among the 500 companies will shift as particular stocks increase or decline in total value.

The 100 largest companies in the S&P 500 represent about 65 percent of the index's total value—about 45 percent of the total value of all U.S. common stocks. The 30 largest companies account for about 40 percent of the value of the index.

30 Companies with Highest Stock Values, S&P 500
(as of April 30, 1993)

Company	Category	Stock Value (Billions)
1. Exxon	Oil and Gas	$79.8
2. General Electric	Conglomerates	$79.7
3. AT&T	Telecommunications	$75.2
4. Wal-Mart Stores	Discount Retailing	$61.5
5. Coca Cola	Beverages	$50.8
6. Philip Morris	Tobacco	$42.0
7. Merck	Drugs and Research	$41.2
8. Du Pont	Chemicals	$35.0
9. GTE	Telecommunications	$32.8
10. Procter & Gamble	Personal Care Products	$32.2
11. Bristol-Myers Squibb	Drugs and Research	$30.6
12. Pepsico	Beverages	$29.3
13. General Motors	Automotive	$28.6
14. IBM	Computers and Peripherals	$27.3
15. Mobil	Oil and Gas	$27.2
16. Amoco	Oil and Gas	$26.8
17. Bell South	Telecommunications	$26.6
18. Chevron	Oil and Gas	$26.5
19. American Intl. Group	Insurance	$26.3
20. Johnson & Johnson	Medical Products	$26.1
21. Ford Motor	Automotive	$25.9
22. Southwestern Bell	Telecommunications	$23.2
23. Bell Atlantic	Telecommunications	$22.8
24. Microsoft	Computer Software	$22.7
25. Disney	Entertainment	$21.7
26. Fannie Mae	Financial Services	$21.6
27. Abbott Laboratories	Medical Products	$21.5
28. Pfizer	Drugs and Research	$21.1
29. Ameritech	Telecommunications	$20.8
30. Amer. Home Products	Drugs and Research	$20.3

Figure 5-9

Figure 5-9 shows the "Big 30" list as of 1993, reflecting a diverse mix of sectors and companies. It shows the companies in order of total market value, beginning with the largest. Each had a total market value of $20 billion or more.

The precise composition of the index adjusts over time to reflect changes in the stock market and the American economy. For example, IBM and General Motors are still in the top 30 but ranked lower in total value than in previous years. Also, note the presence of several pharmaceutical and telecommunications companies, reflecting the growth of business volume and stock trading in these sectors.

The S&P 500 is an evolving index that reflects the growth and decline of particular stock offerings over time. At any point in time it provides a reasonably accurate snapshot of the overall content and performance trend of the U.S. stock market.

How C Fund Money Is Invested

The Thrift Savings Board invests C Fund account balances through the Wells Fargo Equity Index Fund, the nation's single largest stock index fund with total assets exceeding $30 billion. TSP accounts currently represent about 15 percent of the total value of the Wells Fargo Fund, with that share increasing steadily. Under the contract between the Board and Wells Fargo, there is absolutely no risk of TSP money being used to bail out Wells Fargo under any market conditions.

About once a week Wells Fargo processes contributions and withdrawals for its participating investors, including the TSP. All money received is invested in the S&P 500, tracking as closely as possible the ratios of market values among the 500 companies as they shift from week to week. In addition, all dividends paid by companies in the index are re-invested in the index fund. As TSP employee payroll deductions and FERS agency contributions flow into the C Fund, the Board transmits them to the Wells Fargo Fund at the next weekly opening date. Until the next opening date arrives the Board puts C Fund investments in the G Fund, so they continue to accrue earnings during these short waiting periods. At each weekly opening date the Board purchases "units" of the Wells Fargo Index Fund. Each unit represents a proportionate share of all the stocks in the fund, based on their relative total values at the time of purchase.

When the total value of the S&P 500 declines, a given amount of new C Fund money will purchase more Fund units. When total index values increase, that same amount of money will purchase fewer units. Over time the value of each new C Fund purchase—and your account's share in it—will rise or fall with the total value of the S&P 500. As you make your TSP payroll deductions each pay period, whatever portion you have allocated to the C Fund (plus a corresponding share of agency contributions for FERS employees) enters into the purchase process at the next weekly opening date.

Once a month the Thrift Savings Board computes the updated value of your C Fund account balance. Figure 5-10 shows how the C Fund's monthly returns—positive or negative—are calculated.

Monthly Calculation of C Fund Gains or Losses

Capital Gain or Loss in the Value of the S&P 500

PLUS Reinvested Company Dividends (typically about 3 percent of the total value of the S&P 500)

PLUS Short-Term Investments by Thrift Savings Board and Wells Fargo

PLUS Securities Lending Income (Wells Fargo profits by loaning stocks to qualified stock brokers)

LESS Trading Costs (minimized because most TSP "buys" are offset by "sells" from other Wells Fargo clients)

LESS TSP Administrative Expenses

LESS Fund Management Fees Paid to Wells Fargo

Figure 5-10

In 1993 the total of administrative expenses and fund management fees was 0.13 percent, or $1.30 for every $1,000 of C Fund balance. Those expenses are calculated and deducted before the monthly posting of C Fund earnings to your account.

Through this process the portion of your TSP account in the C Fund has a new value each month. Your C Fund account will grow—or decline—in value over time at a rate very close to the total value of the S&P 500. In effect, every pay period you are buying additional shares in the overall performance of the U.S. stock market.

C Fund Investment Returns

Compared to the G Fund, the C Fund historically has demonstrated a potential for higher rates of return—both in the short-term and over longer periods. But this increased earnings potential goes hand-in-hand with a greater degree of volatility as the value of the S&P 500 fluctuates from month to month and year to year.

Annual C Fund Rates of Return, 1988-1993

1988	11.84%
1989	31.03%
1990	-3.15%
1991	30.77%
1992	7.70%
1993	10.13%
Total Return, 1988-1993	**120.14%**
Annual Compounded Return	**14.06%**

Figure 5-11

Let's look first at the recent pattern of annual rates of return for the C Fund. Figure 5-11 shows the C Fund's actual annual rates of return for the period 1988-1993.

These figures reflect two critical aspects of the C Fund that you need to understand in contemplating your TSP investment strategy. On the one hand, the C Fund offers the opportunity for significant investment gains in any given short-term period. In the six years 1988-1993, there were two years in which the annual rate of return for the C Fund was 30 percent or higher. By contrast, the highest annual return for the G Fund during this period was 8.90 percent.

On the other hand, the C Fund also will exhibit sharp fluctuations in performance as it tracks the broad trends of the U.S. stock markets. Periods of robust growth are sometimes quickly followed by periods of much lower returns, or even losses in asset values. The money in your TSP account invested in the C Fund may grow sharply in one year, but grow slowly or even decline in the next.

The period 1989-1991 illustrates this pattern clearly. In both 1989 and 1991 the C Fund recorded annual rates of return of about 31 percent. Between these two years of outstanding growth in values, there was a 3 percent decline in 1990. Taking all three years together, money invested in the C Fund over the entire period grew in value as if the C Fund had average annual earnings of 18.4% over all three years—a very healthy earnings rate even with the poor 1990 performance. But to obtain the total gains of the entire period, investors had to endure the losses in 1990 before realizing the renewed growth in 1991.

The C Fund also experiences sharp fluctuations in performance from month to month. As the stock market moves from relatively strong performance to a period of more modest growth or even decline—or vice versa—it doesn't typically move in a steady path upward or downward. Very good years can include very bad months, weeks, or days. Poor years can include short-term periods of strong growth.

C Fund Monthly Rates of Return, 1988-1993

	1988	1989	1990	1991	1992	1993
Jan.	-0.20%	7.14%	-6.59%	4.55%	-1.89%	0.86%
Feb.	4.82%	-2.51%	1.26%	7.07%	1.29%	1.35%
Mar.	-3.47%	2.21%	2.64%	2.40%	-1.91%	2.09%
Apr.	0.73%	5.14%	-2.52%	0.18%	2.91%	-2.39%
May	1.42%	3.98%	9.44%	4.30%	0.49%	2.66%
June	4.08%	-0.58%	-0.71%	-4.49%	-1.45%	0.32%
July	-0.24%	8.83%	-0.36%	4.63%	4.11%	-0.38%
Aug.	-2.74%	1.98%	-8.65%	2.37%	-2.02%	3.78%
Sept.	4.12%	-0.29%	-4.85%	-1.63%	1.15%	-0.76%
Oct.	2.53%	-2.33%	-0.46%	1.39%	0.42%	2.04%
Nov.	-1.23%	2.05%	6.36%	-3.96%	3.39%	-0.93%
Dec.	1.78%	2.37%	2.72%	11.41%	1.21%	1.20%
Year	**11.84%**	**31.03%**	**-3.15%**	**30.77%**	**7.70%**	**10.13%**

Figure 5-12

Figure 5-12 illustrates the monthly performance of the C Fund for the six-year period 1988-1993.

The volatility of the C Fund is clear when we look at these monthly rates of return. For the 72-months from January 1988 through December 1993, the average monthly rate of return was 1.10 percent, compared to 0.64 percent for the G Fund. But while the G Fund's average movement—up or down—from one month to the next was only 0.03 percent, the average monthly fluctuation of the C Fund was plus or minus 4.41 percent.

It is important for you to understand the C Fund's volatility as you consider your TSP investment strategy. In order to profit from the earnings potential of the C Fund, you have to be comfortable "riding out" periods of poor performance. Or, you have to be very skillful—or fortunate—at determining when to reduce or increase your C Fund investments as these cyclical fluctuations occur.

For example, if we selected the 13 individual months of highest C Fund earnings during the 1988-1993 period, those 13 months achieved combined growth slightly higher than the total C Fund growth for the entire 72-month period. Without these 13 months of exceptionally strong performance, the rest of the period actually had a slightly negative rate of return. Nine of those 13 "high performance" months immediately followed months in which the C Fund's performance was below average.

Overall, 1988-1993 was a period of strong growth for the stock market, even considering the effects of inflation on investment values. Figure 5-13 shows the real rates of return for the C Fund from 1988-1993, the actual rate of return less the underlying inflation rate in each year.

C Fund Real Rates of Return, 1988-1993

Year	C Fund Return	Inflation	C Fund Real Return
1988	11.8%	4.1%	7.7%
1989	31.0%	4.8%	26.2%
1990	-3.2%	5.4%	-8.6%
1991	30.8%	4.2%	26.6%
1992	7.7%	3.0%	4.7%
1993	10.1%	2.7%	7.4%
Total 1988-1993	**120.1%**	**26.7%**	**76.9%**
Annual Compounded	**14.1%**	**4.0%**	**10.0%**

Figure 5-13

While the period 1988-1993 was an exceptionally strong one for the U.S. stock market, it was not unprecedented—the 1950s witnessed a sustained period of even higher real rates of return, about 12 percent per year if you invested in the stock market for the entire decade. For the entire period in which the S&P 500 has tracked stock market performance—since 1926—the average annual real return has been about 7 percent.

The first six years of C Fund performance are neither typical nor atypical of historical stock market patterns. It was a stronger period than the full 1926-1993 timeframe, but it was matched by other periods of five to 10 years during that time. The recent results offer no assurance of what C Fund earnings will look like in the future.

In Chapter Six we'll explore in more detail the long-term earnings patterns and volatility of the stock market and how it might affect your decision-making about investments in the C Fund. And we'll discuss certain factors and situations that might make the C Fund more or less attractive as part of your TSP investment strategy. As you think about the C Fund and whether and how much you might want to invest in it, always keep in mind the major features of the stock index approach:

◇ The C Fund offers the potential for significant investment growth over time, particularly in periods of general economic prosperity and price stability, when investors generally are optimistic and market-wide stock prices climb.

◇ The C Fund poses the risk of short-term and medium-term losses in certain months and years, either through normal market "corrections" or more sustained periods of economic uncertainty and pessimism.

◇ The C Fund's earnings record gives you a basis for projecting your maximum potential account balance based on an aggressive investment strategy.

◇ The C Fund provides a relatively simple, convenient and inexpensive way to "ride" the overall performance of the stock market, without the time demands and brokerage fees involved in constantly picking, monitoring and trading individual stocks or individual mutual funds.

THE F FUND

The F Fund is the Fixed Income Investment Index Fund. The objective of the F Fund is to track the performance of the U.S. bond market. The Thrift Savings Board has contracted with Wells Fargo to manage F Fund assets. F Fund assets are invested in a bond index fund that is similar in operation to the C Fund stock index. Instead of the C Fund's S&P 500 common stock portfolio, the F Fund is based on a mix of government and corporate bonds and mortgage-backed securities.

For many new or "part-time" investors the bond market is the most difficult investment opportunity to understand. While the total dollar volume of TSP investments has grown recently, the F Fund remains by far the least utilized of the three TSP investment funds.

How the F Fund Works

A bond is a debt instrument. An organization borrows money by selling bonds that promise the buyer income. In return for capital, the seller promises to pay a specified interest rate to the buyer for a specified period. The interest (coupon) rate when a bond is issued is determined by current economic conditions and the fiscal soundness of the bond-seller and, sometimes, its capital need.

A bond-seller must compete with all other investment

opportunities to make its offering worthwhile to potential investors. If current inflation and future inflation expectations are relatively low, and the bond-seller has a good track record of meeting its obligations, then a long-term bond may be issued at a relatively low interest rate. On the other hand, if current or future inflation rates concern potential investors or the purpose of the bond is highly speculative or the bond-seller has a poor record, then the bond-seller will have to offer a higher interest rate to make the offering attractive enough to raise the desired amount of capital.

Whatever the specific circumstances and resulting interest rate, a bond transaction concludes with the seller of the bond promising to repay the buyer the original capital and a fixed interest rate over a specified period. As a result bonds serve as "fixed income securities" for the buyer (holder) of the bond.

The F Fund is an index containing government, investment-grade corporate and mortgage-backed fixed income securities. As with the C Fund, the F Fund operates through the TSP buying "units" of an index fund managed by Wells Fargo—in this case the Wells Fargo U.S. Debt Index Fund. The Wells Fargo fund tracks the Lehman Brothers Aggregate (LBA) bond index. The LBA is a portfolio of about 4,600 individual securities designed to reflect the performance of the major U.S. bond markets.

About half of the bonds in the F Fund index are U.S. government bonds, most of which are intermediate and long-term Treasury bonds used to finance the national debt by raising current operating funds through the promise of future payments. About 30 percent of the F Fund represents mortgage-backed securities issued by the three major federal housing financial institutions. They issue bonds to raise the money they lend to American home buyers. The balance reflects high-quality corporate bonds.

The LBA Bond Index

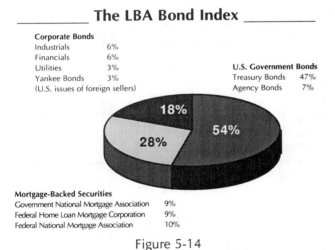

Corporate Bonds
Industrials	6%
Financials	6%
Utilities	3%
Yankee Bonds	3%
(U.S. issues of foreign sellers)	

U.S. Government Bonds
Treasury Bonds	47%
Agency Bonds	7%

Mortgage-Backed Securities
Government National Mortgage Association	9%
Federal Home Loan Mortgage Corporation	9%
Federal National Mortgage Association	10%

Figure 5-14

The F Fund reflects the changes in the value of this bond portfolio. Bonds generate investment earnings in two ways. First, there is the actual interest payable on the bond to its maturity date. The mix of bonds in the LBA ranges in maturity from one to 30 years, and new bonds are added to the LBA as old bonds reach maturity. Second, bonds shift in value over time. In the bond market, individual bonds are constantly being bought and sold, so that each bond has a varying price at different times.

The prices of bonds move in the opposite direction of interest rates. If interest rates are declining, the value of a bond increases. If interest rates are going up, the value of a bond drops. This is a key point to understand about how the F Fund operates.

Let's look at an example to understand this relationship of interest rates and bond values. Let's say that an investor purchases a 20-year, $500,000 bond issued by a corporation or government agency. Under the terms of the bond offering, the buyer will receive an interest rate of 8 percent over the 20-year term of the bond. At the time the bond is purchased this guarantee of 8 percent earnings over a 20-year period is an attractive investment. But if interest rates subsequently start to increase, then the guarantee of 8 percent interest will become relatively less attractive. There may be other more favorable investment opportunities available. The price of the bond will decline.

On the other hand, if interest rates are declining, the bond guaranteeing 8 percent interest will become relatively more attractive to potential bond buyers. Its price will increase. In this way, the bond market continually adjusts the value of future debt instruments.

The F Fund tracks the fluctuating total value of a broad mix of high-quality government and corporate bonds and mortgage-backed securities, based on the changing prices of the bonds and the reinvestment of interest paid on the bonds. Therefore, just like the overall bond market, F Fund earnings will generally be strong when interest rates are declining. F Fund earnings will generally be poor when interest rates are increasing.

F Fund Investment Returns

Figure 5-15 shows the annual rates of return for the F Fund for the period 1988-1993. Over the entire six years the F Fund had a total return of 73.22 percent, equal to annual growth of about 9.6 percent.

Annual F Fund Rates of Return, 1988-1993

1988	3.63%
1989	13.89%
1990	8.00%
1991	15.75%
1992	7.20%
1993	9.52%
Total Return, 1988-1993	**73.22%**
Annual Compounded Return	**9.59%**

Figure 5-15

The period 1988-1993 was a strong one for bond funds. Interest rates were generally declining during the period, driving up the prices of individual bonds and the total value of bond indexes. Over a longer period bond funds may experience negative annual returns.

The potential for negative returns in the F Fund becomes clear when we look at earnings on a monthly basis. Figure 5-16 shows the monthly returns for the F Fund for the 72 months from January 1988 through December 1993.

F Fund Monthly Rates of Return, 1988-1993

	1988	1989	1990	1991	1992	1993
Jan.	-0.06%	1.27%	-1.38%	1.15%	-1.35%	1.88%
Feb.	0.81%	-0.68%	0.21%	0.86%	0.66%	1.73%
Mar.	-0.80%	0.50%	0.01%	0.67%	-0.53%	0.41%
Apr.	-0.46%	2.05%	-0.94%	1.05%	0.67%	0.67%
May	-0.63%	2.42%	2.80%	0.57%	1.84%	0.10%
June	1.97%	3.19%	1.56%	-0.01%	1.36%	1.79%
July	-0.49%	2.06%	1.24%	1.40%	2.00%	0.55%
Aug.	0.33%	-1.48%	-1.42%	2.12%	1.00%	1.72%
Sept.	2.07%	0.37%	0.81%	1.99%	1.15%	0.26%
Oct.	1.68%	2.45%	1.32%	1.09%	-1.30%	0.38%
Nov.	-1.09%	0.86%	2.15%	0.89%	0.01%	-0.84%
Dec.	0.31%	0.16%	1.46%	2.96%	1.54%	0.52%
Year	**3.63%**	**13.89%**	**8.00%**	**15.75%**	**7.20%**	**9.52%**

Figure 5-16

Although bond prices generally do not fluctuate as sharply as stock prices, there is still a substantial degree of volatility. For the 72 months from January 1988 through September 1993, the average monthly rate of return for the F Fund was 0.77 percent. The average fluctuation in earnings from one month to the next was plus or minus 1.20 percent.

Finally, let's look at the F Fund's real rates of return—after accounting for inflation—over the past decade. Figure 5-17 shows the annual real rates of return for the F Fund for the period 1988-1993.

F Fund Real Rates of Return, 1988-1993

Year	F Fund Return	Inflation	F Fund Real Return
1988	3.6%	4.1%	-0.5%
1989	13.9%	4.8%	9.1%
1990	8.0%	5.4%	2.6%
1991	15.8%	4.2%	11.6%
1992	7.2%	3.0%	4.2%
1993	9.5%	2.7%	6.8%
Total, 1988-1993	**73.2%**	**26.7%**	**38.3%**
Annual Compounded	**9.6%**	**4.0%**	**5.6%**

Figure 5-17

When we look at the F Fund's 1988-1993 performance in real—after-inflation—terms, we see a sustained period of generally healthy returns. Every year except 1988 provided real gains, and over the entire period the F Fund had an average annual growth rate of 5.6 percent above inflation.

Some key points to remember when considering investing in the F Fund:

◇ *The F Fund offers a potentially useful "balance" to* **TIP** *the G Fund because the two funds react to current interest rates in opposite ways.* When current interest rates are rising, the G Fund return will generally increase, while the value of F Fund bonds will decline; when current interest rates are dropping, the G Fund return will generally decline, while F Fund values will increase.

◇ Over medium and long holding periods, the F Fund will typically provide somewhat higher returns than the G Fund with less volatile fluctuations than the C Fund.

◇ The F Fund will tend to perform less well in periods of economic uncertainty, particularly in periods in which investors are concerned about current and future inflation and upward interest rate movements.

◇ The F Fund provides a vehicle for investing in the intermediate and long-term government and corporate bond market without the close monitoring and complex trading necessary for an individual investor.

COMPARING THE G, C AND F FUNDS

Investment returns are inherently uncertain. There is no assurance that past patterns will continue in the future. But there are some general patterns and relationships that are worth noting. Let's start by comparing the monthly returns of the three funds since 1988.

Comparison of Monthly Rates of Return, 1988-1993

	G Fund	F Fund	C Fund
Highest Return	0.78%	3.19%	11.41%
Lowest Return	0.45%	- 1.48%	- 8.65%
Average Return	0.64%	0.77%	1.10%
Average Change Month to Month	0.03%	1.20%	4.41%

Figure 5-18

The monthly rates of return for the three TSP investment funds reveal several patterns consistent with comparable investments historically. Let's review the general tendencies of the three funds.

Over extended periods, the G Fund is likely to provide the lowest returns among the three. But it will provide a positive, steady real return with virtually no risk. And in some periods—particularly periods when interest rates are rising or business conditions are uncertain—the G Fund may outperform the C and F Funds for an extended period.

The C Fund is at the other extreme. Over longer periods it is likely to offer the highest returns among the three funds. But there will be very sharp fluctuations from one month to the next. And the C Fund could experience extended periods of poor performance. For example, in 1973-1974 the S&P 500 declined by 35 percent.

In the period June-October 1990, the C Fund experienced five straight months of negative returns and a 14 percent loss for the full five months. However, the stock market and the C Fund immediately recovered from November 1990 through May 1991, posting a gain of almost 31 percent during the seven-month period.

Over time you may obtain somewhat more favorable returns from the F Fund than the G Fund—you gain from increases in bond prices plus the value of interest on the bonds while they are held in the fund. But this somewhat higher earnings potential is accompanied by fluctuating returns from month to month. Relative to the C Fund, the F Fund has recently exhibited lower growth and less fluctuation.

Comparison of Annual Returns, 1988-1993

	Average Annual Rate of Return	Average Change Year to Year	Highest	Lowest
G Fund	8.00%	0.48%	8.90%	6.14%
F Fund	9.59%	5.80%	5.75%	3.63%
C Fund	14.06%	18.80%	31.03%	-3.15%

Figure 5-19

During the period 1988-1993, the average annual rate of return for the G Fund was 8 percent. From one year to the next the average change in the rate of return was only about half a percent. Over the same period the C Fund had an average annual return of 14.1 percent. But the average year-to-year change was almost 19 percent. Healthy growth over the period actually consisted of a diverse cycle of widely fluctuating stock market advances and declines.

Comparisons of Monthly Returns, 1988-1993

G Fund vs. C Fund	G Fund Higher 31 mos.	C Fund Higher 41 mos.
G Fund vs. F Fund	G Fund Higher 30 mos.	F Fund Higher 42 mos.
C Fund vs. F Fund	C Fund Higher 40 mos.	F Fund Higher 32 mos.

Figure 5-20

The F Fund has occupied a middle ground between the G and C Funds with respect to rates of return and year-to-year volatility. The F Fund, on average, earned somewhat higher rates of return than the G Fund, but with higher fluctuations from year to year. Compared to the C Fund, the F Fund showed lower earnings and less volatility.

Looking closely at how the three funds performed relative to one another on a month-to-month basis offers some additional insights. Figure 5-20 looks at relative performance among the three funds.

Remember, these comparisons are for a fairly brief period. And in any event, the important point is not the exact count of how many times each fund outperformed the others—those patterns will vary. The essential point is that none of the funds consistently outperforms the others from one month to the next. *All three funds will exhibit periods* TIP *of relative strength and weakness. Don't attach great importance to what happens in any short period of months.*

To take the point further, examine how many months during 1998-1993 the return for each fund was the best of the three funds, the worst of the three, or fell in the middle. Figure 5-21 also shows what the funds' average returns were in those situations.

Which Fund Did Better or Worse Each Month

January 1988 - December 1993

	G Fund	C Fund	F Fund
Had the Highest Return	16	38	18
Average in Those Months	+ 0.65	+ 3.75	+ 1.49
Had the Middle Return	28	6	38
Average in Those Months	+ 0.63	+ 0.20	+ 0.84
Had the Lowest Return	28	28	16
Average in Those Months	+ 0.65	- 2.04	- 0.09

Figure 5-21

Let's look first at the G Fund. It provided the highest return in 16 of the 72 months, the lowest return in 28 months, and it fell in the middle 28 times. The exact numbers are not particularly important. The noteworthy figures are the G Fund's average returns in those three sets of months. In the 16 months when the G Fund had the highest return, its average return was 0.65 percent. In the 27 months when the G Fund had the lowest return, its average return was the same—0.65 percent.

Compared to the C and F funds, the G Fund does not have "strong" or "weak" months. It is a reflection of the interest rates that investors in intermediate and long-term government securities require to make locking up their money in those securities worthwhile. The G Fund rate will move up and down as investors assess economic conditions and adjust their expectations about how much return is necessary to justify the investment. It reflects shifting expectations and the return needed to compensate for future uncertainties.

That's certainly not the case for the C Fund. The C Fund reflects the advances and declines of the stock market. It also turns on economic expectations and uncertainties, but in a marketplace that reflects the—sometimes quickly—shifting judgments of buyers and sellers. While G Fund interest rates typically rise or fall gradually, the changes in the C Fund are more frequent and pronounced.

Suggestions of strength in the economy as a whole, or in a particular sector of the market, lead some investors to buy. If those investors are market leaders, their decisions spawn a buying trend, pushing stock prices up. Likewise on the downside: Signs of weakness lead to major sell orders, dragging prices down. This leads others to fear major losses, producing additional selling to escape more extensive damage. No one wants to miss out on what the others know, at least until they determine that maybe the others were wrong.

The result? The stock market—and therefore the C Fund—has frequent short-term swings up and down. From January 1988 through December 1993, the C Fund had either the highest or the lowest monthly return of the three TSP funds in 66 of the 72 months. The growth of the C Fund was quite favorable over the period as a whole. But the growth trend rests on a constantly shifting foundation.

As with the C Fund, the F Fund frequently fluctuates upward and downward. But unlike the C Fund, which provided either the highest or lowest return in 66 out of 72 months, the F Fund shows a more moderate pattern of returns. During the 72 months from January 1988 to December 1993, the F Fund provided the "middle" return about half the time—in 38 of the 72 months. In most of these months, the F Fund and the C Fund moved in similar directions—both earned higher returns than the G Fund or both earned lower returns than the G Fund.

Now let's turn to a comparison of real—after inflation—rates of return among the three funds. All three of the TSP investment funds earned high real rates of return over the past decade. The average real rates of return from 1988-1993 were 4 percent for the G Fund, 5.6 percent for the F Fund and 10.1 percent for the C Fund. The G Fund provided steady, mildly fluctuating real returns in a range from 2-5 percent. The C Fund's real returns varied widely in a range from -9 percent to +27 percent. The F Fund fluctuated within a range from -1 percent to +12 percent.

Comparison of
____ Real Rates of Return, 1988-1993 ____

	G Fund	F Fund	C Fund
Highest Return	4.7%	11.6%	26.9%
Lowest Return	3.4%	- 0.5%	- 8.6%
Average Return	4.0%	5.6%	10.1%

Figure 5-22

The G Fund and C Fund are fundamentally different investment approaches. The G Fund typically provides a steady, modest and predictable stream of investment earnings. The C Fund offers potentially higher earnings power over time, but you must endure the risk of periodic losses along the way. The F Fund combines the stability of interest earned on fixed-income securities and the uncertainty of market fluctuations in the prices of those securities.

The rates of return achieved by the TSP investment funds from 1988 through 1993 offer no assurance about future rates of return for any of the three funds. But they do illustrate some fundamental lessons about how potential return and potential risk operate in each of the three funds. Developing an effective investment strategy depends on making informed and prudent judgments about the future, not assuming that past patterns will necessarily repeat themselves. In looking at the pattern of TSP investment performance over the past decade, you should focus on the basic characteristics and tendencies of the three funds, not on precise earnings levels that may or may not provide an accurate barometer of future earnings.

Now that we've looked at how the three TSP investment funds operate and their recent earnings patterns, let's move to planning and carrying out an effective TSP investment strategy. As we do that, you should keep in mind the basic characteristics of each of the three funds.

HOW YOU ALLOCATE
YOUR TSP INVESTMENTS _____

There are two ways in which you can allocate your TSP savings among the three funds. First, during any TSP open season, you can use Form TSP-1 to allocate your future payroll deductions to each of the three funds. This is the same form you use to designate the TSP contributions you want deducted from your paycheck each pay period.

Appendix 5 provides a specimen copy of this form. At the top of the form you indicate your desired contributions, as a percentage of pay or a fixed dollar amount. In the next section, there are boxes for each of the funds, in which you list how you want your contributions divided, in 5 percent increments, among the three funds. Complete this section carefully and make sure your three allocations total to 100 percent. For example, if you wanted half your deductions to go to the G Fund, and the rest to be split evenly between the C and F Funds, you would enter 50 percent, 25 percent and 25 percent in the three boxes going across the page.

Figure 5-23 shows a FERS and a CSRS employee making two particular investment allocations.

You have the opportunity to designate the investment of your payroll deductions twice a year during TSP open seasons. One open season runs from May 15 through July 31, the other from November 15 through January 31.

Investment Allocation of TSP Payroll Deductions

	FERS Employee	CSRS Employee
Annual Salary	$39,000	$39,000
Earnings per Pay Period	$1,500	$1,500
TSP Contribution	5% of pay	5% of pay
Employee Contributions	$75.00	$75.00
Agency Contributions	$75.00	$0.00
Total Contributions	$150.00	$75.00
Allocated to G Fund	50%	20%
Allocated to C Fund	25%	60%
Allocated to F Fund	25%	20%
Amount to G Fund	$75.00	$15.00
Amount to C Fund	$37.50	$45.00
Amount to F Fund	$37.50	$15.00

Figure 5-23

You also have the opportunity to reallocate the investment of your total account balance. You do this by filing Form TSP-30. See Appendix 5 for a specimen copy. You may file a Form TSP-30 up to four times a year. If your form is received by the 15th of the month, your reallocation will be effective the last day of the month. For example, a form received on or before August 15 will become effective August 31. A form received any day from August 16 through September 15 will become effective September 30.

Figure 5-24 shows an employee reallocating the investment of the total TSP account balance.

Reallocation of $50,000 TSP Account Balance

	G Fund	C Fund	F Fund
Original Allocation of Contribution on TSP-1	50%	25%	25%
Current Account Balance	**$23,000**	**$14,000**	**$13,000**
Percentage of Total Account	46%	28%	26%
Requested Allocation on TSP-30	50%	25%	25%
Interfund Transfer	+$2000	-$1,500	-$500
New Allocation of Account	**$25,000**	**$12,500**	**$12,500**

Figure 5-24

In the example in Figure 5-24, the employee has used an interfund transfer to restore an original investment strategy. The original goal was to have half the account in the safer G Fund, and the rest split evenly between the more risky C and F Funds. In our example the C and F Funds had somewhat higher returns than the G Fund, shifting the distribution of the total account. The employee files Form TSP-30 to reallocate the account, restoring the original investment profile.

Reallocation also can be used to shift to a different investment strategy, as shown in Figure 5-25.

Reallocation of $50,000 TSP Account Balance

	G Fund	C Fund	F Fund
Original Allocation of Contribution on TSP-1	50%	25%	25%
Current Account Balance	**$23,000**	**$14,000**	**$13,000**
Percentage of Total Account	46%	28%	26%
Requested Allocation on TSP-30	60%	40%	0%
Interfund Transfer	+$7,000	+$6,000	-$13,000
New Allocation of Account	**$30,000**	**$20,000**	**$0**

Figure 5-25

In the example in Figure 5-25, the employee has switched strategies. The original goal was to have half the account in the safer G Fund, and the rest split evenly between the more risky C and F Funds. In our example, the employee concluded that increasing the amount of C Fund investments offers higher growth potential. However, to offset the greater fluctuation of the C Fund returns, the employee decided to compensate by increasing the G Fund allocation at the same time.

Note: These particular investment allocations are shown only as examples. They are not recommended allocations. You have to make up your own mind about how you want to invest your TSP funds at various times. In Chapter Six we'll discuss some suggested approaches to defining a personal TSP investment strategy.

A PROFILE OF ACTUAL TSP INVESTMENT ALLOCATIONS

When the TSP was established, employee investment decisions were restricted. CSRS employees had to direct all their contributions to the G Fund, and FERS employees could only invest limited amounts in the C and F funds. Those restrictions were removed in 1991. Since then, all TSP participants have been able to allocate their new contributions and accumulated account balances among the three funds. There have been some general patterns worth noting.

The overall investment patterns of FERS and CSRS have become similar. Since the allocation restrictions were lifted, the general pattern has been a gradual but steady reallocation of TSP investments. Employees as a whole—CSRS and FERS alike—moved money from the G Fund to the C and F Funds.

Overall Use of G, C and F Funds
(Year-End Figures)

	Percentage of Contributing TSP Participants with:			
	All Money in G Fund		Some Money in C or F Funds	
	FERS	CSRS	FERS	CSRS
1991	57%	75%	43%	25%
1992	46%	52%	54%	48%
1993	39%	41%	61%	59%

Figure 5-26

The G Fund remains the predominant investment focus of TSP participants, but to less of an extent than in the past, as Figure 5-27 illustrates.

Investment of New TSP Contributions
(Year-End Figures)

	Percentage of New Contributions Invested in:		
	G Fund	C Fund	F Fund
1991	83%	13%	4%
1992	69%	23%	8%
1993	60%	30%	10%

Figure 5-27

Again we observe a movement of investments toward the C and F Funds, with their percentage shares more than doubling during the time. But the greater share of total account balances remains in the G Fund, as shown in Figure 5-28.

Distribution of TSP Account Balances
(Year-End Figures)

	Percentage of Total Balances Invested in:		
	G Fund	C Fund	F Fund
1991	88%	9%	3%
1992	80%	15%	5%
1993	72%	21%	7%

Figure 5-28

There is a difference between how new contributions are invested and how total account balances are invested. About 40 percent of new contributions are invested outside the G Fund, but only 29 percent of total balances are invested outside the G Fund. There is, however, some reallocation of accounts taking place. On balance, as Figure 5-29 shows, these interfund transfers have moved money from the G Fund to the C and F funds.

There is only about one interfund transfer per year for every 15 TSP participants. And, assuming that some employees transfer their funds more than once a year, still fewer participants apparently are using the interfund transfer mechanism each year.

Summary of Interfund Transfer Activity

	Total Number of Interfund Transfers	Movement of Funds ($ Millions)		
		G Fund	C Fund	F Fund
1991	128,419	- $528	+ $409	+ $119
1992	135,803	- $562	+ $436	+ $126
1993	135,847	- $631	+ $476	+ $155

Figure 5-29

These figures profile how your fellow employees are managing their TSP investments. But what they're doing is not necessarily what's best for you. In Chapter Six we'll consider some possible approaches to designing, monitoring and adapting your own TSP investment strategy.

5 THINGS TO DO

1. Start reading the business section of your newspaper, or a financial magazine, on a regular basis. The best way to become familiar with investments is by gradually absorbing the language and measurements of the financial world.

2. Move from your general learning toward a focus on each of the three TSP investment funds. Your goal: An understanding of intermediate and long-term interest rates (G Fund), stock indexes (C Fund) and intermediate and long-term bonds (F Fund). Learn about their earnings patterns and how and why they shift over time. See Chapter Six for some basic guidance.

3. Build a knowledge base that works for you. Don't get absorbed in one or a million investment theories and suggestions if you don't really understand the basis of the discussions. Build your personal understanding at your own pace.

4. As you improve your understanding of how and why the three TSP funds work, start thinking about what each of them can or cannot accomplish for you. Are you looking for maximum growth potential or a guaranteed minimum result? What's the timeframe for your TSP decision-making? How comfortable are you with risk? How does that affect your opportunities?

5. Trust your own opinion and judgment before anyone else's. Use others to confirm or review your own notions if you wish. But don't adopt someone else's insights or suggestions simply because you think they know more than you do. First of all, they may be wrong. Second, if you follow someone else's lead, you won't be in much of a position to monitor your results and reassess your decisions.

BUILDING YOUR TSP INVESTMENT STRATEGY

⟨6⟩

The following is a framework, not a blueprint. Our goal is to spotlight the information, schedules and choices that you may want to consider in building your TSP strategy. Throughout the discussion we will offer you options to tailor a specific approach based on your preferences.

For example, we'll give you basic guidelines for doing "ballpark" projections of your retirement income potential. Then we'll provide more detailed information if you want to do more precise calculations. You'll learn some important historical tendencies of the three TSP funds and then look more closely at how to build and adjust a TSP investment portfolio. You may decide to adopt a "low maintenance" TSP strategy, a "high maintenance" approach, or something in between. You may decide to devote minimum "upkeep" time to the TSP at some stages of your career, then become more active and focused at other times. That is your choice. This chapter will help you establish long-term goals, monitor progress toward those goals and understand the tools available to you along the way.

ESSENTIAL ELEMENTS OF AN EFFECTIVE TSP STRATEGY

The two pillars of the TSP are time and money. A careful TSP strategy pays attention to both, understands how they interact and uses them advantageously. A careless TSP strategy—or no strategy at all—wastes time and money.

To be careful—and successful—in your TSP planning does not require your every waking hour. Indeed, you may use the TSP effectively while spending only a few hours a year plotting your course. Successful TSP planning involves understanding how the program operates, assessing your goals and preferences, and adjusting to personal and financial developments as they unfold. With a basic strategy, you'll be able to monitor and anticipate events, identify key decisions and choices, and understand the potential consequences.

Let's begin with the concept of a "TSP Time Line." A TSP Time Line, depicted in Figure 6-1, is a lifelong calendar of the most important goals and choices you will face in using the TSP to your maximum financial advantage.

_____ Your TSP Time Line _____

Long-Term Strategies

What Are They?
> Your long-term strategies define the broad shape of your financial path from now to retirement. The long-term is a point of view, not a specific number of years. You can set or reset long-term strategies. From wherever you are now until retirement is the long-term.

Essential Question:
> How do I get from here to there?

Primary Goal:
> Plotting a course that will generate substantial retirement income with an acceptable level of risk

Key Elements:
> Estimating the potential range of your account growth
> Translating your potential savings into retirement income
> Defining a basic TSP investment strategy

Medium-Term Tactics

What Are They?
> Your medium-term tactics are the decisions you make along the way to ensure long-term success and maintain a balance with interim financial needs. They help you sustain progress and identify your "room to move."

Essential Question:
> What do I need to do to stay on track with my original plan?

Primary Goal:
> Identifying whether you are behind or ahead of your long-term savings schedule, and rethinking your financial choices accordingly.

Key Elements:
> Using TSP "checkpoints" to monitor your account growth
> Building mid-career financial needs into your TSP strategy
> Fitting your TSP account into your total savings portfolio

Short-Term Operations

What Are They?

Your short-term operations are mechanisms you use to understand when and how to change course in response to events and trends.

Essential Question:

Has something happened that I need to respond to?

Primary Goal:

Responding effectively to significant changes in market conditions.

Key Elements:

Gathering information and interpreting it accurately

Understanding market trends, market corrections and market-timing

Developing and implementing short-term adjustments

Figure 6-1

If you keep this basic TSP Time Line in mind, you'll be in a position to focus on the decisions that matter when they matter most. This will help you maintain steady and consistent control over your TSP account and maximize its advantages over time.

TSP LONG-TERM STRATEGY

The primary focus of the TSP is long-term retirement saving. As a TSP participant you always have a long-term strategic horizon—from now until the point at which you use your TSP account balance as retirement income.

It doesn't matter if you've just started your federal or postal career, are getting close to retirement, or somewhere in between. You still have a long-term time horizon that defines your total potential TSP account growth. The horizon may span 40 years or a much shorter period, but the essential point of reference remains the same. Your long-term retirement plans—definite or "best-guess"—provide the framework for your TSP planning and strategies.

Focusing on a long-term TSP time horizon is a key starting point regardless of your career plans. If you stay in federal or postal work straight through to retirement, your TSP account will in most cases be a substantial portion of your total retirement income package.

But even if you leave federal or postal service a long-term planning horizon is important. When you leave the government your TSP account is still a key piece of your retirement income potential, whether you keep the account in place for continued investment or "roll it over" into another savings plan. Establishing a long-term TSP focus will help you maintain that focus as you continue to build your retirement savings after you leave federal or postal service.

Whatever your age, career plans and retirement targets, your primary long-term goal remains the same: substantial savings growth with acceptable risk. The TSP has several built-in features that will help you meet this goal—convenient payroll deductions, monthly compounding of investment earnings and tax-deferred savings growth. Your long-term goal is to use those features effectively according to your personal circumstances and preferences.

Let's look at three key elements that will help you develop a successful long-term TSP strategy.

➤ **Key Long-Term Strategy #1:** Estimating the Potential Range of Your TSP Account Growth

Few things are as uncertain as your future savings potential. How will your career and earnings develop over the years? What will future economic conditions be like? How will the various financial markets perform under those conditions?

But all these uncertainties don't diminish the value of long-term retirement and TSP planning. You may not know exactly what's going to happen in the future. But the better you understand the likely range of what might happen, the more you'll be able to turn whatever events unfold to your best possible advantage.

Start by estimating what your final TSP account will be under various scenarios. These scenarios might include different combinations of events you can control and those you can't. You can control your general career path, how much you contribute to the TSP, how you invest your account among the three TSP funds and when you retire. You can't control the exact timing and size of salary increases, actual performance of TSP investment funds, future inflation and the purchasing power of your savings.

Even though these and other uncertainties may change your TSP outlook over time, you can still base your long-term strategy on a solid foundation. You can look first at the factors within your control—they'll define the basic structure of your TSP account growth. Then, for the factors outside your control, you can explore "best case" and "worst case" scenarios that capture the range of your likely TSP savings potential.

Three variables determine the growth of your TSP account:

◇ The amount of contributions flowing into your account every pay period,

◇ The length of time you make those contributions, and

◇ The rate of compounded investment earnings over that time.

You control the first two variables directly. You can also control the third variable to some extent through your TSP investment decisions.

The absolute first step in plotting a long-term TSP strategy is to take an early reading of the potential growth of your TSP account. There's no need to get obsessive about making an exact calculation—it would be silly to worry down to dollars and cents when so many events and variables lie between your decisions now and your ending

TSP balance years down the road.

But just because a precise calculation is impossible, that doesn't mean you should forget about long-term measurements. Don't react to the uncertainty of the future by saying "Well, I don't know how much my account will grow, so I'll just keep saving and the money will keep piling up." You need to have a basic idea of where your account is headed and what's waiting at the end of the journey.

We're going to start by giving you a fairly simple way to get a "ballpark" estimate of what your TSP account will be when you reach retirement. Appendix 2 (FERS employees) and Appendix 3 (CSRS employees) provide detailed tables to project your TSP account growth.

To get a general picture of how the two key factors—investment growth rate and years of compounded earnings—affect your potential account growth, review the numbers in Figure 6-2. It shows account estimates based on $1,000 in total contributions to your TSP account each year. You can estimate your account potential by comparing your total annual contributions to the $1,000 benchmark. For example, if your contributions equal $3,000, multiply the estimates by three. Estimated account balances are based on annual growth rates ranging from 3 percent to 10 percent.

As you review the annual growth rates to think about your projected account balance, keep an important point in mind. *Over the long haul, two factors will accelerate your account growth—real investment returns (over and above inflation) and real salary growth (over and above inflation).* For example, if your TSP investments earn 7 percent in a year and inflation is 3 percent, then the real investment gain is 4 percent.

Future TSP Account Balances in Today's Dollars

For Every $1,000 in Total Annual Contributions
Ending Account Balances in Thousands

Years in TSP	Annual Real Growth Rate (above inflation)							
	3%	4%	5%	6%	7%	8%	9%	10%
5	5	6	6	6	6	6	6	6
10	12	12	13	14	14	15	16	17
15	19	21	22	24	26	29	32	35
20	27	31	34	39	44	49	56	64
25	37	43	50	58	68	80	94	111
30	49	58	70	84	102	125	153	189
35	62	76	95	119	151	192	246	318
40	77	99	127	166	219	292	392	529

Figure 6-2

Similarly, if your salary goes up just because of a general annual cost-of-living adjustment, there is no real salary growth. Your salary has just kept pace—more or less—with inflation. But if you receive step or grade increases, then your salary goes up in real terms, above basic cost-of-living adjustments.

Three percent annual growth would be a conservative assumption. Investment earnings and pay raises will usually achieve that level, even if you don't receive substantial promotions during your career. Annual growth of 10 percent is a very optimistic assumption. You would have to achieve favorable investment returns and frequent step and grade increases. As a reference point, the historical real growth rate (above inflation) of the S&P 500 (C Fund) is 7 percent.

In our example, if the employee is in the TSP for 20 years and the real account growth is 4 percent per year, then the ending balance will be about $31,000 in today's dollars. If the employee is in the TSP for 30 years and real growth is 7 percent per year, then the ending balance will be about $102,000.

Note that if you're in the TSP for only a few years, investment returns do not affect your ending balance dramatically. Your total account growth is determined largely by the amount of contributions flowing into your account. As your investment period lengthens, differences in investment returns begin to affect your balance more substantially.

Possible Account Growth Scenarios

Conservative—4 Percent Annual Real Growth
This represents the historical pattern of long-term gains from low-risk investments like the G Fund, plus fairly modest growth in your salary during your career. If you invest conservatively or if the stock market hits a poor stretch or if you don't get the rapid promotions you were hoping for, you'll still be in a position to obtain a 4 percent real growth rate.

Realistic—7 Percent Annual Real Growth
This reflects the average real return from common stocks since 1926. It corresponds to what you could realize if you invest in the C Fund and the long-term performance of the stock market continues in the future. The longer your TSP investment period, the higher the probability that your C Fund returns would be close to the long-term pattern of 7 percent real growth.

Optimistic—10 Percent Annual Real Growth
This represents an optimistic potential return based on heavy investment in the C Fund, sustained stock market strength and (1) aggressive, well-timed movement of your TSP account among the C, F and G Funds to "time" movements in the stock and bond markets, and/or (2) a rapid promotion career path. You may want to use this scenario to estimate maximum growth potential. But you should not count on achieving this level of growth, and you should recognize that attempting to achieve it through "market-timing" may backfire—your own timing skills aside, the TSP is not well suited to quick account switching.

Figure 6-3

You can get a rough picture of your potential account growth by comparing the amounts in Figure 6-2 to the approximate amount of your total annual contributions to the TSP, including any matching contributions. To project more carefully based on your current account balance and future contribution plans, use the tables in Appendix 2 (FERS employees) or Appendix 3 (CSRS employees).

What rate of annual growth should you use in estimating your long-term account growth? There is no correct answer to that question; investment performance is inherently uncertain. But Figure 6-3 provides some benchmarks that you might find useful.

Give some thought to these three hypothetical scenarios before estimating your potential TSP account growth. We suggest using the 4 percent annual growth as your low-end estimate and 7 percent annual growth as your high-end estimate, with the 10 percent figure reserved for "what-if" speculation. Always remember that the hypothetical scenarios are for estimating purposes only. There is no assurance that your actual TSP investment performance will end up being at any particular point within this range, or within this range at all.

➤ **Key Long-Term Strategy #2:** Translating Your Potential TSP Savings into Retirement Income

In the previous section we discussed how to project your future TSP account balance. This enables you—at any point during your career—to estimate the total amount of retirement savings you may be able to accumulate through the TSP.

The next step in your long-term TSP planning is to know how that estimated account balance translates into retirement income. In Chapter Seven we'll look in detail at your choices when you actually use your TSP account as retirement income. In this section we want to give you a general sense of your projected account's retirement income value.

For your long-term TSP planning we suggest you focus on what your estimated TSP account balance will be worth if you use it to purchase an annuity. An annuity guarantees you a steady stream of monthly payments from the time you purchase it until you die. If you are married an annuity can also provide continuing payments to your spouse after your death.

When you purchase an annuity a formula determines the future monthly payments equal to the value of your TSP account balance. The annuity is calculated to "spend down" your account balance, based on: the total amount of your account balance; how old you are when you purchase the annuity; the average life expectancy for a person that age, and an interest rate index used to estimate continued earnings on your account balance during the annuity payment period.

If you elect an annuity option that includes continued payments to your surviving spouse, then your spouse's

age and average life expectancy also will affect the calculation.

When estimating your potential annuity payments use **TIP** *your TSP estimated account balance under conservative growth scenarios. This will give you a picture of extra retirement income that you can count on achieving.* It's an estimate that you can safely plan on as you consider the full range of your financial needs and choices. If you end up enjoying higher account growth, so much the better. But it's only prudent to estimate your retirement income using growth rates that you have a reasonable chance of achieving.

Remember that the numbers in Figure 6-4 are broad estimates for your long-term TSP and retirement planning. Exact actual amounts will depend, for example, on average life expectancies and interest rates at the time you retire, and on the specific type of annuity you elect.

Translating TSP Account Balance into Lifetime Retirement Income

**Annual Retirement Income
from $100,000 Account Balance**

| Age You Start
Receiving Income | Approximate Annual
Retirement Income |
|---|---|
| 55 | $7,000 - $8,000 |
| 60 | $8,000 - $9,000 |
| 65 | $9,000 - $10,000 |
| 70 | $10,000 - $11,000 |

Figure 6-4

You may wonder why the income amounts increase so gradually as the age you start receiving benefits increases. Keep in mind that this table reflects a fixed account balance of $100,000. If you wait to first obtain your TSP account balance until a later age, your account will continue to gain investment earnings. As a result, your retirement income would increase because of the increased value of your account.

➤ **Key Long-Term Strategy #3:** Defining a Basic TSP Investment Approach

A sound TSP investment strategy consists of three essential elements. First, an understanding of your investment goal. Second, a grasp of the nature of investment risk and how to take it into consideration. Third, a commitment to developing and implementing an investment strategy. With these three elements as a foundation, you cannot go far wrong. Your investment strategy may be substantially different from your neighbor's. But it will be solidly rooted and make sense for you.

As you consider your long-term investment strategy, understand three fundamentals: your attitude toward risk and return; the relationship between risk and time, and how to use risk and time as investment tools.

First, explore your personal preferences and attitudes toward potential risk and potential return. Your strategy has the same goal as everyone else's: maximum investment returns with an acceptable level of risk. But only you can define what level of risk you can accept, and how large the potential gains have to be to make the risk worthwhile. There is no one "correct" TSP investment strategy. The best TSP strategy for you will depend on your goals, age, other savings and investments, and your personal preferences.

Beware of claims that a particular investment or investment strategy is "better" than another. Think about this for a moment. At any point in time, all investment opportunities compete with one another for an available pool of investor dollars. If an investment has a negative feature, such as a high degree of risk, it must compensate with a positive feature, such as a potential for above-average returns.

A high risk, low return investment will be unable to attract investor dollars. Certain stocks or bonds may appear to be low risk, high return investments for short periods of time, but again the market will take over. Investors will chase after this "dream" opportunity, driving the price higher. Eventually the potential for future income will become less attractive relative to the current market price—new investors will back away, and current holders will sell off. Investment markets, like markets for goods and services, respond to the laws of supply and demand.

TIP In short, there is no such thing as a free lunch. *If you want to enjoy the possibility of higher long-term gains, you pay in the form of enduring the possibility of short-term loss. If you want to enjoy the comfort of a relatively certain outcome, you pay in the form of generally lower gains.*

These concepts directly apply to your choice of TSP investments. The G Fund will typically provide steady, predictable returns, but over time those returns will be lower than the C and F funds. The C Fund will offer the highest potential gains in a given period, but with the highest possibility of loss during that time. The F Fund will typically occupy a middle ground—potentially more profitable but riskier than the G Fund, generally less risky but less profitable than the C Fund.

When all is said and done, developing a personal TSP investment strategy comes down to making an informed judgment about the price you attach to risk and the potential gains entailed in assuming risk. The potential gains are determined by the specific investments involved—in the case of the TSP, the broad-based stock (C Fund) and bond (F Fund) markets and medium and long-term government securities (G Fund).

You may find it useful to begin by asking yourself a series of questions:

◇ Are you counting on realizing at least a certain minimum outcome? For example, do you absolutely have to have a certain amount in your TSP account at a certain point in time?

◇ How great a value do you attach to potential gains above your minimum goal? For example, if you can reasonably count on saving $100,000 with little or no risk, how important would it be to try to save $125,000, $150,000 or $200,000 instead? How much larger would the potential gain have to be to take on the risk of short-term losses?

◇ Would you prefer to establish a basic investment strategy and not worry about it? Or are you willing to take the time and thought to be more adaptive to changing circumstances?

◇ Is there a fixed timeframe that defines your goals? For example, if your goal is to save $100,000 within 30 years, will you take on more or less risk at various points during the 30-year period?

The sooner you address your personal attitudes toward risk and return, the sooner you'll begin the self-education process necessary to build a sound and profitable TSP investment strategy.

When you think about these questions, pay attention not only to your answers but also to the process you use to arrive at those answers. Were your initial reactions analytical or instinctive? Was your first impulse to decide or calculate?

Did you make definite decisions that you would stick with, or did you find yourself thinking, "It depends on other factors?" Is that a good answer or a bad answer? "It depends" might be a good answer if you are weighing alternative investments in terms of specific goals or constraints. It's a bad answer if you don't want to take the time to define your goals, don't understand the basic features of the TSP investment funds or view investment returns as essentially random results that you can't control.

Let's review some of the personal circumstances you may want to consider as you focus on your TSP investments. Your overriding goal might be to achieve a definite minimum target—for example, an extra amount of monthly retirement income that you feel you need to have to feel secure about your retirement. If so, you might incline toward an investment strategy that will almost certainly achieve that goal regardless of market fluctuations.

But a minimum goal might not be that important. You may not need your TSP account to build an adequate retirement income. You're more interested in potential gains that could increase your flexibility regarding when to retire, where to live after you retire or other financial options. You might look at strategies with somewhat higher risk and higher potential growth.

Constraints might be as important as goals. If your TSP account is a large portion of your entire lifetime savings, you might want to build a base of small gains until you have more leeway to play with. But if your TSP account is only a portion of a broader savings portfolio, you might be more willing to take risks.

Now consider whether you want to be relatively active or passive in the management of your TSP account. If you're prepared to be fairly active in your account management—adapting your strategy to changing circumstances—you can probably afford to take on a higher level of risk at any one point in time. By monitoring your account growth relative to long-term and mid-stream targets, you'll be in a position to assess when you can take on additional risk without endangering baseline expectations.

On the other hand, your approach to your TSP account may be more passive. Your inclination is to lock into a basic strategy and stick with it. There's nothing wrong with this approach. But it means you have to be more careful at the outset in projecting your expected outcomes. You can lock in a fixed strategy that includes a low, medium or high degree of investment risk. You should, however, be sure to look closely at the range of potential results your fixed strategy is likely to generate.

If you're going to adopt a passive approach, don't lock into a strategy until you've checked to be sure it will likely achieve a long-term outcome that falls within a range of acceptable results. For example, don't commit to 100 percent investment in the G Fund if its relatively modest returns won't achieve your long-term TSP account target. Similarly, don't commit to substantial C Fund investments without thinking about the possibilities for below-average results over the timeframe you've defined.

If you want to define and stick with a long-term TSP investment profile, take the time to develop a strategy that virtually guarantees your minimum expectations. Then assess your attitude toward additional potential growth—and the associated risk.

A final element in developing your TSP investment is the timeframe in which you're operating. In general, the longer the period before you need to use your TSP funds, the more you can trade short-term risk for potentially superior long-term returns. The closer you are to using your TSP account, the more cautious you have to be about the possibility of short-term losses.

Summary of Factors Affecting Your TSP Investment Strategy

	You Design a TSP Strategy That Includes	
	Lower Risk **Guaranteed Returns**	**Higher Risk** **Potential Returns**
Income Target	Defined minimum goal you must achieve	More discretionary retirement income
Other Savings	Low—TSP is most of your long-term savings	High—TSP is part of a broad portfolio
Other Investments	Have higher degree of risk (stocks, mutuals)	Have lower degree of risk (money markets)
Timeframe	Will count on TSP account balance soon	Many years before using TSP account

Figure 6-5

Before turning to specific aspects of the TSP investment options that may affect your strategic decisions, let's review the personal factors that define your strategic thinking. Figure 6-5 shows a range of factors that might affect the level of investment risk you might seek in your TSP account. For each factor, the table shows what considerations might lead to a lower-risk or higher-risk TSP investment strategy.

Only you can define how these and other factors should affect your personal TSP investment strategy. If you begin by focusing on how your TSP account fits into your overall savings goals, resources and timeframes, you can interpret information about the TSP investment funds more effectively. Our focus now is on an underlying long-term investment strategy. We'll discuss middle-term adjustments and short-term decision-making later. For now we want to continue to concentrate on defining your basic strategic framework.

Once you've identified your basic attitude toward return and risk, it's time to consider the relationship between risk and time. Let's look at the three TSP investment funds to build this understanding. We'll start with the shortest TSP investment timeframe—a single month—to observe investment returns and their fluctuations. Then we'll look at longer timeframes to see how time affects risk.

In Chapter Five we looked at the operation of the three TSP investment funds. We also reviewed their actual rates of return since January 1988, summarized in Figure 6-6.

Monthly Rates of Return for TSP Investment Funds, 1988-1993

	G FUND	C FUND	F FUND
Average Monthly Return	0.64%	1.10%	0.77%
Highest Monthly Return	0.78%	11.41%	3.19%
Lowest Monthly Return	0.45%	-8.65%	-1.48%
Average Change in Return Month to Month	0.03%	4.41%	1.20%

Figure 6-6

There is no assurance that future returns from the funds will closely resemble the figures shown here. What's important is the pattern of the figures and the general relationships among the three funds.

When we look at average monthly returns we find that the C Fund produced significantly higher average earnings than the G Fund and F Fund. If we look back over a longer historical period the same general pattern holds. For example, over the period 1976-1993 the S&P 500 (C Fund) had an average monthly return of 1.21 percent compared to 0.87 percent for the LBA Bond Index (F Fund) and 0.82 percent for G Fund-related securities. For the period 1961-1992 the average monthly return for the S&P

500 was 0.89 percent, compared to 0.66 percent for G Fund related securities. Notice that the average "spread" between the C Fund and the other two funds has been higher during the past five years than it was during longer historical periods.

But regardless of the exact size of the average C Fund "spread" over particular time periods, the general tendency is the same. The C Fund—over reasonably long periods—has in the past outperformed the other two funds in terms of average monthly returns. When we shorten the time period and focus on any particular month, we find a very different story. The overall tendency of the C Fund to outperform the G and F funds on an average basis does not mean that the C Fund provides the best returns in any particular period. The C Fund often underperforms the other two funds over shorter periods, sometimes significantly so. During 1988-1993, when the C Fund was averaging a gain of 1.26 percent per month, actual returns in any individual month ranged from an 11.41 percent increase to an 8.65 percent decrease. And, if we look at typical movements from one month to the next, we find that the C Fund didn't move gradually from strong periods to weak periods. Instead, it fluctuated sharply from one month to the next. The average change in the C Fund return from one month to the next was 4.78 percent.

Let's look at the 60-month period from January 1988 to December 1992 more closely. During those 60 months the C Fund earned a higher monthly return than the G Fund 34 times. The G Fund outperformed the C Fund in 26 months. The reason the C Fund averaged a 1.26 percent return per month compared to the G Fund average of 0.67 percent was not because the C Fund regularly performed better. The C Fund's average was higher because many of its "better than G Fund" months involved major gains. They were offset by major losses in many other months, but the balance was substantially positive.

Any C Fund investments you made for the entire 1988-1992 period proved profitable. But in almost half the individual months they were less profitable than G Fund investments. And there were stretches of up to 18 months in which the G Fund provided a higher return.

These monthly returns for 1988-1992 provide a backdrop to your understanding of short-term market risk. If you had $10,000 invested in the C Fund at any point in time, your monthly returns ranged from a gain of $1,141 to a loss of $865. By comparison $10,000 invested in the G Fund always gained, within a relatively narrow range of $54-$76 in any given month.

In hindsight you know that the risk of short-term C Fund losses would have been worth enduring. You know that if you had hung in there and didn't panic in the face of setbacks, you would have enjoyed an average gain on your $10,000 of $126 per month in the C Fund, instead of $67 in the G Fund and $78 in the F Fund. But the key point is that you only knew that in hindsight. It's the uncertainty of the result looking ahead that defines the risk.

Would you risk losing $865 in a given month if you didn't know what the longer-term outcome was going to be? The answer to that question depends a great deal on your personal situation, goals and preferences. But that does not mean that you can't think about risk in a systematic way. Future investment results are uncertain, but that doesn't mean they're random.

When you think about how much risk you want to build into your TSP account, think about the range of potential gains and losses in your specific context. A sensible risk for you is not necessarily a sensible risk for someone else. Don't let someone else define what is or is not a sound investment decision unless that judgment reflects your personal circumstances.

In particular, try to take account of risk and rewards within the overall context of your TSP time line. Because an absolutely critical point for you to understand is that time and risk are related. Your TSP time line may substantially shift your risk calculation at various points.

Let's look at this concretely by examining the real rates of return—after inflation—for the S&P 500 for the period 1926-1993. Again, the past does not ensure the future—there is no assurance that future investment returns will repeat past tendencies. But by looking at the entire 67-year period of S&P 500 measurements, we can gain some insights into past stock market patterns and the relationship between risk and time. When we calculate the year-to-year growth of the S&P 500 over the 67-year period, we observe a consistent and very important pattern.

For the entire period 1926-1993 the S&P 500 had an annual real return of 7.06 percent. If you invested in the S&P 500 over the entire period, your total gain at the end of 1993 would have amounted to the equivalent of earning a little more than 7 percent each year, over and above inflation.

___ Standard & Poor's 500, 1926-1993 ___

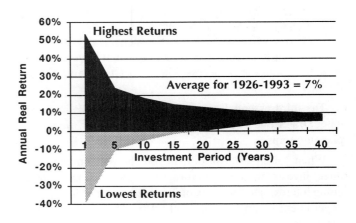

Figure 6-7

But, as we've already seen, this hardly means that the S&P 500 gained 7 percent every year. Figure 6-7 shows the range of annual returns for varying amounts of time within the overall 67-year period. For example, there were 67 one-year periods. In those individual years S&P 500 real returns ranged from 53.48 percent to a negative 38.67 percent. When we shift to five-year periods, the range of annual returns narrows—the highest five-year performance was 23.77 percent per year for five years, while the worst average return was a negative 9.92 percent. And so on as we look at ever-longer "holding periods."

Over holding periods of 20 years or longer, the average rates of real return were always positive. And, over periods of 30 years or longer, the average real rate of return always exceeded 4 percent per year.

Understanding Figure 6-7 is vital if you want to use the TSP C Fund successfully and confidently. It highlights the difference between short-term fluctuations and long-term trends. And it puts the relationship between risk and return in sharp focus.

At any point in time your C Fund investments involve a high degree of risk. From 1926-1993 the stock market suffered losses in nearly half of all individual months and in 20 out of 67 calendar years. *If you invest in the stock market—through an index fund similar to the C Fund, a mutual fund or by selecting individual stocks—avoiding temporary losses is impossible.*

If historical patterns hold true, there are three ways to reduce the chance and size of losses on your C Fund investments. First, you can plan on holding C Fund investments for long periods. Second, you can attempt to time your entries to and exits from the C Fund, maximizing your holdings during upswings and minimizing your investments during downturns. Third, you can blend the two approaches—taking a generally long-term view toward your C Fund investments while attempting to reduce your loss exposure in the short-term.

We'll look in more detail at short-term risk management later in this chapter. The essential point from a long-term perspective is that determining the appropriate level of risk for your TSP investments does not have to be an uninformed decision. You can look at the tradeoff between risk and expected return systematically. And if you do so early in your TSP time line, you will very likely achieve long-term success with reduced anxiety along the way.

The third essential consideration in your TSP investment strategy is your understanding of risk and time as planning tools.

When you invest TSP dollars you choose from among three investment opportunities. The G Fund pays the going interest rate for a mix of intermediate and long-term government securities. The fund reflects the rates paid on securities with varying maturities—for example, five years, 10 years, 15 years, 20 years and 30 years to maturity. At any time the G Fund interest rate will reflect expec-

tations about inflation over the periods from purchase to maturity, plus a real above-inflation return to attract investors.

As a result, G Fund rates tend to shift gradually. The G Fund is an average of the rates on government securities bought and sold at varying times. As old securities reach their maturity dates and new securities are auctioned by the Treasury, the G Fund average for all securities shifts up and down in a gradual pattern. The primary driving force will be future inflation expectations.

This explains why the G Fund paid a relatively high real rate of return from 1988-1993—an average of 4 percent annually. In response to the high inflation of the late 1970s and early 1980s, interest rates climbed sharply during that period. As inflation was brought under control, intermediate and long-term interest rates declined, but gradually. As a result, while inflation was down to 3 to 4 percent per year in the late 1980s and early 1990s, intermediate and long-term interest rates were still in the range of 6 to 9 percent.

Now let's look at the F Fund. The F Fund, like the G Fund, also revolves around intermediate and long-term fixed-income securities. There are two differences. One difference is that the F Fund reflects a mix of Treasury, corporate and mortgage-backed securities—not just the Treasury securities of the G Fund. But remember that all these fixed-income securities compete with one another for investors, and the slim chance of corporate or mortgage defaults does not significantly increase the interest rates necessary to attract buyers.

The other difference between the F Fund and the G Fund is between interest rates and market value. The G Fund pays the average interest rate for a mix of securities. The F Fund pays the change—plus or minus—in the market value of those securities, plus the reinvestment of interest earned while the securities are held.

We discussed in Chapter Four how the market value of fixed income securities is sensitive to current interest rates. To recap, if an investor holds a bond paying 8 percent for 20 years and current interest rates are rising, the 8 percent bond becomes less attractive. The investor may or may not sell it off to replace it with a 9 percent bond, but even if the investor holds onto the bond there aren't going to be a lot of bidders knocking on the door to buy it. As a result, its market price will decline. On the other hand, if current interest rates are falling, the opportunity to lock in an 8 percent interest rate for 20 years becomes more attractive. Buyers will come and the price of the 8 percent bond will rise.

If you grasp this relationship, several conclusions follow logically. If you want to use the F Fund and the G Fund effectively at different points in time, you need to understand these basic concepts:

◇ During periods when current interest rates are stable, F Fund and G Fund returns will be roughly comparable. Both will earn the interest on a mix of intermediate and long-term securities, and there will be little buying or selling affecting the market price of F Fund securities.

◇ When current interest rates are rising, the F Fund will earn a lower rate of return than the G Fund. The rising interest rates will be gradually driving up the average G Fund rate, while driving down the market value of the F Fund's securities.

◇ When current interest rates are falling, the F Fund will earn a higher rate of return than the G Fund. The declining interest rates will be gradually driving down the average G Fund rate, while driving up the market value of the F Fund.

◇ Over long periods, the F Fund can be expected to have slightly higher returns than the G Fund. Periods of rising interest rates will favor the G Fund. Periods of falling interest rates will favor the F Fund. Over long periods involving interest rate movement in both directions, the total long-term returns may not differ substantially. But the F Fund will be likely to have somewhat higher returns over time because changes in market value are supplemented by interest paid on securities while they are held. Those somewhat higher returns will also involve the risk of losses and larger short-term fluctuations.

We've described the relationship between the G Fund and the F Fund in some detail for an important reason. We're focusing at this point on your long-term TSP investment strategy. We'll look at medium-term and short-term adjustments later in this chapter. For now we want to concentrate on your development of a baseline, long-term investment strategy.

From a long-term perspective, you do not face an important choice between the G Fund and the F Fund. You can reasonably expect the F Fund to pay a slightly higher rate of return than the G Fund over long time periods. But you will also encounter higher short-term fluctuations in the F Fund compared to the G Fund.

You may decide on a long-term strategy that includes substantial or minimal G Fund investments and substantial or minimal F Fund investments. But both are going to be sensitive to interest rate movements over the long term.

Your much more important choice from a long-term perspective is how much of your TSP account you devote to the C Fund. History suggests that the C Fund is likely to provide higher potential for long-term growth and a significantly higher degree of risk, particularly in the short-term, compared to either of the other two funds. *Your essential long-term strategic choice is how much of your account you want to invest in the C Fund.*

Only you can assess the returns and risks of C Fund investments relative to your goals, circumstances and preferences. But the more informed your assessment is, the better your chances of achieving higher long-term savings growth within a comfortable range of risk.

There are two major issues you should focus on. First, how much would the C Fund's typically higher average

long-term returns increase your final TSP account balance? Second, how much would the C Fund's larger short-term losses threaten your projected long-term results? In general, the length of your future TSP investment period is the most important factor in answering both questions.

The typically higher returns of the C Fund will dramatically increase your TSP account growth over long investment periods. Figure 6-8 shows the growth of two TSP accounts over a 40-year period. Account A earns a 4 percent real rate of return with low risk. Account B earns a 7 percent rate of return reflecting historical C Fund (S&P 500) patterns with a higher degree of risk. Both accounts have a total $2,000 of new contributions each year. In this example, it doesn't matter whether the $2,000 is all employee contributions (CSRS) or a mix of employee and agency contributions (FERS).

Growth of Two TSP Accounts over a 30-Year Investment Period

Based on $2,000 in New Contributions Each Year

TSP Account Balance After	Account A 4% Real Return	Account B 7% Real Return	Account B Higher by
5 years	$11,000	$12,000	$1,000
10 years	$24,600	$28,800	$4,200
15 years	$41,000	$53,000	$12,000
20 years	$61,200	$87,000	$25,800
25 years	$85,800	$135,200	$49,400
30 years	$115,800	$203,600	$87,800

Figure 6-8

Over the entire 30-year period, Account B steadily gains more value compared to Account A. But it takes some time before the differences in total account balances become substantial. If the investment mix needed to pursue 7 percent real growth involves more risk than the investments that will yield 4 percent, is the risk worth it?

The expected length of your investment period is a key variable in answering that question. Over a five-year period you're taking on the risk in the expectation of gaining $1,000, only 10 percent more than what you expect from the lower-risk strategy. But over a 30-year period you're taking on the risk in the expectation of gaining $87,800, over 75 percent more than your lower-risk expectation.

So the ratio of risk to reward generally lessens as your investment period lengthens because longer investment periods increase the likelihood that any short-term losses you encounter will be overcome by gains in the future.

Build your long-term TSP investment strategy on a three-part foundation—your financial goals, your personal attitudes toward risk and an understanding of how risk and time interact. Above all, ask the questions that matter to you and rely on yourself to develop the answers.

MEDIUM-TERM TACTICS _____

In the previous section we looked at the three essential elements of a long-term TSP strategy—assessing your account's potential growth, translating account projections into expected retirement income and building an investment strategy sensitive to your goals and the relationship between risk and time. Together they provide the road map guiding you toward your TSP goals. It's vitally important to base your TSP participation on realistic measurements of your savings potential and investment choices.

It's equally important to be prepared to review your progress and, when appropriate, adjust your original strategy. Medium-term tactics are the assessments and adjustments you make to sustain your long-term TSP strategy and balance it with other financial goals.

Why are medium-term tactics important? First of all, like any other significant aspect of your life, your retirement income deserves your attention. It's easy and tempting to make some basic long-term decisions and let them ride: "I'm putting aside 5 percent of pay and my investments seem to be doing pretty well—everything must be fine." Still, it's worth double-checking from time to time. You don't just buy a car. You fill it with gas, check the oil, rotate the tires and listen for funny noises. You don't just send your child off to a new school. You check out the neighborhood, meet with the teachers and know exactly when the report cards arrive. It only makes sense to give your retirement savings the same careful treatment.

Second, you want to be in a position to spot—sooner rather than later—that you're not on track to meet your targets. When you first started participating in the TSP, or when you first took the time to sit down and figure out where your account was headed, you probably defined some general expectations. Perhaps now you've brought those expectations into sharper focus. For a variety of reasons, your original strategy may not be progressing as well as you anticipated. Your TSP investment earnings may not be as high as you expected. You may not have received the promotion you were counting on. Your spouse's earnings or retirement coverage may have changed for the worse. Time to take another look at your long-term prospects.

Third, you need to know if you're doing better than you expected. Being able to judge that your retirement savings are ahead of schedule is important. Peace of mind is a precious commodity. But you also want to be able to act on that knowledge by balancing your long-term retirement goals with other financial needs. Your TSP contributions involve sacrificing current consumption for a long-term savings goal. It's possible to oversave for the long-term at the expense of current needs. If you're running ahead of your long-term goal, you want to be able to see that and perhaps adjust your balance of savings and consumption accordingly. But if you choose to cut back on your savings, be sure to continue to monitor your investment's performance so that you stay on your long-

term plan. It's your money. Manage it so you can pursue as many of your goals as possible.

Let's look at each of these three elements in turn: reviewing where you are; adjusting your strategy when you're behind schedule, and thinking about alternatives if you're exceeding your long-term targets.

> ➤ **Medium-Term Tactic #1:** Use TSP Checkpoints to Monitor Your TSP Account and Your Savings Goals

Make TSP checkpoints a standard part of your financial planning. At least once a year, set aside time for a thorough review of your TSP account and how it fits into your overall financial goals. The two TSP open seasons each year, when you may change investment levels or allocations, offer natural times to do this.

The first time you do this you may find it time-consuming and a little perplexing. But don't get discouraged. It may take a while before you become comfortable with the issues and calculations involved in your personal money management. But it's time well spent. Self-education is an important element in getting the most out of your TSP opportunities. And the time you spend assessing your TSP account will add to your understanding of your personal finances and investment opportunities.

Set the scene properly. It's your money and your retirement. Conduct your checkpoints at home, in comfortable surroundings, with the time available to ponder all your goals without pressure or distractions. This is not for your lunch hour, car pool or subway ride.

What goes into a thorough TSP checkpoint? Several topics are essential. You may have additional issues that arise from your personal circumstances.

Checkpoint 1: Update Your TSP Account Projection. Use tables in Appendix 2 (FERS employees) or Appendix 3 (CSRS employees) to bring your account projection up to date. If your retirement or career expectations have changed since you last reviewed your TSP account, adjust your projections accordingly. For example, if you had been planning on retiring at age 65 but now think you might be interested in retiring earlier, look at your account from your revised perspective. Or, if you are rethinking your career plans, look at your account in terms of when you might consider leaving federal or postal employment.

Checkpoint 2: Look at Your Potential Account in Terms of Potential Future Income. It may be satisfying to expect to have $100,000, $250,000 or some other large amount balance in your long-term projections. Large lump sum amounts always look impressive. But take the time to translate that into a real income pattern so that you have some perspective on what you're building.

Although you will have several options for withdrawing your TSP money, for this purpose estimate what your projected account balance will be worth as a lifetime annuity. Why? Because building a secure, regular stream of income is the first step in retirement planning. Layering your projected TSP annuity income on top of other expected retirement benefits will give you a good overall view of your prospects. You can think about other uses of your TSP account once you've looked at your monthly retirement income. Don't worry about exact dollars and cents—just compute a ballpark estimate of your annuity amount.

Checkpoint 3: Compare Your Projections to Previous Estimates. If you check your TSP account status every year, you're going to get some variations in your estimates. You have an approximate notion of expected investment performance, but your actual investment returns won't exactly match your long-term expectation in any particular year. So don't get too worried if your current account is not quite what you expected it to be. Conversely, don't get too excited if it's running a little ahead of your previous projections.

Look instead for significant differences or consistent patterns. If your account balance is much higher or lower than you expected it to be, take some time to understand why this happened. This is important. If your account is larger than your previous projections, it may be simply that the stock market (C Fund) had a particularly good stretch. Or, the G Fund may be tracking on top of a relatively high inflation—high interest rates don't necessarily mean substantially higher real growth. Similar short-term events may push your account balance below your previous projections. Don't let temporary conditions automatically dictate a major change in your goals or strategies.

But differences between your previous and current estimates may in some cases be significant. Your account balance may be consistently falling behind your projections with each passing year. This may mean your TSP investment mix is not suited to produce the results you originally expected.

Checkpoint 4: Assess Any Shifts in Your TSP Investment Mix. At some point you'll probably decide on a basic long-term TSP investment strategy. You may adjust it from time to time in response to market conditions, but there is an underlying "investment mix" that you've established.

For example, you may decide that you want to stake a substantial portion of your account on expected long-term stock market growth. But you also want to have a steadier component to temper the effects of short-term fluctuations. You end up with a basic long-term strategy of allocating 60 percent to the C Fund, 30 percent to the G Fund and 10 percent to the F Fund. Your expectation is that over the long-term this investment will achieve about a 5 percent annual real rate of return. Combined with 1 percent real salary growth you expect an annual account growth rate of 6 percent per year.

When you check your TSP investments, look at two questions. First, does the current allocation of your account balance reflect your intended strategy? Second, how is your investment mix actually performing compared to your original expectations?

Over time, the distribution of your account among the three funds will shift as each fund's performance varies from month to month and year to year. If one fund has particularly strong or weak returns in a certain period, you may end up with an investment that's strayed quite a bit from your original plan, as illustrated in Figure 6-9.

Example of Shift in TSP Investment Mix, 1988-1993

Based on $2,000 Total Annual Contributions

	C Fund	F Fund	G Fund	Total
Original Allocation on Form TSP-1	60%	10%	30%	100%
Annual Contributions	$1,200	$200	$600	$2,000
Total Contributions	$7,200	$1,200	$3,600	$12,000
Earnings:				
1988	$71	$4	$26	$101
1989	$581	$42	$82	$705
1990	-$115	$44	$143	$72
1991	$1,458	$124	$192	$1,774
1992	$569	$80	$227	$876
1993	$928	$133	$244	$1,305
Balance, End of 1993	$10,692	$1,627	$4,514	$16,833
Allocation, End of 1993	63.5%	9.7%	26.8%	100%

Figure 6-9

By the end of 1993 the investment allocation differs somewhat from the original allocation—about 64 percent of the total account is in the C Fund, compared to an original 60 percent allocation. The G Fund share declined from 30 percent to about 27 percent.

As you move forward into a longer TSP investment period with larger account balances, the effects of short-term movements of the funds will become more dramatic. Your total account will be larger compared to incoming contributions, and the effects of different investment returns will become greater. Use your TSP checkpoint to compare your current TSP investment mix with your original long-term strategy. By keeping the shares of your account in each fund consistent over time, reallocation of your account will help you automatically respond to market trends. For example, you will be moving money into the C Fund when stock prices have fallen and removing money from the C Fund when stock prices have increased. This will provide a ballast against short-term market fluctuations. The same principle applies to the F Fund with respect to fluctuations in bond prices.

Checkpoint 5: Review Mid-Career Developments and Financial Needs. You may encounter situations that affect your TSP contributions or investments. First, there may be an anticipated financial expense that you have to meet, such as the cost of a child's education. Second, you or your spouse's career expectations may shift. You may contemplate taking a job outside the government. Your spouse's retirement benefits may change.

If you're anticipating a known financial need, use the TSP as one of your planning tools. The first step is to determine whether the anticipated expense qualifies under the TSP loan program. Then you can consider the advantages and disadvantages of using a loan from your TSP account or securing financing from other sources. Chapter Seven will walk you through the details of the TSP loan program. In this section we simply want to highlight the major questions you might want to incorporate into your TSP checkpoints:

◇ How much money will you need and when will you need it?

◇ Could a TSP loan be part of your financing?

◇ Will your projected account balance and resulting eligible loan amount be enough?

◇ Do you need to shift your TSP investment mix to protect against possible short-term losses, so your expected loan amount is secure?

◇ Will you be able to take on TSP loan payments—or payments to another financing source—without reducing your TSP salary deductions?

◇ If you do expect to have to scale back your TSP contributions temporarily, how will those reductions affect your long-term TSP planning?

Ideally, you'll be in a position to review these questions well in advance of the actual need. This will give you the time to assess your options carefully and make sensible adjustments to your overall financial plan.

If you're thinking about possible career changes, this too should be an element in your TSP review. What kinds of retirement benefits will your potential new employer provide? Is there a savings plan comparable to the TSP at the job you're considering? If you leave federal or postal service, what will you do with your TSP account?

As you explore and evaluate possible career opportunities, be sure to factor into the equation possible effects on your retirement income. Some jobs may offer benefits comparable or superior to the government. In other cases a career change may reduce your retirement income opportunities. That doesn't necessarily mean you shouldn't make the career change. There may be other advantages to the new job that make up for less attractive retirement benefits. The important thing is to be aware of the retirement implications and—if you do leave the government—start building a revised long-term strategy as soon as possible.

For example, you may be thinking about setting up your own business, or joining a new or small firm that has minimal benefits. If so, start thinking about your TSP account and what part it might play in your transition to a new situation. You may want to accelerate your TSP account growth to help you gain the security and comfort

you need to be able to think seriously about an enticing career opportunity. Or, if you're considering retiring from the government in your mid-fifties and setting up your own business, look closely and realistically at your expected income during the first few years. Will your CSRS or FERS pension be enough to live on while you get your business going, or should you supplement it with income from your TSP account?

Checkpoint 6: Look at Your TSP Account as Part of Your Overall Savings Portfolio. Early in your career your TSP account may be your only major source of long-term savings. But as you move through your career, you may start to develop other savings instruments—growing equity in your home, an IRA, mutual funds, stock and bond portfolios and so on.

When you review the status of your TSP account, spend some time thinking about how the TSP fits within your overall savings. In particular, pay attention to the following issues:

◇ What is the overall investment strategy of your total portfolio?

◇ Have you used different savings vehicles to diversify your investment mix, or are you stacking low-risk or high-risk approaches on top of one another?

◇ If you want to diversify your investment profile, which savings vehicles should you use for higher risk and growth potential?

◇ Double-check the liquidity of each part of your portfolio so you'll know the easiest and least expensive ways to obtain quick access to some of your savings under different circumstances.

There is no perfect investment portfolio and no fixed blueprint for how the TSP should fit within your overall savings. However, one important point to keep in mind is that the TSP is distinctly suited to long-term savings growth. The tax deferred treatment of contributions and investment earnings, restrictions on when and how you can withdraw your account balance, the tax penalty on early withdrawals and the fact that you can only adjust your TSP investment allocations on a fixed monthly cycle—all these factors differentiate your TSP account from other savings opportunities.

If as you progress through your career you begin to build a range of investments, think carefully about which ones are best suited to various financial tasks. For example, if you have a $30,000 TSP account and $20,000 in other savings, think of your investment strategies in terms of the full $50,000 portfolio. If your preferred investment mix is 80 percent higher-risk and 20 percent lower-risk, that translates to $40,000 and $10,000 respectively. Decide on the best places to locate the $40,000 in higher-risk investments. Look at the track records of earnings and fluctuations, but also consider your ability to manage and move the money in response to changing market conditions. Also consider tax treatment and liquidity of the various investment options.

You might also want to link the growth of your various savings accounts with the financial goals they are supporting. Within an overall $50,000 portfolio, think about how much of the total is for retirement purposes, how much for other defined financial needs, and how much for more discretionary and flexible goals. The planned use of your savings may affect your desired risk profile at various times.

By reviewing these TSP checkpoints from time to time, you'll be able to monitor your account growth effectively. Make it a regular part of your TSP planning, perhaps in conjunction with one or both TSP open seasons each year. As it becomes a regular part of your financial planning, you'll be able to tailor your TSP review to your individual needs and circumstances.

➤ **Medium-Term Tactic #2:** Identifying and Adjusting If Your Account Growth Is Below Expectations

If you use TSP checkpoints to monitor your account growth, you'll be able to identify situations in which your balance is not as high as you expected it to be. Knowing that you're lagging behind your original projections is important in and of itself. But equally important are being able to identify why you're below your target and knowing how to determine whether adjustments are necessary.

To understand what you should be looking for and how to interpret what you find, look at the example given in Figure 6-10. It illustrates what might happen when $3,000 in total contributions annually enters your account, either through solely your own investments (CSRS employee) or a combination of personal and agency contributions (FERS employee).

TSP Account Balance Is Lower Than Expected

Annual TSP Contributions:		$3,000
Expected Real Growth (Above Inflation):		7% per year
Projected TSP Balance After:	5 years:	$18,000
	10 years:	$43,200
	15 years:	$79,500
	20 years:	$130,500
	25 years:	$202.800
	30 years:	$305,400
Actual Account Balance after 10 Years:		$38,700
Actual Growth Rate, Years 1-10:		5% per year

Figure 6-10

In this example, you expected a real growth rate—over and above inflation—of 7 percent per year on a $3,000 annual contribution. As a result, you projected your account to grow as indicated. But in Year 10 you realize that you've fallen substantially behind your target. Your account balance is $38,700, not the $43,200 you expected. Your future financial projections and plans may have to be redrawn.

What to do in this situation? First and foremost, don't panic. Review your account to identify exactly what happened and what—if anything—you should do about it. Don't jump to seemingly obvious, but possibly incorrect conclusions: "I need to contribute more, I need to get better returns, I need to work longer to afford to retire, I need to do something!" Well, maybe you do, maybe you don't.

What are the possible reasons for your shortfall? Let's take up several so that you understand what to look for if and when you encounter a shortfall in your TSP account.

There Was a Decline in Your Investment Returns. You based your TSP account projections on a 7 percent annual growth rate. You invested your entire TSP account in the C Fund, hoping that it would match its long-term real growth rate from 1926-1992. You get to Year 10 and find out the growth rate has been only 5 percent and you're $4,500 below your expectations. What happened?

What may have happened is that the C Fund experienced a sharp short-term decline within an overall pattern of solid performance. For the first nine years the C Fund performed as you expected it to. There were upswings and downturns, but for the entire nine-year period the annual growth rate was 7 percent over and above inflation. At the end of Year 9 your account balance was about $37,500 and you were progressing nicely toward your 10-year projection of $43,200.

All of a sudden, the stock market has a poor stretch during Year 10. Instead of matching its long-term trend of 7 percent real annual growth, the C Fund has a 5 percent negative return that year. You temporarily lose about $1,800 from your account balance, offset by $3,000 in new contributions, for a net gain of only $1,200 during Year 10, rather than the $5,700 you were hoping for.

So you're $4,500 behind your target, but do you have a problem? Probably not. You're expecting to stay in the TSP for years to come, plenty of time to recoup the losses. Is there any reason to think that one bad year on the stock market means your original long-term expectations were incorrect? Again, probably not. That's just how the C Fund and the stock market function.

Your Expectations Don't Match Your Investment Mix. You started off investing your entire account in the C Fund. Over the first five years your account growth more or less kept pace with your expectations. But you didn't like the way the C Fund moved sharply up and down from month to month and year to year. So starting Year 6 you changed your TSP investment mix from 100 percent in the C Fund to 50 percent in the C Fund, 25 percent in the F Fund and 25 percent in the G Fund—a sensible thing to do if the C Fund fluctuations made you uncomfortable. One precondition for a good investment portfolio is that it allows you to sleep at night.

OTIP *But if you do make any major changes in your TSP investment mix, you have to revisit your long-term account growth expectations. In general, if you shift from a higher-risk mix to a lower-risk mix, your annual growth rate will decline. It's not realistic to expect to enjoy the safety of lower-risk investments without giving up some of your growth potential.*

There's historical evidence to support an expectation of 7 percent annual real growth from the C Fund. There is no assurance that you'll match that expectation, but there's ample reason to have that expectation. On the other hand, there is no historical evidence to support an expectation of 7 percent real growth from either the F Fund or the G Fund. You may get that level of growth in short spurts, but it would be unrealistic to expect it consistently. A more reasonable expectation for the G Fund would be 3 percent real annual growth, and for the F Fund perhaps 4 percent real annual growth.

The reason for the shortfall in your account at Year 10 was that you never adjusted your growth expectations to reflect your revised investment mix. Your new investment mix performed fairly close to what historical patterns would suggest. Your investments aren't off, your projections are.

You Expected Your Salary to Grow More than it Actually Did. If you're contributing a designated percentage of pay to the TSP, your account growth results from your investment earnings and salary increases. When you project future account growth, think about investments and pay increases in real terms, above inflation.

In our example of an account shortfall at Year 10, what may happened is that your TSP investments performed more or less as expected, but your promotions and salary increases didn't. Let's say you began participating in the TSP with $3,000 in annual contributions—for example, a FERS employee earning $30,000 and contributing 5 percent of pay ($1,500), together with 5 percent agency contributions (another $1,500). Your total contributions when you first started in the TSP were $3,000 a year.

You decided to invest your entire TSP account in the G Fund. You projected the G Fund to earn a 3 percent annual real return. Then, on top of your expected investment returns, you added expected growth to your account from future salary increases. You estimated that grade and step promotions would increase your salary—in real terms— by about 4 percent per year. As a result, you based your TSP account projections on a total of 7 percent real annual growth—3 percent from investment earnings, plus 4 percent from salary increases.

In our example, that means you projected your salary to increase from $30,000 in Year 1 to about $42,700 in Year 10 (4 percent real growth for nine years). To put it in perspective, that would be roughly equivalent to moving from a Grade 9, Step 3 to Grade 12, Step 2 between Year 1 and Year 10.

That may have been a perfectly reasonable expectation

during Year 1. But, unfortunately, things didn't work out that way. Instead, your real salary growth averaged out to only 2 percent per year for the nine years. Instead of your salary moving from $30,000 in Year 1 to about $41,100 in Year 10, it only increased to about $35,900. Instead of reaching Grade 12, Step 1, your promotions only carried you to Grade 11, Step 1.

As a result, your annual TSP growth rate was 5 percent instead of the 7 percent you originally projected. Your G Fund investments matched your expectations, but your salary growth was not as rapid as you had hoped it to be.

These are a few examples of why and how your actual TSP account balance may not match your previous estimates at a particular time. *If you encounter a short-term* **TIP** *loss due to poor investment returns, make sure you look at your investment returns from a long-term perspective before making any hasty decisions about changing your TSP investment mix.* You may have a momentary account shortfall that has no real significance for your future growth potential. Are your investments truly off track compared to your expectations, or are you simply taking your measurements right after a market downturn that future returns will overcome?

Or, were your expectations unrealistic? If you encounter a mismatch between your account expectations and your investment mix, then you've got some thinking to do. If you're comfortable with your investment mix and want to stick with it, you need to reassess your future account projections accordingly. Whatever your particular TSP investment mix, base your account projections on a realistic look at historical patterns for that mix. History is no guarantee; but it's the best available guide.

You may decide that you're not happy with scaling back your expectations to match your investment mix. You've identified the shortfall, recognized that you made a mistake earlier in assuming too high a return from your investment mix, and now you want to do something about it. If so, you need to start from where you are now and look ahead to your ultimate long-term TSP target.

First, look at possible shifts in your investment mix. At your current rate of contributions to the TSP, how high an average annual investment return would you need to reach a target 10, 15 or 20 years down the road? In many cases, only a slight improvement in your investment returns may be needed to get back on course. For example, let's say you originally planned on earning 5 percent returns for 30 years. If you discover 15 years down the road that you've only earned 4 percent, think about what it likely would take to earn 6 percent for the remaining 15 years. How much would you have to redesign your investment allocations? Use the tables in Appendix 2 (FERS employees) or Appendix 3 (CSRS employees) to estimate what your future returns would have to be to get back on course toward your long-term target.

Modest improvements in investment performance, compounded over time, will often get you back on track and may involve only modest adjustments toward higher-risk options. But if you have a substantial shortfall and only a limited time period for future investment gains, don't go chasing rainbows. Don't revise your projections based on potential future investment returns that are unrealistic and that have no basis in historical patterns. Don't say: "Well, I'm behind where I want to be, but 10 years of 10 percent real returns and everything will be fine again." Don't plan on investment returns that you have a poor chance of achieving. If your original long-term target is that important, increase your contributions. If you're already investing the maximum in the TSP, you'll have to do the extra saving elsewhere.

If you encounter salary growth below your expectations, look at your future career opportunities and TSP growth potential. Scale your TSP expectations to an honest assessment of your career path. You may decide to tighten your belt and make higher percentage contributions to the TSP to make up for your pay not being as large as you hoped it would be. But that could be difficult. Take the time to measure realistically where you are in your career now, where you can confidently plan on getting to in the future and what that means for your long-term TSP savings potential.

➤ **Medium-Term Tactic #3:** Identifying and Adjusting If Your Account Growth Is Above Expectations

So much for the bad news. Let's turn now to a more pleasant prospect. You review the status of your TSP account and find that you're ahead of schedule. For example, after 15 years you expected to have an account balance of $79,500, and—lo and behold—it's actually $95,000.

Before you get too excited, be sure to go through the same series of "reality checks" that we walked through in the previous section on account shortfalls. Make sure you understand why your account is outpacing your expectations before you make any decisions about adjusting your long-term savings behavior.

First, look for exceptional short-term investment returns. You may be ahead of your target simply because of a relatively brief period of high real interest rates in the G Fund, strong stock market performance in the C Fund or short-term declines in interest rates that drove up bond prices and F Fund returns. Any or all of these short-term results may have little to tell you about how your investments will perform in the future. Indeed, just when you're about to count up how much "ahead of the game" you are, the financial markets may be entering into a new cycle of corrections that will undo some of your gains. So maintain a realistic sense of long-term investment returns and your retirement savings potential.

Second, double-check your investment mix and the expectations you attach to it. It could well be that when you originally projected your TSP account growth you were overly conservative in your assumptions about what your particular investment mix would earn. You may have thought that the G Fund would just barely keep ahead of inflation when, in fact, you can reasonably expect it to earn up to a 3 percent real annual return on a fairly steady long-term basis. Or you may have started in the TSP when the stock market was churning up and down, but over time it has returned to its historical pattern of about 7 percent real growth per year.

Find out if the strong investment earnings you've enjoyed thus far are consistent with your investment mix's likely long-term results. If they are, and you were overly cautious in your previous projections, then you might be in a position to rethink your future projections and how you allocate your current income to current consumption, TSP savings and other investments.

Third, take stock of your career path, looking backward and forward. One of the reasons your TSP account may be larger than you expected it to be is that you've received promotions sooner than you anticipated. Before you readjust your future TSP account expectations or rethink your overall financial plan, take a full-career picture.

Let's say that you expected to reach Grade X in 10 years. Instead you reach Grade X in five years. That's good. But be realistic about where your career is headed from here. You may have reached a career target sooner than you thought you would, but does that mean you'll proceed substantially beyond that position in the future? Or will your rapid promotions be followed by a period in which you've "topped out" at a certain level?

Your "fast track" may slow down and you may want to view your current TSP "surplus" as protection against slower salary growth in the future. But if you strongly believe more promotions will follow and you'll stay comfortably ahead of your TSP goals, you might be in a position to balance your TSP contributions against other financial opportunities.

If you conclude that you're ahead of your TSP projections and it's not a short-term event that will be undone in the future, what should you do? First of all, you could obviously do nothing, stay on your current course, and look forward to a larger pool of retirement savings than you had expected. Nothing wrong with that.

But you may decide to adjust your overall financial planning. Why? Because your TSP savings are, like any other use of your money, a choice that involves tradeoffs with other financial needs and opportunities. If you are running ahead of your long-term TSP goals, and you're confident that you'll continue to track ahead of schedule, look at your alternatives.

For example, suppose your target was to have $15,000 in additional retirement income at age 60, and you think you're going to reach that goal safely even with conservative TSP investment returns. You may consider scaling back on your TSP contributions, to have more money for current spending or to shift some of your savings to other investments that are more flexible and liquid than the TSP. You may end up building up these investments until retirement anyway. But you'll have the freedom to manage those investments and dip into them from time to time as you see fit.

SHORT-TERM OPERATIONS

It bears repeating that the TSP has a distinctly long-term orientation. It's structured to help your savings grow over the long haul. It's not the kind of investment you can "micro-manage" as you might a portfolio of mutual funds or individual stocks, moving from one investment to another in response to changing market conditions. But effective use of the TSP and its investment options does involve some attention to short-term decisions and adjustments. It's important that you understand the opportunities you have to respond to changing market conditions and fund performance. It's equally important that you appreciate the limitations on your range of actions.

Most important of all, you have to be sure that you are collecting and interpreting information correctly. Investment strategies—when you establish them for the long-term and when you fine-tune them for the short-term—are only as solid as your understanding of the information and logic underlying your decisions. So let's start our discussion of your short-term TSP operations with a basic, but potentially confusing, question—how can you keep track of your TSP investment returns?

> **Short-Term Operation #1:** Knowing How to Monitor the TSP Investment Funds

Twice a year—shortly before each TSP open season—you receive your individual account statement. It includes a month-by-month recap of the money that has flowed into and out of your TSP account during the past six months. One statement covers the period from November through April of the following year. The other statement covers the period from May through October. Your ending account balances on one statement should match the beginning balances on the next statement.

The statement is divided into three sections, showing your balances for the G Fund, the C Fund and the F Fund separately. Review it carefully to make sure it corresponds to your records. Mistakes can happen. For example, check to be sure there's an entry for every pay period. Match the contribution amounts against your pay stubs. Check to see that the total contributions to all three funds equal your designated contribution—as a percentage of pay or as a flat dollar amount.

If you're a FERS employee, remember that your account statement shows the combined total of your contributions and those made by your employing agency. Check to see that the matching formula is applied properly and your total contributions are accurate.

You can also use your account statements to check on the current status of your investment mix. You're looking for two things. First, make sure that your total contributions are distributed properly across the three funds. The distribution of your contributions should reflect your most recent filing of Form TSP-1 during a previous open season. For example, if your designated distribution for your new contributions is 50 percent to the G Fund, 40 percent to the C Fund and 10 percent to the F Fund, check to see that this distribution matches the money shown flowing into each fund on your account statement.

Second, you can use your account statement to calculate the investment mix for your total account balance. As the investment returns of the three TSP funds vary over time, the portions of your total balance in each fund will shift. When you receive your account statement, divide the ending balance of each fund by the total of all fund balances. You may find that the investment allocation of your account balance—as opposed to your new contributions—has shifted substantially. You may want to reallocate your investments to bring them back in line with your intended investment mix. You can do this by filing Form TSP-30, Request for Interfund Transfer.

If you have obtained a loan from your TSP account, check to be sure the disbursement of the loan and your pay period loan payments are entered on your statement accurately. Just like a statement from your bank, your semi-annual TSP statement is an official record of your transactions. If there are any discrepancies, address them now rather than later.

Your semi-annual TSP account statements provide thorough documentation of how your account has functioned over the preceding six months. How do you keep track of what's happening to your TSP account and investments between statements? You can always call the TSP Inquiry Line—(504) 255-8777—to obtain the most recent rates of return, your current account balance and your eligible loan amount. But you also can use your own information-gathering to stay abreast of your TSP investments.

Tracking your TSP investment performance on your own will help you build knowledge for informed investment decision-making. You'll gradually learn about the full range of financial issues involved in managing your TSP account to your best advantage. Second, the Inquiry Line can only give you an updated snapshot of where you are in the TSP the moment you call. It tells you what's happened to your investments and account balance in the past month, but it can't give you any perspective on what might happen in the months and years to come. Rely on the Inquiry Line for current, dollars-and-cents checks on your account status. Rely on yourself for the information you need to monitor and evaluate your TSP savings as part of your overall financial planning.

Where should you start? If you haven't done so already, *make a few minutes with the business section of* **TIP** *your daily newspaper part of your daily ritual.* You don't need to calculate day by day the exact movements of the

Vested in the 1% automatic agency contributions

Total flow of money into each fund from contributions, loan disbursements and repayments, and interfund transfers

THRIFT SAVINGS PLAN
PARTICIPANT STATEMENT

For the period:
11/01/92 through 04/30/93

TSP-8-A

Name: Mary Smith

Social Security Number: 123-45-6789

Date of Birth: 01/01/60

Retirement Coverage: FERS (K)

Separation Status: Not separated

Total Service Required for Vesting: 3 Years from 04/27/86 (TSP Service Computation Date)

Personal Identification Number (PIN): 0001 for the TSP Inquiry Line 504-255-8777

		Employee	Agency Automatic (1%)	Agency Matching	Total
G FUND	Beginning Balance	5,000.00	1,000.00	4,000.00	10,000.00
	Transactions This Period	3,203.02	1,340.14	5,354.78	9,897.94
	Earnings This Period	267.01	68.82	275.26	611.09
	Ending Balance	8,470.03	2,408.96	9,630.04	20,509.03
F FUND	Beginning Balance	2,500.00	500.00	2,000.00	5,000.00
	Transactions This Period	2,430.49 –	483.62 –	1,935.55 –	4,849.66 –
	Earnings This Period	3.36	0.76	3.14	7.26
	Ending Balance	72.87	17.14	67.59	157.60
C FUND	Beginning Balance	7,500.00	1,500.00	6,000.00	15,000.00
	Transactions This Period	4,695.63 –	704.80 –	2,819.28 –	8,219.71 –
	Earnings This Period	348.08	74.42	297.76	720.26
	Ending Balance	3,152.45	869.62	3,478.48	7,500.55
TOTAL ACCOUNT BALANCE	Beginning Balance	15,000.00	3,000.00	12,000.00	30,000.00
	Transactions This Period	3,923.10 –	151.72	599.95	3,171.43 –
	Earnings This Period	618.45	144.00	576.16	1,338.61
	Ending Balance	11,695.35	3,295.72	13,176.11	28,167.18

Money transferred into G Fund

Total of investment earnings for all six months

Source of Contributions / **Total**

Rates of Return* (Numbers in parentheses are negative)		1992 November	December	January	1993 February	March	April	Last 12 Months (May '92 – Apr '93)
	G Fund	0.56%	0.58%	0.58%	0.49%	0.52%	0.51%	6.95%
	F Fund	0.01%	1.54%	1.88%	1.73%	0.41%	0.67%	12.94%
	C Fund	3.39%	1.21%	0.86%	1.35%	2.09%	(2.39%)	9.37%

MARY SMITH
123 MAIN STREET
ANYTOWN, STATE 54321

For detailed information about Activity Code A, C, V, or Y, see your agency employing office.

Figure 6-11

$5,000 Loan disbursed–withdrawn proportionately from the three investment funds

New investment allocation after Interfund Transfer–75% G Fund, 0% F Fund, 25% C Fund

Interfund Transfer–$12,948.52 into the G Fund from the C and F Funds

Allocation of new contributions–40% G Fund, 35% F Fund, 25% C Fund

New contributions each pay period–5% employee, 1% automatic, 4% matching

Investment earnings for January

Loan Payments—$50 each pay period–restored proportionately to the three investment funds

DETAIL OF ACCOUNT ACTIVITY

For the period: 11/01/92 through 04/30/93   TSP-8-A

Name: Mary Smith   Social Security Number: 123-45-6789   Date of Birth: 01/01/60

Activity Code	Payroll Office	Pay Date	Process Date	Source			Investment Fund			
				Employee	Agency Automatic (1%)	Agency Matching	G Fund	F Fund	C Fund	Total
MONTH-END BALANCE OCT 1992				15,000.00	3,000.00	12,000.00	10,000.00	5,000.00	15,000.00	30,000.00
D	47000016	11/10/92	11/10/92	57.69	11.54	46.15	46.16	40.38	28.84	115.38
D	47000016	11/25/92	11/25/92	57.69	11.54	46.15	46.16	40.38	28.84	115.38
E				282.85	56.56	226.28	56.50	0.37	508.82	565.69
T				0.00	0.00	0.00	12,948.52	5,081.13 –	7,867.39 –	0.00
MONTH-END BALANCE NOV 1992				15,398.23	3,079.64	12,318.58	23,097.34	0.00	7,699.11	30,796.45
D	47000016	12/09/92	12/10/92	57.69	11.54	46.15	46.16	40.38	28.84	115.38
D	47000016	12/23/92	12/23/92	57.69	11.54	46.15	46.16	40.38	28.84	115.38
E				114.49	22.89	91.58	135.05	0.61	93.30	228.96
L				5,000.00 –	0.00	0.00	3,731.21 –	13.02 –	1,255.77 –	5,000.00 –
MONTH-END BALANCE DEC 1992				10,628.10	3,125.64	12,502.46	19,593.50	68.35	6,594.32	26,256.17
D	47000016	01/06/93	01/06/93	57.69	11.54	46.15	46.16	40.38	28.84	115.38
D	47000016	01/20/93	01/20/93	57.69	11.54	46.15	46.16	40.38	28.84	115.38
E				69.83	20.46	81.90	113.19	2.03	56.97	172.19
MONTH-END BALANCE JAN 1993				10,813.31	3,169.15	12,676.66	19,799.01	151.14	6,708.97	26,659.12
D	47000016	02/03/93	02/03/93	57.69	11.54	46.15	23.08	0.00	92.30	115.38
D	47000016	02/17/93	02/17/93	57.69	11.54	46.15	23.08	0.00	92.30	115.38
P			02/28/93	100.00	0.00	0.00	74.33	0.56	25.11	100.00
E				78.43	22.76	91.10	97.65	2.60	92.04	192.29
C	47000016			0.00	1.70	0.00	1.40	0.25	0.05	1.70
MONTH-END BALANCE FEB 1993				11,107.12	3,216.69	12,860.06	20,018.55	154.55	7,010.77	27,183.87
D	47000016	03/03/93	03/03/93	57.69	11.54	46.15	23.08	0.00	92.30	115.38
D	47000016	03/17/93	03/17/93	57.69	11.54	46.15	23.08	0.00	92.30	115.38
D	47000016	03/31/93	03/31/93	57.69	11.54	46.15	23.08	0.00	92.30	115.38
P			03/31/93	150.00	0.00	0.00	110.71	0.84	38.45	150.00
E				105.39	30.08	120.33	105.21	0.62	149.97	255.80
A	47000016	09/02/92		23.07 –	0.00	0.00	17.30 –	0.00	5.77 –	23.07 –
MONTH-END BALANCE MAR 1993				11,512.51	3,281.39	13,118.84	20,286.41	156.01	7,470.32	27,912.74
D	47000016	04/14/93	04/16/93	57.69	11.54	46.15	23.08	0.00	92.30	115.38
D	47000016	04/28/93	04/28/93	57.69	11.54	46.15	23.08	0.00	92.30	115.38
P			04/30/93	100.00	0.00	0.00	72.97	0.56	26.47	100.00
E				32.54 –	8.75 –	35.03 –	103.49	1.03	180.84 –	76.32 –
MONTH-END BALANCE APR 1993				11,695.35	3,295.72	13,176.11	20,509.03	157.60	7,500.55	28,167.18

Activity Codes

D = Deposit	T = Interfund transfer	C = Earnings correction	O = Court-ordered payment
E = Earnings	F = Forfeited nonvested monies	Y = Earnings correction transfer	W = Withdrawal
L = Loan	R = Restored amounts	V = Reversal of earnings correction	M = Minimum distribution
P = Monthly loan payment summary	A = Adjustment	B = Declared abandoned	N = Refunded excess deferral

Monthly earnings are calculated by multiplying the rate of return for the month shown by the sum of your prior month-end balance and one-half of the total of deposits and loan repayments during the month shown. Earnings are credited at the end of the month shown. Adjustments, earnings corrections, forfeitures, loans, restored amounts, and withdrawals affect your account for the calculation of earnings at the end of the month shown. Interfund transfers also affect your account at the end of the month shown. **Pay date** is the date reported by your payroll office for deposits and certain adjustments. **Process date** is the date deposits and loan payments were processed to your account by the TSP recordkeeper.

Figure 6-12

three TSP investment funds. But stay aware of the general movements and patterns of the three funds. And in the process you'll develop—at a pace and level of detail you define—a sense of how, why and when different financial markets function.

There are two elements of the business news you might want to review on a regular basis. First, become familiar with the direct numerical reports on daily movements in various financial markets. It's not that you're particularly worried about day-to-day movements—after all, the TSP functions on a monthly investment cycle. Rather, you want to become comfortable reading and interpreting the daily market performance reports so that you build an understanding of what's happening and why.

You may learn something today about how financial markets work and not have to use that knowledge to make a TSP investment decision until months or years down the road. But *if you start learning today you'll increase the chance that when a key TSP decision point arrives, you'll have the knowledge you need to respond effectively and profitably.*

Second, find in your newspaper's business section the article that provides a summary of the previous day's financial activity. It's usually presented as a brief account of what happened in various markets and how those daily movements relate to longer-term patterns expectations. Most major newspapers run such a story every day, in a consistent format and in more or less the same place. This article will help you sift through the numbers that tell you what happened and help you understand why various movements occur and how they interact with one another. If the newspaper you read doesn't provide this type of report, find another newspaper.

You don't have to subscribe to the Wall Street Journal and Business Week, Fortune, and Money magazines to manage your TSP account effectively. On the contrary— littering your mind with excessively detailed information about all the daily market movements will probably hurt rather than help. Instead, steadily develop an understanding of how the three TSP investment funds connect to the financial markets they reflect. With the TSP, you don't have to micro-manage a complicated investment portfolio. You just have to track three basic financial barometers and—when necessary—be in a position to make informed and confident decisions when you see the barometers moving in particular directions.

Let's turn to each of the three TSP investment funds and what you should be looking for when you scan your daily newspaper. There is—surprisingly—no newspaper so far that's had the good sense to track TSP movements in detail for a potential readership of 2,000,000 participants with collective investments of $20 billion. But most newspapers present market reports that will enable you to monitor fund movements.

Monitoring the G Fund. The G Fund pays an interest rate equal to the earnings on all Treasury securities with maturities of four years or longer. The rate, calculated monthly, is a composite based on the value of all outstanding medium-term and long-term securities. The exact composition of the securities portfolio in the G Fund will shift over time. But there are some general benchmarks you can use to track how the G Fund is behaving.

The current "maturity mix" of the G Fund is 14 years. That means that when you take all the securities in the G Fund—5-year, 7-year, 10-year, 20-year and 30-year securities, for example—they combine to form a portfolio with an average maturity of 14 years. The average maturity will shift over time, but not enough to affect your ability to monitor important G Fund trends.

Examine your newspaper's business section to see how it presents information about Treasury securities. Virtually all newspapers list the current earnings rate for 30-year bonds. Some, but not all, present daily information on 5-year, 7-year and 10-year Treasury securities. The G Fund will typically pay an interest rate between the 10-year and 30-year rates. The 10-year rate is probably the best single G Fund barometer because it's the closest to the average maturity of the G Fund securities.

Remember that the rates you see in the newspaper are annualized rates. To translate that into an approximate monthly G Fund return, divide by 12. For example, let's say the newspaper reports that the yield on 30-year Treasury bonds is 8.16 percent and the yield on 10-year Treasury notes is 7.80 percent. The monthly G Fund return will probably fall in the range between 0.65 percent (7.80 percent divided by 12) and 0.68 percent (8.16 percent divided by 12). Watch the movements in the rates and you'll have a good sense of the short-term direction—up or down—of G Fund interest rates.

Monitoring the C Fund. Almost all newspapers report on the previous day's movement in the S&P 500. Many newspapers include a calculation of the S&P 500's movement over the past three, six or 12 months. And, financial magazines frequently describe S&P 500 trends.

Reports in the newspaper, on radio or on television that are based on the Dow Jones Industrial Average do not correspond exactly to movements in the S&P 500. But in general the Dow and the S&P 500 move in similar directions. The Dow frequently will move more sharply up or down in percentage terms, because it tracks a smaller number of stocks and can be affected more significantly by the changes in the stock prices of a few companies. Dow reports provide an approximate guide to movements in the C Fund. Find a news source that tracks the S&P 500 specifically.

The S&P 500 is expressed as a composite index value. You want to become familiar with how movements in the S&P 500 value translate into approximate returns from the C Fund. Simple division provides the answer. For example, suppose that between April 1 of Year 1 and April 1 of Year 2 the S&P 500 value moved from 450 to 500. That would represent a gain of 50 points from a base of 450.

Divide 50 by 450 and you find that the index gained 11.1 percent over the course of the 12 month period. If the index value then moved from 500 back down to 490 during April of Year 2, there would be a one-month loss of 2.0 percent—10 points down divided by the 500 point starting value.

Note, however, that the composite index value of the S&P 500 does not exactly match the performance of the C Fund. In particular, the index value does not include the value of reinvested stock dividends. The C Fund—through the actual portfolio of stocks managed by Wells Fargo—does include the additional value of reinvested dividends. So, as dividends are paid and reinvested over the course of the year, actual C Fund returns will generally be higher than the returns suggested by the movement of the index. The extra value of reinvested dividends may be as much as 3 percent per year. Nonetheless, the S&P 500 index value reported in your daily newspaper is a good barometer of short-term movements and approximate C Fund returns.

Many newspapers regularly report on S&P 500 movements over various periods, such as total movement the previous day, the previous month, the previous three months and the previous year. The advantage of these reports is that they help you interpret daily and monthly fluctuations within a broader perspective. They may reassure you during momentary downturns and temper your excitement during upswings. Find a publication that reports S&P 500 movements over multiple time periods and in a consistent format.

Monitoring the F Fund. Of the three TSP investment options, the F Fund is the most difficult to understand and monitor for many TSP investors. Remember, the F Fund reflects the performance of major sectors of the U.S. bond market. Bond prices move in the opposite direction of yields, depending on the magnitude of the change. So if the yields of intermediate and long-term securities decline, the F Fund gains. If the yields rise, the F Fund loses.

Most newspapers provide information about the performance of bond indexes. Some detail the movements of a corporate bond index, some focus on a government bond index, some provide both. In most instances, corporate bond indexes and government bond indexes will move in similar directions. Many newspapers will present a bond index that includes movement over the past day, the past month and the past year. Some will provide a graph detailing all movements over the past year.

Remember, you're looking for an index that tracks the composite value of bond prices—not bond yields. Like the S&P 500, a bond index value provides a measuring stick to calculate movements and returns, not a direct expression of earnings like an interest rate. If the bond index is at 5000 and then moves up to 5100, that movement represents a 2.0 percent gain—100 divided by 5000.

Look in your newspaper for a composite index of bond prices. It won't precisely reflect the composition of the F

Fund. But it probably will give you a good indicator of directional shifts. Periods of increasing index values will match with periods of favorable F Fund returns. Likewise, declining index values will reflect periods of generally poor F Fund performance. The index in your newspaper may be more or less volatile than the F Fund as its value moves up and down. But it will still give you a very easy and quick read on F Fund patterns.

Figure 6-13 illustrates typical reports in newspaper business sections to give you some pointers on what to look for as you track the three TSP investment funds. Your regular newspaper probably provides a similar set of measurements.

> **Short-Term Operation #2:** Understanding Market Trends, Market Corrections and Market-Timing

In the previous section we gave you some tips regarding how to monitor movements in the three TSP investment funds. What will you gain from taking the time to stay abreast of market movements?

First, you'll develop an understanding of how and why stock prices (C Fund), bond prices (F Fund) and interest rates (G Fund) behave the way they do. Second, you'll develop increasing confidence in your own observations and judgments. Instead of basing your investment decisions on the latest fashionable theory or hot tip from the lunchroom financial expert, you'll become equipped to gather and digest information on your own.

Third, you'll be in a better position to understand the differences between market trends and market corrections. This will improve the quality of your investment decision-making and reduce your anxieties as you watch the markets dancing about. Remember, *an effective investment* **TIP** *strategy meets two important tests—it puts you in a position to realize quality returns on a sustained basis and it allows you to sleep at night.*

Understanding the market trends and market corrections associated with each of the three TSP funds will help you sort through the "noise" of temporary and potentially misleading developments. It will also enable you to bring your understanding of investment risk into clearer focus.

What do we mean when we refer to market trends and market corrections? A market trend is a sustained upward or downward movement in an investment's value. A particularly prolonged period of strong growth is called a "bull market." A prolonged period of decline and loss is called a "bear market." In some periods there may be no discernible trend at all. Investors are buying and selling stocks and bonds, but the net effect of these transactions on overall market values is small. During these periods of buying and selling within a narrow range of prices, the market is said to be "churning."

A market correction is a short-term market movement in the opposite direction of the prevailing trend. For example, the stock market may exhibit generally strong growth

The following examples are illustrative only. They do not reflect patterns during any particular time period.

THE G FUND. Look for a section listing Treasury yields. If your newspaper provides the rate for 10-year Treasury notes, that's the single best benchmark for monitoring G Fund returns and trends. If the 10-year rate is not provided, you can still use other rates to get a rough picture of G Fund patterns. For example, if your newspaper reports the 5-year and 30-year rates, the G Fund rate will almost always fall between the two. In this example, the 10-year rate is 6.84%, up 0.96% over a year ago and 1.6% higher than it was 6 months ago. This trend should correspond closely to G Fund movements during that period–generally up over the past year, but yesterday's drop may be a sign of a future downward trend.

Treasury Securities	Yesterday	6 Months ago	1 Year ago
3-month T-bill	3.56% +.01	2.90%	2.81%
6-month T-bill	3.89% -.01	3.02%	2.89%
10-year Note	6.84% -.20	5.24%	5.98%
30-year Bond	7.14% -.16	5.90%	6.86%

THE C FUND. Most business sections present the Dow Jones Industrial Average in graphic form. The Dow is based on only 30 stocks and has a much higher numerical scale than the S&P 500. The Dow and the S&P 500 typically move in the same direction, so you can use the Dow picture to quickly gauge general stock market trends. But if you want to monitor the C Fund more closely, look for specific S&P 500 reports, either in a table or in an article summarizing the day's market activity. Keep in mind that the index value does not include the value of reinvested dividends. In this example, the past 6 months have witnessed a mix of relatively modest fluctuations, with an overall upward trend and gains of about 3%.

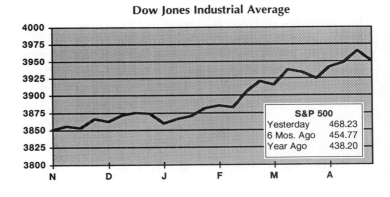

THE F FUND. Your newspaper may carry a pictorial report on a particular bond index. This graph shows the movements in bond values over time for a particular model bond portfolio. Such an index will give you a basic idea of bond market trends as interest rates and bond prices change over time. Remember, however, that the index you see in your paper is based on a group of bonds that are not the same as the collection of bonds in the F Fund. You can use the Bond Index in your paper to watch general bond market patterns, but not as a barometer of actual F Fund returns. In this example, bonds gained about 10% in value from November through May, then entered a period of minimal fluctuations.

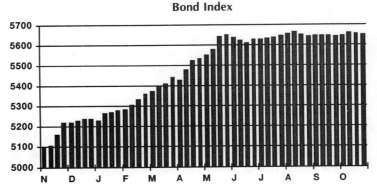

Figure 6-13

over a nine-month period, but have several short periods of decline during the generally upward trend. These corrections may occur because some investors decide to sell their stocks while prices are favorable—you'll see this referred to as "profit-taking" in the business reports.

Corrections may also develop when investors become concerned that prolonged growth has driven prices up to levels that can't be sustained. In their view, the market has "topped out" and it's time to sell. Sometimes the "topping out" of a market is indeed the signal of a newly emerging trend in the opposite direction. But frequently it's only a temporary reversal, and the original trend continues on after the brief correction in the opposite direction.

As you take the time to learn first-hand about market movements, you'll develop a more focused sense of how and when trends develop and corrections occur. Is there any sure-fire method for determining when a trend is beginning? Definitely not. Even the shrewdest investors and the most successful investment advisers are frequently wrong. They sometimes foresee trends that don't materialize, and they sometimes discount as temporary corrections what turn out to be significant reversals of trend. If the pros are wrong as often as they are, *don't naively think that you're going to do better and "time" the market to perfection. It's not going to happen.*

Is the TSP well suited to spotting and responding to market trends? Yes and no. The TSP provides you with a certain advantage through its use of broad-based, index-oriented investments. This means that if you anticipate a period of strong growth in one of the funds, and you're correct, you'll be in a position to obtain the average, market-wide results of that trend. You don't have to worry about picking exactly which stocks or bonds have the best chance of doing well.

Riding the average of the market means you may not realize as high a rate of growth as you would from correctly picking individual winners. But neither will you suffer the extreme losses possible when individual stocks perform poorly. In the TSP, you'll gain the overall growth of the market as a whole, with lower risks and transaction costs than a managed portfolio of selected stocks or bonds. Note that this advantage is essentially the same as that offered by broad-based mutual funds.

But the TSP has a distinct disadvantage if you're trying to "time" the market and respond to emerging trends. It operates on a fixed monthly investment cycle. You can't call the TSP to buy or sell on a moment's notice as you could call the manager or broker of a mutual fund.

Let's say you decide to move more of your account into a particular fund to increase your gains from an anticipated upward trend. If you file your interfund transfer by the 15th of the month, your investment reallocation will be effective on the last day of the month—at least 15 or 16 days later. If you miss the 15th of the month deadline, your interfund transfer will take place on the last day of the month after that—as much as 47 days later.

If the information you acted on turns out to be the signal of a lengthy bull market, no problem. You'll miss out on half a month to a month and a half of the early stage of the gain. If indeed it's a prolonged growth trend, the transfer will still be to your advantage. But if it was just a short-lived upward movement, you may have missed it by the time your funds are reallocated. In fact, the movement may be strongly in the opposite direction by the time your transfer takes effect.

The C Fund typically earns its long-term growth through recurring cycles of up and down movements. The long-term growth results from the fact that the ups are slightly more frequent and tend to be larger than the downs. In short, the market is constantly correcting itself in the short-term while an underlying pattern of long-term growth in value is moving forward. The F Fund follows a similar pattern with less extreme fluctuations and a generally lower long-term growth pattern.

In the 72 months from January 1988 through December 1993, the C Fund had only three sustained, consistent market trends that lasted more than three months. Two were strong growth periods, one was a period of substantial losses.

The Three Major Market Trends in the C Fund

Period	Number of Months	Total Gain or Loss
June 1989 - October 1989	5	- 14.4%
November 1989 - May 1990	7	+ 30.9%
September 1992 - March 1993	7	+ 10.9%

Figure 6-14

The period from September 1992 through March 1993 offered seven consecutive months of C Fund growth. But, despite its steady upward trend, this period wasn't dramatically stronger than the overall C Fund performance for the entire 72-month period. The average monthly gain during this seven-month period of growth was 1.50 percent, compared to 1.18 percent for the entire 72-month period. A very good stretch of growth, to be sure, but not as dramatic as the other two C Fund trend periods.

Let's look at those two periods—one strongly up, the other strongly down—more closely. Notice that the extended downturn from June through October 1989 was followed immediately by the compensating upward trend from November 1989 through May 1990. That's a continuous 12-month period consisting of a major five-month downturn and an even more dramatic seven-month upswing.

Could you have been very sharp and foreseen these two trends correctly and on time? In short, could you have emptied out your C Fund account in time to avoid the 14.4 percent loss, and then put your money back in to the C

Fund in time to enjoy the 30.9 percent gain? Possibly, but highly unlikely.

The downturn started in June of 1989, but in that month the C fund only dropped by 0.71 percent. That was followed in July by another very small decline of 0.36 percent. Now go back two months. In May of 1989 the C Fund posted a walloping 9.44 percent gain, the second-best individual month in the history of the TSP.

If you gained 9.44 percent in one month, would you be likely to empty out your C Fund account after a modest loss in the next one or two months? Or would you wait for a more compelling signal that a true downturn had begun? If you waited past July 15 of 1989 to move your money out of the C Fund, then your money was still in there for August's 8.65 percent loss, the worst single month in the history of the TSP. If the August losses didn't really start piling up until the middle of the month, and you didn't get your transfer in by August 15, then your money was still in the C Fund for September's 4.85 percent loss.

See the problem? If you're going to time the markets using the TSP's fixed monthly investment cycle be careful about monitoring fund movements and timing your interfund transfers. Of course, if you're constantly trying to give yourself enough lead time to be out of the fund before an expected downturn, you'll end up missing out on months of positive growth just before the downturn. Is it impossible to win at this game? No, it's not impossible. But recognize the perils and play at your own risk.

> **Short-Term Operation #3:** Developing and Implementing Short-Term Adjustments

Because of its monthly investment cycle, the TSP puts you at least 15 days behind investors who can buy and sell stocks and bonds at a moment's notice. That's not a criticism of the TSP. It's simply a recognition of the fact that the TSP serves different purposes than other, more flexible investment accounts. *The TSP exists to provide a convenient, tax-deferred vehicle for long-term gains. That is its mission. It's not designed for micro-management and finely-tuned market timing.*

But that doesn't mean that you should simply lock into a long-term investment allocation and ride the market waves from here to retirement. There are sensible opportunities available for using short-term adjustments to sustain and enhance your long-term results. The trick is to craft your short-term adjustments with the proper tools.

First, use the tool of "dollar-cost averaging" to accomplish—automatically—some of what more complicated market-timing tactics might achieve. The goal of market-timing is to realize every investor's dream—buying low and selling high. The problem with market-timing, beyond its general hazards, is that it's particularly difficult to execute through the TSP. Again, the lags between your buy and sell decisions and when they become effective will diminish your gains and—in some cases—lead to complete mis-timing and losses.

Start with the basic step of reallocating your account balances to restore your original investment mix. For example, if you have 50 percent of your account in the C Fund and the stock market has a period of particularly strong earnings, more than 50 percent of your account is now in the C Fund. It has grown faster than the other two funds. So you're exposed to more risk than you originally intended.

Equally important, we've seen that over time the stock market gains through a constant cycle of upswings and downturns—some prolonged, but most of them brief and subject to market correction. On balance, over time, periods of strong performance increase the likelihood of a subsequent period of poor performance, and the opposite is also true—a bad period increases the chance of a coming upswing. It is the nature of the beast—advance-correct-advance-correct.

By reallocating your account back down to 50 percent after gains—or back up to 50 percent after downturns—you'll automatically move money into the fund when prices are low and more likely to climb, and out of the fund when prices are high and more likely to fall. Call it "passive market-timing" if you like. It won't generate the dramatic spurts of properly guessing a major stock market surge and pouring all your money into the C Fund. But it will—simply and painlessly—add to the growth of your account over time.

Second, if you haven't already, set a basic strategy that you're comfortable with as a starting position. Then pay close attention to market movements and their underlying causes. Look for patterns that are consistent and make sense. In particular read and understand what you can about how investors in general behave and how different financial markets interact. Then you can start developing your own approach to an important investment goal—understanding when the market is moving in response to strong and important underlying factors, and when it is simply surging in response to an illusory crowd psychology.

Millions of people invest billions of dollars in stocks and bonds. Some of them make sound judgments based on their best guess interpretation of significant data. Others follow hunches or hitch a ride on the judgments of others. Successful investors, over time, are those who understand the difference between real advances and declines driven by economic reality, and illusory advances and declines driven by herd behavior.

In particular, *be on the lookout for the connections between broad, everyday financial developments and the movements of the three TSP investment funds.* Understanding these connections, even in a relatively simple form, will serve you better than trying to keep up with the latest hot investment theory. Markets behave erratically, to be sure, but the movements still rest on a logical foundation. Forget about gimmicks, but also don't give in to the view that investment results are essentially random. Find the connections that you understand, test them against reality and—if you choose to—use them in your TSP account.

For example, review financial magazines and books to collect a broad overview of the different theories various advisers have for how and why markets behave the way they do. Eliminate the ones that can't be expressed in relatively simple language. It will almost always be a mistake to try to use market adjustments based on concepts and measurements you don't truly understand.

Don't spend too much time with tactics that don't suit the TSP. Any investment guidance that assumes you can move money in and out of your funds instantaneously probably won't work as well—and may fail altogether—when you try to implement them though the TSP's monthly cycle. You'll be on much sounder footing concentrating on tactics based on information and measurements that are simple and readily available. Take the time to develop your own indicators and theories to determine when you might want to move money into or out of a particular fund. Fairly simple theories applied consistently won't yield perfect results—no theory will. But using a framework you understand and can monitor will serve you well.

Want a relatively simple place to begin? Watch interest rates. They are an important cog in the entire machinery of the financial markets. Interest rates reflect the return necessary to make it worthwhile for a lender to give money to a borrower for a particular length of time. Other investment opportunities compete with interest rates to attract investors' dollars. In general, when interest rates are dropping, bond prices are rising. The same holds true in reverse—when interest rates are rising, bond prices will drop as current yields adjust upward to keep up with interest rate movements. Because the G Fund reflects the yield of intermediate and long-term securities, while the F Fund reflects the prices of intermediate and long-term bonds, it is logical to expect the two funds to move generally in opposite directions. And, since long-term interest rates represent a major element in corporate debt financing and capital investment decisions, it's also logical to suppose that the G Fund and the C Fund will move in opposite directions as well.

Let's conduct a brief test of this theory. Figure 6-15 shows four periods of significant, steady shifts in the G Fund's long-term interest rates—both up and down. For each period, let's look at the returns from each of the three TSP funds during the indicated period.

These limited data seem to support our hypothesis. But obviously you'd want to look at longer periods to test the theory. You'd also want to review the financial literature for similar or conflicting arguments.

Do we offer this as a suggested basis for your short-term TSP investment decision-making? Absolutely, positively not. We offer it as an example of the kind of information-gathering and theory-testing you might want to explore as you consider whether, when and how to engage in short-term adjustments of your TSP investment strategy.

G Fund Movements and C & F Fund Returns

March 1988 - August 1988: G Fund Rates Rising
Returns: G Fund: + 4.3%   C Fund: - 0.4%   F Fund: -0.1%

April 1989 - August 1989:   G Fund Rates Dropping
Returns: G Fund: + 3.6%   C Fund: +20.6%   F Fund: +8.4%

March 1990 - October 1990: G Fund Rates Rising
Returns: G Fund: + 6.0%   C Fund: - 6.3%   F Fund: +5.4%

September 1991-February 1992: G Fund Rates Dropping
Returns: G Fund: + 3.7%   C Fund: + 6.1%   F Fund: +6.3%

Figure 6-15

SOME POSSIBLE TSP INVESTMENT STRATEGIES

The best TSP investment strategy is one that can achieve your financial goals and leaves you comfortable about the balance of potential rewards and risks. Your best strategy may be very different from your neighbor's, and it may change from one stage of your career to the next.

This section summarizes the results that various TSP investment strategies would have achieved during the six years from 1988 through 1993. They are examples only, and do not exhaust the range of strategies you might consider. As we've said several times before, there is no assurance that the 1988-1993 returns will correspond to future returns under any of the examples.

Strategy: Maximum Growth Potential

Objective: To pursue potential growth from investment in the stock market (C Fund), which historically has outperformed the bond market (F Fund) and long-term interest rates (G Fund).

Investment Mix

C Fund: 100%   F Fund: 0%   G Fund: 0%

Performance, 1988-1993

Average Annual Return:	14.1%
Average Annual Real Return:	10.1%
$1 Invested in 1/88, Value 12/93:	$2.21
Real Value After Inflation	$1.78

Range of Returns Over

	1 Month	3 Months	6 Months	12 Months
High Return	12/91	12/90-2/91	11/90-4/91	9/88-8/89
	11.41%	14.99%	25.46%	35.26%
Low Return	8/90	8/90-10/90	4/90-9/90	10/89-9/90
	- 8.65%	- 13.48%	- 8.26%	- 9.13%

This Strategy Might Suit You If:

◇ You're taking a long-term view and want maximum growth potential

◇ You need maximum returns to meet a specific financial goal, and the near-term stock market outlook is favorable

This Strategy Might Not Suit You If:

◇ You're getting closer to withdrawing your TSP balance—or taking a TSP loan—and you want to avoid short-term losses

◇ The rest of your savings are substantially tied to stock market performance

Strategy: Growth and Diversity

Objective: To blend substantial stock investments with long-term securities to be more diversified under varying market conditions.

Investment Mix
C Fund: 70%   F Fund: 15%   G Fund: 15%

Performance, 1988-1993

Average Annual Return:	12.5%
Average Annual Real Return:	8.5%
$1 Invested in 1/88, Value 12/93:	$2.03
Real Value After Inflation	$1.63

Range of Returns Over

	1 Month	3 Months	6 Months	12 Months
High Return	12/91	12/90-2/91	11/90-4/91	9/88-8/89
	8.52%	11.32%	19.57%	27.97%
Low Return	8/90	8/90-10/90	4/90-9/90	10/89-9/90
	- 6.16%	- 9.00%	- 4.56%	- 4.11%

This Strategy Might Suit You If:

◇ You're focusing on long-term growth, but you'll give up some growth potential to reduce the size of short-term fluctuations.

◇ You're generally upbeat about the stock market, but you want to cover yourself during periods when fixed income investments perform better.

This Strategy Might Not Suit You If:

◇ You're investing for the long haul and can afford to ride out the full extent of potential C Fund fluctuations.

◇ You believe both stocks and bonds will perform poorly over an extended period.

Strategy: Conservative "Interest Rate Hedge"

Objective: To base your account for the most part on long-term interest rates, balancing the F Fund and G Fund to cover yourself whether interest rates are rising or falling.

Investment Mix
C Fund: 20%   F Fund: 40%   G Fund: 40%

Performance, 1988-1993

Average Annual Return:	9.8%
Average Annual Real Return:	5.8%
$1 Invested in 1/88, Value 12/93:	$1.75
Real Value After Inflation	$1.40

Range of Returns Over

	1 Month	3 Months	6 Months	12 Months
High Return	12/91	5/89-7/89	2/88-7/89	10/90-9/91
	3.71%	6.51%	9.29%	15.9%
Low Return	8/90	9/93-11/93	7/93-12/93	1/93-12/93
	- 3.76%	1.38%	2.87%	6.14%

This Strategy Might Suit You If:

◇ You want a basically conservative portfolio, but are willing to endure some market risk.

◇ There's no particular pattern to expected interest rate movements, so blending the F Fund and G Fund is a good way to insure that you realize gains whether rates generally move up or down in the future.

This Strategy Might Not Suit You If:

◇ You think that by moving 60 percent of your account out of the G Fund, you significantly increase your growth potential. You've still got 80 percent of your account tied to fixed income securities. Over the long haul, that mix will likely be outperformed by strategies that emphasize the C Fund.

◇ You are very confident that interest rates will move strongly in a particular direction during a certain time period. If rates are high and you expect them to drop dramatically, your hedge probably won't earn as much as a more heavy F Fund commitment. If rates are low and you expect them to rise sharply, the hedge probably won't earn as much as a more heavy G Fund commitment.

Strategy: Extreme Caution

Objective: To protect yourself against any chance of losing any principal at any time, even if it means sacrificing growth potential.

Investment Mix
C Fund: 0%   F Fund: 0%   G Fund: 100%

Performance, 1988-1993

Average Annual Return:	8.0%
Average Annual Real Return:	4.0%
$1 Invested in 1/88, Value 12/93:	$1.59
Real Value After Inflation	$1.27

Range of Returns Over

	1 Month	3 Months	6 Months	12 Months
High Return	3/89	3/89-5/89	12/88-5/89	6/88-5/89
	0.78%	2.31%	4.54%	9.22%
Low Return	11/93	9/93-11/93	7/93-12/93	1/93-12/93
	0.45%	1.38%	2.87%	6.14%

This Strategy Might Suit You If:

◇ You simply cannot cope with sharp market fluctuations and any exposure to short-term losses.

◇ You're comfortable with your account level and want to "lock it in" to preserve the principal value between now and when you use the funds.

This Strategy Might Not Suit You If:

◇ You overestimate the growth potential and safety of G Fund returns by not counting the effects of inflation.

Watch out for periods when long-term interest rates lag behind short-term inflation levels.

◇ Your other investments are mostly conservative. A portfolio dominated by money market funds, CDs and the G Fund may leave you very disappointed down the road.

5 THINGS TO DO

1. Build a realistic range of possible TSP outcomes. Where will you end up with your current contributions and conservative investment and salary growth assumptions? What's your high-end potential if you increase your contributions to the most you can possibly afford, and have more optimistic investment earnings and career advances?

2. Take this range of outcomes and think about it carefully in terms of tradeoffs involved. Compare higher contributions to the current uses you might have for that money. Think about the extra gains from higher investment earnings, compared to the potentially higher risks involved in realizing those earnings. Your conclusions will depend largely on your personal circumstances and preferences, and that's exactly as it should be.

3. Figure out a TSP account checkpoint process that works for you. Make it a consistent part of your overall financial planning.

4. Become accustomed to monitoring financial developments on a regular basis. Not so that you can quickly start making drastic changes in course, but to gradually become a more informed and confident TSP investor.

5. Explore financial magazines and books for information and theories that might help you realize higher returns from your TSP investments. But read these claims and arguments with a skeptical eye. Look for logical, time-tested theories, not the latest "how to beat the market" sales pitch.

⟨7⟩ THE TSP LOAN PROGRAM

An important feature of the TSP is the availability of loans from your account. The TSP loan program allows you to build up your investment account over the course of your federal or postal career, but retain some access to your funds to meet important financial needs along the way.

This chapter describes how the TSP loan program operates, including what purposes you can borrow money for, how much you can borrow, how to apply for loans and loan repayment terms. We'll discuss how the loan program can be an important factor in your personal TSP investment strategy and how TSP loans compare with other possible financing sources.

Our goal is to help you understand the TSP loan program and how it might fit into your long-term TSP planning. Before you apply for a TSP loan, be sure to review the TSP Loan Program booklet, available at your employing agency.

OVERVIEW OF THE TSP LOAN PROGRAM

You can obtain a loan from your TSP account for four purposes—buying a primary residence, paying educational expenses or medical bills, or coping with sudden financial hardship. Depending on your account balance, you may borrow from $1,000 to $50,000. You can have two loans outstanding at the same time, except when your first loan is for financial hardship.

Loans for purchase of a primary residence are repayable over a period of up to 15 years. Educational, medical and hardship loans have a four-year maximum repayment period. In later sections we'll look closely at how you apply for a TSP loan and how to calculate your potential loan amounts and payments.

The availability of TSP loans is in a sense a two-edged sword. On the one hand, the assurance that your money will be accessible for important mid-career financial goals encourages participation in the TSP and long-term savings. Many employees undoubtedly save more retirement income because of the added "comfort level" that loan

programs provide. On the other hand, some employees may focus excessively on the loan programs and neglect or diminish the long-term, retirement-oriented goals of tax-deferred savings plans.

In deciding whether and how much to invest in the TSP, the availability of loans from your account may be important to you. It may also influence how you choose to allocate your account among the three TSP investment funds. For example, let's suppose you are anticipating a loan from your TSP account to help finance a new home or a child's college education. You may decide to move temporarily to a more "conservative" investment mix—heavily weighted toward the G Fund—immediately before you apply for the loan. You don't want to risk a sudden short-term loss in the C Fund or F Fund that would reduce the amount you can borrow.

If you want to meet your short-term financial needs while continuing a growth-oriented TSP investment strategy, plan accordingly. Recognize that short-term fluctuations in the C Fund or F Fund could affect your potential TSP loan amount. If necessary, identify sources of additional financing if the amount you can borrow from the TSP is not quite as large as you originally planned.

If you expect to take a loan from your TSP account at some future point, it's important to consider your loan expectations within the broader context of your long-term savings and retirement goals. For example, if you are age 35 and investing in the TSP to reach a particular retirement income goal, loans from your TSP account may help you finance several important interim goals along the way. But you should plan your contribution and investment strategies to compensate for the anticipated loans and protect your long-term retirement goals. Later on we'll walk through several specific cases to see how you balance loans and effective long-term account growth.

The next few sections concentrate on the mechanical details of the TSP loan program. After we see how the program works, we'll discuss how loans fit into your overall TSP strategies and how TSP loans compare to other sources of financing.

QUALIFYING EXPENSES

You can borrow from your TSP account for any of the following four categories of qualifying expenses:

Purchase of a primary residence. You may borrow from your account to help finance a house, condominium, cooperative unit, townhouse, boat or mobile home which is not used on a transient basis. You must be buying or building your primary residence. But you cannot use a TSP loan for renovations or to refinance or prepay an existing mortgage. And, TSP loans don't cover purchases of vacation homes, rental or investment properties, or the purchase of land only.

If you're considering a TSP loan as part of your home financing, remember two important factors. First, unlike a regular mortgage, the interest payments on a TSP loan are not tax deductible. Second, the TSP requires proof that you are purchasing a specific primary residence. There is no guarantee that a TSP loan will be disbursed by a specific closing date. If you are planning to use a TSP loan as part of your home financing, be sure to time your purchase and your loan application carefully.

Education expenses. TSP loans generally cover education expenses—tuition, books, lodging—associated with primary, secondary, college and graduate schools for you, your spouse and your dependents. TSP loans do not cover courses given by organizations whose primary function is not formal instruction, such as museums or professional associations. TSP loans do not cover expenses for institutions who primarily provide day care or custodial care.

A wide range of educational expenses—for you or members of your family—can qualify for a TSP loan. But there are some areas in which you should be sure to obtain information and guidance before assuming a loan will be available. Certain professional, vocational or certification programs may not qualify. You may be unsure whether a particular program for your child constitutes education (eligible for a TSP loan) or day care (not eligible). Get information and clarification from the Thrift Service Office sooner rather than later.

Medical expenses. You can use a TSP loan to pay for medical expenses that are generally recognized as deductible for federal income tax purposes, such as doctor and hospital bills or prescribed medical supplies and devices. Loans cover medical expenses for you, your spouse and dependents. TSP loans generally cover any medical expenses deductible under the federal income tax. The exact boundaries of allowable expenses may vary somewhat from year to year. But you can generally expect to qualify for a loan to cover significant uninsured expenses for you or your family, such as dental fees or co-payments for surgery and hospitalization costs.

Financial hardship. You may qualify for a hardship loan if your regular monthly expenses exceed net monthly income after taxes and retirement deductions and you don't have other available financial assets. You also may qualify if you have certain extraordinary expenses that you cannot cover with one month's net income or available financial assets.

The financial hardship category covers unforeseen events that suddenly and significantly worsen your household's financial situation. Such events could include, for example, major uninsured losses, your spouse losing his or her job, or a disabling illness or injury that abruptly reduces your family's income. You will have to document that your normal monthly expenses exceed your monthly income or that you face certain extraordinary expenses larger than one month's net income. The hardship loan application includes a worksheet with the exact calculations involved in documenting financial hardship.

These qualifying categories enable you to use the TSP loan program to help finance a wide range of anticipated or unforeseen expenses. If you expect to apply for a loan, obtain the TSP Loan Program booklet from your employing agency and read it carefully. By understanding loan requirements and procedures in advance, you'll minimize last-minute surprises or complications.

When you take out a TSP loan you are "borrowing" your own money and your repayments go back into your TSP account. But even though your loan payments go back into your account, you are still effectively paying an interest cost on the loan—the investment earnings you lose while you gradually repay the loan and replenish your account. And, your TSP loan repayments are not tax deductible. A conventional mortgage with tax deductible interest payments will continue to be the most tax-favored means of financing the bulk of your home purchase costs.

Always keep in mind that the loan program is for a specific set of documented expenses. It does not provide for ready access to your account balance under any and all circumstances.

As you chart your current and future TSP situations, you may want to identify future points when the loan program might be useful to you and your family. For example, if you hope to buy a house in five years or your daughter will be attending college 10 years down the road, you'll want to factor these predictable events into your TSP investment planning.

ELIGIBILITY AND APPLICATION PROCEDURES

To receive a loan from your TSP account balance you must meet all of the following eligibility requirements:

◇ You must be a current employee in a pay status. Federal or postal employees who retire or separate from government service are not eligible to receive loans, even if they continue to have a TSP account balance after separation. Employees temporarily in a non-pay status are not eligible to apply for a loan during the non-pay period. If you already have a TSP loan and then enter into a non-pay status, you may continue to carry the TSP loan. In a later section we'll explain how temporary non-pay status affects repayment of your loan.

◇ You must have at least $1,000 of your contributions and earnings in your TSP account to receive a loan. The minimum loan amount is $1,000. The maximum loan amount you can apply for will range from $1,000 to $50,000, depending on your account balance at the time of your application. The next section describes the loan calculation process in detail.

◇ Your loan amount and repayment schedule must be such that your net government paycheck—after loan payments, retirement contributions and all other deductions—is equal to at least 10 percent of your basic pay.

◇ For educational, medical or residential loans you must submit Loan Application Form TSP-20. You obtain Form TSP-20 from your employing agency office and send it to the TSP Service Office. We've included a specimen copy of Form TSP-20 in Appendix 5, so you can anticipate the information you'll need to provide. The form includes the address of the TSP Service Office.

Form TSP-20 requires the following major categories of information—purpose of the loan, requested loan amount, loan repayment period (one to four years for educational and medical loans, one to 15 years for residential loans), your pay schedule (biweekly, monthly, other) and information about your spouse if you are married. Do not submit additional documentation with Form TSP-20.

The TSP Service Office will inform you of additional requirements after receiving your application. Of course, you should have ready any bills, receipts, invoices and agreements that describe your educational, medical or residential expenses. If you request a loan amount higher than the amount you are eligible for, the TSP Service Office will reject your application unless you indicate you want the maximum loan allowed. The next section helps you estimate the loan amount you're eligible for depending on your TSP account balance.

◇ For a financial hardship loan you submit Hardship Loan Application Form TSP-20-H. You can obtain Form TSP-20-H from the TSP Service Office by mail or phone.

Because hardship loans address pressing financial situations, you'll need to supply more detailed documentation immediately. The required information will include your monthly income, monthly expenses, financial assets, extraordinary expenses, requested loan amount, loan repayment period (one to four years), pay schedule and current earnings and leave statement.

For a hardship loan it's important to indicate on your application form that—if it turns out you're not eligible for your requested loan amount—you want the maximum loan possible. If you don't, you risk rejection of your requested amount and a financially difficult delay while you submit a new application.

◇ If you are a FERS employee your spouse must consent to the loan application. If you are a CSRS employee the Thrift Service Office will notify your spouse of the loan application.

TSP loans are not instantaneous. You should allow about two months between filing your TSP loan application and receiving a check for the loan amount. During this period the Thrift Service Office processes your application and assembles a loan agreement package. This package includes a Loan Agreement/Promissory Note indicating the loan amount, interest rate, repayment period and the payment amount. It also provides loan account identification for correspondence during the life of the loan.

When you receive the Loan Agreement/Promissory Note you have three choices:

◇ Accept the terms of the loan. Complete and return the Agreement within 45 days from its issue date. Send it to the TSP Service Office and include all requested documentation and your most recent earnings and leave statement.

◇ Modify the terms of the loan. Check the cancellation block on the Agreement and submit a new application to the TSP Service Office requesting a different loan amount or repayment period. In other words, do not change the agreement. Cancel and reapply.

◇ Cancel the loan. Check the cancellation block and send the canceled agreement to the TSP Service Office.

You can help make the loan processing as speedy as possible by applying for an amount you're eligible to borrow, requesting the maximum eligible amount as a "backup," and returning the Loan Agreement/Promissory Note and any other required documents promptly. Remember to sign and date all documents carefully.

CALCULATION OF MAXIMUM LOAN AMOUNTS _____

Stay aware of your potential TSP loan amounts over the course of your federal or postal career. If you are planning to use a TSP loan to finance a future expense, you'll want to plot your projected account growth and—if necessary—adjust your contributions or investments to meet your future loan target. It's also prudent to keep abreast of what your TSP loan potential would be in the event of an unforeseen financial need. Your TSP account provides an important "rainy day" fund that can help you and your family cope with financial emergencies.

The amount you can borrow from your account increases as your account balance grows. Remember that the maximum loan amount under any circumstances is $50,000 and there is a $1,000 loan minimum. The following rules apply in determining the amount you can borrow from your TSP account:

◇ You can never borrow more than the amount of your contributions and associated investment earnings.

◇ If your contributions and earnings are $1,000-$10,000 and you have not had an outstanding loan during the previous 12 months, you can borrow up to the full amount of your contributions and earnings.

◇ When your contributions and earnings are more than $10,000 or you have had an outstanding loan during the previous 12 months, a three-part formula determines the maximum amount you can borrow. The formula can be fairly complicated, depending on your circumstances. The TSP Inquiry Line—(504) 255-8777—provides your current potential TSP loan amount, updated monthly. Appendix 1 describes the full range of TSP Inquiry Line services. If you want to be able to estimate on your own what your potential loan amount will be at some future point, you'll want to know the three-part formula. Figure 7-1 shows you how to estimate your maximum loan amount if you have not had an outstanding loan during the previous 12 months.

_____ Maximum TSP Loan Amounts _____
Employee with No Outstanding Loan in Previous 12 Months

Your Contributions and Earnings Are	Your Vested Account Balance Is	You Can Borrow Up to
Less than $1,000	Any amount	Not eligible for loan
$1,000 - $10,000	Any amount	100% of contributions and earnings
$10,000 or more	Less than $20,000	$10,000
$10,000 or more	$20,000 - $100,000	The Smaller of: 100% of contributions and earnings or 50% of vested balance
$50,000 or more	$100,000 or more	$50,000

Figure 7-1

The most complicated loan amount calculations occur when your own contributions and earnings are $10,000 or more and your vested account balance is in the range of $20,000-$100,000. Your maximum loan amount is the smaller of your contributions and earnings or one-half your vested account balance. For example, if your vested account balance is $40,000 and the value of your own contributions and earnings is $25,000, your eligible loan amount would be $20,000—half of the $40,000. If the total vested balance is $40,000 but your contributions and earnings are only $15,000, then your eligible loan amount would be $15,000.

◇ If you are a CSRS employee and your contributions and earnings are greater than $20,000, the 50 percent of vested balance amount will apply. Your entire account consists of your contributions and earnings, so you are always fully vested in your entire account balance. Thus, 50 percent of your vested balance will be a smaller amount than 100 percent of your contributions and earnings.

◇ If you are a FERS employee, remember that you are not vested in your agency's automatic 1 percent of pay contributions until you have completed three years of service. This may slightly reduce your potential loan amount during your initial three years.

◇ If you are a FERS employee, the relationship between 100 percent of your contributions and earnings and 50 percent of your vested account balance depends on the pattern of your TSP contributions and the resulting matching contributions over time. If you have consistently contributed more than 5 percent of pay, in most cases 50 percent of your vested balance will be the smaller amount—your contributions and earnings make up more than half of your account.

If you have consistently contributed less than 5 percent of pay, 100 percent of your contributions and earnings will usually be the smaller amount—your contributions and earnings make up less than half of your account. If you have always contributed exactly 5 percent of pay, then the full amount of your contributions and earnings will be equal to 50 percent of your total vested account balance. If your contributions have varied over time, whether 100 percent of your contributions and earnings or 50 percent of your vested account balance is the smaller amount will depend on the exact pattern of your contributions.

TSP LOAN REPAYMENT TERMS _____

The repayment periods for TSP loans depend on the purpose of the loan. If you obtain a loan for purchase of a primary residence you may select a repayment period from one to 15 years. Under the other three categories—educational expenses, medical expenses or financial hardship—you may select a repayment period from one to four years. Within these ranges you may choose a specific repayment period that best suits your circumstances. For example, if a two-year loan makes the payments too high, but you don't want to stretch the loan over a full three years, you might choose something in between—two years and six months, for example.

You must repay TSP loans through substantially equal payroll allotments every pay period. *You always have the* 🔑 *option of prepaying the entire outstanding account balance—partial prepayments are not allowed. You may also reamortize the loan—shortening or lengthening the original repayment period—once during the life of the loan.* The upper limits of four years (educational, medical, financial hardship) and 15 years (primary residence) always apply.

You cannot temporarily suspend your payments unless you enter a non-pay status. If this occurs and loan payments are not made for more than 90 days, you must either reamortize the loan or prepay the entire loan balance.

The interest rate on a TSP loan is the most recent G Fund interest rate at the time your application is received. This rate will apply for the life of the loan. If G Fund rates are moving up or down sharply as you near your expected loan application, be sure to pay attention to where the rates are likely to head. If you expect G Fund rates to rise or continue rising, apply for your loan as soon as possible to avoid higher loan payments. If you expect rates to drop or continue dropping, think about delaying your application to reduce your payments. Don't get too cute, because long-term interest rates typically shift gradually. But if there's a clear and strong trend in long-term interest rates, you may want to adapt your loan planning accordingly.

After you apply for a loan the TSP Service Office will send you a Loan Agreement/Promissory Note specifying the loan amount, interest rate, repayment period and resulting payroll allotment amounts. You have a 45-day period in which to accept the terms. If you do not complete, sign and return the Loan Agreement/Promissory Note and all other requested information within the 45-day period, the loan offer is canceled and you must reapply. If this happens, the interest rate for your loan will be the latest G Fund rate at the time your new application is received.

Approximate Loan Payments Every Bi-Weekly Pay Period for Each $1,000 Borrowed

26 Payments Per Year

Years to Repay	TSP Loan Interest Rate				
	6%	7%	8%	9%	10%
1	$39.75	$39.95	$40.15	$40.35	$40.60
2	$20.45	$20.65	$20.85	$21.10	$21.30
3	$14.05	$14.25	$14.45	$14.65	$14.90
4	$10.85	$11.05	$11.25	$11.50	$11.70
5	$8.95	$9.15	$9.35	$9.60	$9.80
6	$7.65	$7.85	$8.10	$8.30	$8.55
7	$6.75	$6.95	$7.20	$7.45	$7.65
8	$6.05	$6.30	$6.55	$6.75	$7.00
9	$5.55	$5.75	$6.00	$6.25	$6.50
10	$5.10	$5.35	$5.60	$5.85	$6.10
11	$4.80	$5.00	$5.25	$5.50	$5.80
12	$4.50	$4.75	$5.00	$5.25	$5.50
13	$4.25	$4.50	$4.75	$5.05	$5.30
14	$4.05	$4.30	$4.55	$4.85	$5.10
15	$3.90	$4.15	$4.40	$4.70	$4.95

Figure 7-2

Figure 7-2 shows your approximate bi-weekly loan payments for a $1,000 TSP loan at interest rates ranging from 6 percent to 10 percent. To estimate your payments for loans of varying amounts, multiply the figures by the amount of your loan in thousands of dollars. For example, payments for an $8,000 loan would be eight times the figures listed below. Payments for a $22,350 loan would be 22.35 times the amounts listed in figure 7-2.

If you are on a weekly, semi-monthly, or monthly pay schedule, your loan payments each pay period will differ from those in Figure 7-2. To estimate your loan payments each pay period, find the appropriate loan term and interest rate, then multiply the payment by the factor for your pay schedule.

Weekly (52 payments per year)	Multiply by 0.50
Semi-monthly (24 payments per year)	Multiply by 1.08
Monthly (12 payments per year)	Multiply by 2.17

For example, if you are paid monthly and take a four-year TSP loan of $10,000 with 7 percent interest, your approximate monthly loan payment would be $239.80— $11.05 per $1,000, times 10 for a $10,000 loan, times the 2.17 factor (from the table).

If you are considering applying for a TSP loan—soon or at a known date in the future—it will be worth your while to plot your expected loan possibilities as far in advance as possible. You won't know exactly your potential loan amount, applicable G Fund interest rate and resulting repayment amounts until you actually file your loan application. But by paying attention to your TSP account balance, the movement of G Fund interest rates and your overall household finances, you will be able to borrow from your TSP account more effectively.

WHAT HAPPENS IF YOU CAN'T REPAY YOUR LOAN

A TSP loan represents a temporary use of your own savings. This has certain advantages, the most important being that you cannot encounter any legal actions to recover any unpaid amounts. But there are some specific consequences and complications involved if you are unable to make your scheduled loan payments.

You repay your loan through an agreed schedule of payroll allotments. The Loan Agreement/Promissory Note specifies your repayment obligations. Remember, you cannot choose to suspend your payroll allotments—they are binding for the entire period of the loan. You can pay faster than originally scheduled if you want, either by— once only—reamortizing the loan to shorten the repayment period or by prepaying the entire outstanding loan balance. You can pay slower than originally scheduled by—once only—reamortizing the loan to lengthen the repayment period within the upper limits of four years or 15 years, depending on the type of loan.

⊙TIP But *you cannot temporarily stop your scheduled payments by choice. Your regular loan payroll allotments stop only under narrowly specified circumstances and with clearly defined consequences.* The following are the situations that may interrupt or alter your scheduled loan payments:

◇ You go on leave without pay. Your agency must confirm to the TSP that you have entered an approved non-pay status and the approved period of that status. During that period, your payroll allotments stop. If you miss loan payments for fewer than 90 days your loan payment schedule will be extended under the existing terms of the loan. If you miss payments for more than 90 days but less than a year, you must reamortize your loan.

If you are in an approved non-pay status for more than a year, you must prepay the outstanding balance of the loan within a year of entering non-pay status. If you don't prepay the loan you are subject to a "taxable distribution" of the outstanding balance. This means that the amount of your money (principal and accrued interest) that you've not paid back to your account is deemed by the IRS to have been paid to you as current taxable income. If this occurs you will—in most cases—be subject in addition to a 10 percent "early withdrawal" tax penalty because in effect you've taken tax-deferred savings as income before retirement.

◇ You are on leave without pay to work for an employee organization or an IPA (intergovernmental transfer) assignment. Your loan payments continue. Contact the TSP Service Office to make necessary arrangements for the transfer of your payroll allotments.

◇ You transfer to a new agency or payroll office. Your loan payments continue. To avoid missing payments you should inform the TSP Service Office of your transfer and inform your new payroll office that you are repaying a TSP loan. If you miss loan payments for more than 90 days you will have to reamortize your TSP loan. If your transfer changes your pay period schedule, notify the TSP Service Office as soon as possible. You will receive a reamortization package that adjusts your loan payments to reflect your new pay cycle.

◇ You leave federal or postal service. You must repay the full amount of the outstanding loan balance. You will receive a payment notice and instructions, and you must pay the full amount within 90 days of the notice date. If you fail to pay up within 90 days, the outstanding principal and any unpaid interest will be declared a taxable distribution from your account. Your unpaid loan amount is reported to the IRS as taxable income for the year the distribution occurs, usually subject to an additional 10 percent early withdrawal penalty. Note: An unpaid loan may also delay your withdrawal of the rest of your TSP account balance.

◇ You die. The outstanding principal and interest becomes a taxable distribution to your estate. There is no early withdrawal penalty. The outstanding amount cannot be prepaid.

That—particularly the last—is the bad news. The good news is that there are certain things you can do to make your TSP loan process as advantageous as possible. Let's review them.

LOAN PLANNING AND YOUR OVERALL TSP STRATEGY _____

You may end up at the end of your federal or postal career without ever needing to apply for a loan from your TSP account. Or you may know in advance that you want to use the TSP loan program—possibly several times—as an integral part of your long-term financial planning.

Whatever your circumstances, you should be at least generally familiar with how TSP loans work—to be better prepared for an unexpected emergency or to lay the groundwork for a future loan. And as you become more certain about a future loan application and approach the actual point you'll need the funds, you should focus and refine your planning for maximum financial advantage.

The following are some factors you may want to consider as part of your TSP loan planning:

◇ Always have an approximate estimate of your current eligible loan amount. Your maximum potential loan amount grows as your TSP account balance accumulates over time. To be prepared for unforeseen financial needs, you should know roughly how much "crisis money" you can draw upon for medical expenses or other sudden hardships.

This doesn't mean you have to go through an elaborate recalculation every pay period. But you should at least call the **TSP Inquiry Line**—(504) 255-8777—once a year or so to check your eligible loan amount. And, preferably, you should understand the loan formula well enough to be able to gauge the growth of your eligible loan amount over time.

◇ If planning a future loan, estimate your projected eligible loan amount. You may know the likely timing of an educational or residential loan several years in advance. For example, if you have an eight-year-old daughter you may expect her to face college tuition costs in about 10 years. Or you and your spouse may be planning to buy a house in three years.

For known and important financial purposes such as these, it's advisable that you take the time to project your TSP account balance and the resulting eligible loan amounts. This is not difficult as long as you keep in mind that you are estimating approximate amounts, not computing to the penny. To estimate the future growth of your eligible loan amount, use the tables in Appendix 2 (FERS employees) or Appendix 3 (CSRS employees) to project your future account balance.

These calculations will give you a reasonably accurate projection of your future eligible loan amounts. You can then chart the actual growth of your TSP account to measure whether you're on track to meet one or more specific loan target points. The accuracy of your estimates will depend on your actual pattern of future TSP contributions and on how close your actual TSP investment returns are to your estimates. It may be useful to reassess your projections at least every year.

Tracking your eligible loan amount compared to your future loan target can help you make the most of your long-term financial opportunities. If you are planning a future residential loan, the knowledge that you are on target to meet a down payment may give you greater flexibility in negotiating advantageous mortgage terms. If you end up moving substantially ahead of your original target, that knowledge may even alter your plans regarding the size or location of the home you plan to buy.

Of course you may find yourself tracking behind your projected loan target. This might occur because you were unable to continue your expected level of TSP contributions, or if actual investment returns did not meet your estimates. Even in this case, though, you will benefit from your loan planning and tracking. You'll spot potential shortfalls sooner rather than later and give yourself more time to adjust your TSP contributions or investments, your overall household finances or your loan expectations.

◇ *Try to structure your loan so that you can afford to continue your regular TSP contributions.* This is key. The TSP loan program is a relatively simple and convenient source of financing. You are borrowing your own money and repaying it to your own account. All the principal and interest return to your TSP account as you make your repayments, automatically reentering the tax-deferred savings process.

But there is still a definite cost involved in taking a loan from your TSP account. The cost is the compounded investment earnings you forego over the life of the loan. Your account balance gradually returns to its pre-loan equivalent as you repay the principal and interest back to your TSP account.

You will pay an added cost if your loan payments force you to reduce your pay period contributions to your TSP account. And, if you are a FERS employee, you will pay a steep cost if your loan payments force you to eliminate TSP contributions that are also generating agency matching contributions.

If you are a FERS employee contributing more than 5 percent of pay to the TSP, try to maintain your contribution level. But if you have to reduce your contributions because of the loan payments, make every effort to maintain at least a 5 percent of pay contribution to keep maximum agency matching contributions.

If you are a FERS employee contributing 5 percent of pay or less to the TSP, it is very important for you to maintain your contribution level and matching contributions. In fact, if you are contributing less than 5 percent of pay, you should consider increasing your contributions to the 5 percent level. The additional matching contributions will help you preserve your short-term account balance and your long-term compounded growth potential.

CSRS employees do not face the extra cost of losing matching contributions. But if you are counting on your TSP account as a retirement supplement or for other financial purposes, it's just as important to you to protect the current value and growth potential of your TSP account.

◇ Adjust your TSP investment strategy to reflect your loan planning. For most federal and postal employees the TSP is a long-term proposition. It's specially designed to serve retirement income goals and long-term tax-deferred capital growth. Even if you don't expect to continue your federal or postal career straight through to retirement, your TSP account retains its long-term focus.

How do TSP loans fit into your investment strategy? The expectation of a future loan creates an interim financial target within the longer timeframe of your retirement savings. In effect, you have temporarily shortened the time interval between current investment decisions and your expected use of the funds. As a result, you may want to shift temporarily to a more conservative investment mix shortly before your expected loan application.

You don't necessarily have to move your entire account balance into the G Fund. But you should measure how large a temporary C Fund or F Fund loss you could endure without jeopardizing your desired loan amount. If necessary, shift your investment mix so that the portion of your total account exposed to short-term risk is such that, even if a short-term loss occurs, your targeted loan amount will remain intact. On the other hand, if you want to maintain your current investment strategy, plan for the possibility of downward fluctuations. Anticipate a potentially lower eligible loan amount and—if you have to— identify additional sources of financing to supplement a somewhat smaller TSP loan.

If you have a more substantial cushion over and above your desired loan amount, you may proceed with your current investment mix. But keep an eye on short-term C Fund and F Fund movements. The more flexible your loan needs and resulting account targets, the more you can ride out market fluctuations without jeopardizing essential short-term goals. The more fixed the financial need and amount, the more careful you should be about protecting your eligible loan amount.

COMPARING TSP LOANS AND OTHER LOAN SOURCES

TSP loans offer certain advantages and disadvantages compared to other potential loan sources. The primary advantage is that, because you are borrowing your own money, you do not face demanding qualification requirements. You need to demonstrate the qualifying expense that you are using the loan to finance—purchase of a primary residence, educational or medical expenses, or financial hardship. But you do not need to go through an examination of your financial qualifications and credit-worthiness.

The major disadvantage is that repayment provisions are not very flexible. You can reamortize your TSP loan once during the term of the loan, in order to shorten or lengthen the repayment period. Or, you can repay the loan in full at any time. But you cannot prepay a portion of the outstanding balance, as you can with other loans—prepayment of a TSP loan is an all or nothing proposition. And, if you leave government service you must pay the entire outstanding TSP loan balance within 90 days. If you cannot repay the full amount, the outstanding balance is deemed to have been paid to you as income from your account, and is taxable income.

Figure 7-3 highlights some of the essential features of TSP loans compared to two other potential loan sources—second mortgages or home equity loans, and consumer loans from a bank or credit union. In general, if you qualify for a second mortgage or home equity loan, and you can afford the upfront "points" and processing charges, this route will likely be preferable to a TSP loan. Because the interest you pay is tax-deductible, the effective cost of the loan is lower. But *you need to review carefully the interest rate, your tax savings and the cost of the upfront charges*. If you are in doubt about the true cost of the loan because you don't understand the tax savings or the effect of the upfront charges, it may be worth your while to consult a financial adviser before deciding between a mortgage/equity loan and a TSP loan.

On the other hand, TSP loans will in most cases be superior to consumer loans from a bank or credit union. Again, the primary issue is which loan source has the lower effective cost. In this instance, consumer credit rates will almost always be higher than the G Fund interest rates payable on TSP loans.

However, there may be situations in which the amount you can borrow or repayment flexibility favor the consumer loan, or a combination of a consumer loan and a TSP loan. Typically, though, cost considerations will make the TSP loan superior to a consumer loan. Remember, though, that you may be able to obtain a consumer loan for a wide range of financial needs, while TSP loans are restricted to a specific set of qualifying expenses described above.

A word of caution. Don't be confused by the difference between borrowing your own money through a TSP loan, compared to borrowing someone else's money through a mortgage, line of credit or consumer loan. Interest is interest and you will face a loan cost, regardless of the loan source. In a TSP loan, the cost of the loan is the interest you are not earning while your funds are withdrawn from your account. In a commercial loan, your cost is the interest you pay to the lender, less the tax savings if the interest is deductible. But in either case your loan cost is based on the rate of interest, whether you incur this cost in the form of interest not earned or interest paid.

Comparison of TSP Loans and Other Loan Sources

	Amount You Can Borrow	Length of Loan	Interest Rates	Repayment Restrictions	Tax Treatment
TSP Loans	$1,000 to $50,000, depending on your account balance	To buy a primary residence—1 to 15 years. Other loans—1 to 4 years.	G Fund rate when you apply for the loan. 1988-1993, 5.625%-9.375%	Can prepay in full. Cannot partially prepay. Full repayment within 90 days if you leave federal service.	Interest not deductible. If you leave federal service and do not repay in full, unpaid amount is taxable income.
Mortgages, Home Equity Loans and Lines of Credit	Varies, based on equity in appraised value of home	Up to 30 years for mortgages, home equity loans may be revolving line of credit	Fixed or variable, rates 1988-1993, 6%-11%, including effective cost of upfront charges	Can accelerate payments. Loans require payment of upfront charges.	Interest paid is tax-deductible.
Unsecured Consumer Loans	Varies, based on purpose and amount you qualify for	Varies, typically 1-4 years	Varies, typical rates 1988-1993, 10%-15%	Can accelerate payments or repay in full.	Interest not deductible.

Figure 7-3

5 THINGS TO DO

1. Always try to have an approximate idea of your maximum loan amount from your TSP account. Even if you don't face any known financial needs, it will be good to know the amount you can count on if you face sudden medical or other expenses.

2. If you anticipate needing a TSP loan at some point, estimate your expected account growth up to the time you'll apply for the loan.

3. If your anticipated loan period is several years away, check your TSP investment strategy and investment returns. Adjusting your strategy may help you increase your maximum loan amount by the time the qualifying expense occurs.

4. As you approach the date of your loan application, review your TSP investment mix to make sure the amount you want to borrow will be there when you need it. If short-term fluctuations in the C or F funds would threaten the loan amount you need, you might want to move some of your account to the G Fund temporarily, for greater stability.

5. Stay current on G Fund interest rates and the interest rates for other potential loan sources. This will help you measure the costs of alternative loan sources and, if you have some flexibility in when you apply for the loan, repay the loan at the lowest possible cost.

◇8 WITHDRAWING YOUR TSP ACCOUNT BALANCE

This is where all of your careful TSP planning finally pays off. In this chapter you'll learn what choices you have for withdrawing your TSP account balance and using it as retirement income. We'll look at what options you may select from under different circumstances, how you can vary the size and duration of your payments, tax issues you may want to consider, and implications for your spouse or other survivors. We'll also point out when particular options might be more or less advantageous.

You can withdraw your TSP account when you separate from federal or postal service. Or, in most cases, you can choose to leave your account in place, and then withdraw it at a later date. While you are a federal or postal employee you can only draw on your account through the TSP loan program. You cannot actually withdraw any of your account until you separate from service. And once you have separated, you can only obtain TSP funds through a withdrawal. You are no longer eligible to draw loans from your account. Planning your withdrawal strategy is an important last step in your TSP decision-making.

SUMMARY OF OPTIONS FOR WITHDRAWING YOUR ACCOUNT BALANCE

When you leave federal or postal service you'll have the following options for withdrawing your TSP account balance:

◇ Transfer your account balance to an Individual Retirement Account (IRA) or other eligible retirement plan. A transfer enables you to continue tax-deferred treatment of your account balance. If you transfer the account to an IRA or certain other qualified plans you will also retain control over the investment of your account. It does not work the other way around. You cannot transfer IRA money into your TSP account at any time. Note: If you leave the government and are not eligible for retirement benefits—in most cases, if you do not have at least five years of service—then you must transfer your TSP account balance.

◇ Receive your balance in a single lump sum pay-

ment. You can receive your account as a single payment at or after the point when you're eligible to begin receiving your federal/postal retirement benefits. In many cases receiving the balance as a lump sum will increase the taxes you pay on your TSP income. However, if you have a specific investment opportunity or other financial goal that requires a large liquid cash reserve, this option may be advantageous.

◇ Receive your balance in a series of equal monthly payments. This payment option also can begin any time at or after you're eligible to receive retirement benefits. You can designate the number of payments, such as 60 payments over five years, 120 payments over 10 years or 180 payments over 15 years. You can designate the amount of the payments, such as $250, $500 or $1,000 each month. Or, you can have the TSP compute monthly payments based on your account balance and the average life expectancy for someone your age. Whatever designation you make, you will receive payments until your account balance has been exhausted. This option may be useful to design a "bridge" income that fits well with other retirement income sources.

◇ Use your balance to purchase a lifetime annuity. An annuity guarantees you monthly payments for the rest of your life. You may also elect to have your spouse or another survivor continue to receive payments after your death. The actual payment depends on the amount of your balance, the type of annuity you elect, average life expectancy and interest rates at the time you purchase the annuity. This option provides the security of a steady stream of income for you and your survivor.

The options available to you will depend on your retirement eligibility at the time you separate from federal or postal service. You will fall into one of three categories:

◇ Not eligible for retirement benefits. In most cases you will not be eligible for retirement benefits if you leave the government with less than five years of credited service.

◇ Eligible for deferred retirement benefits. You leave government with the five years of service required for retirement eligibility, but before the age when you can start receiving the retirement benefits. For example, if you leave at age 45 with 20 years of service, you will be eligible for deferred benefits at age 60 (CSRS) or at the FERS minimum retirement age. The FERS minimum retirement age—which applies for those with 30 years of service—is 55 until the year 2002, after which it begins to climb by two months per year in coordination with the gradual rise in the age of unreduced benefits under Social Security. The age will reach 56 in 2009, where it remains until the year 2020. Beginning in 2021 it rises by two months per year, reaching 57 in the year 2026.

◇ Eligible for immediate retirement benefits. You leave government meeting the age and service requirements to begin receiving retirement benefits immediately. For example, you are age 55 or older with at least 30 years of service, age 60 with 20 years of service or age 62 with five years of service. Or, under a reduction-in-force or other early retirement opportunity, at age 50 with 20 years of service or any age with 25 years of service.

Figure 8-1 summarizes the withdrawal options available, depending on your retirement eligibility status at the time you separate. Note: If you have a break in service of less than 31 full days, you are not considered separated and are not eligible to withdraw your TSP balance.

Summary of Eligibility for TSP Account Withdrawal Options

Retirement Status When You Leave Government

	Not Eligible for Retirement Benefits	Eligible for Retirement Benefits	
		Deferred	Immediate
Transfer to IRA or Qualified Employer Plan	Yes	Yes	Yes
Lump Sum Payment	No	Yes—when you can receive your retirement benefits	Yes
Series of Equal Payments	No	Yes—when you can receive your retirement benefits	Yes
Purchase Life Annuity	No	Yes	Yes
Defer Withdrawal Choice	No	Yes	Yes

Figure 8-1

If you choose to defer your withdrawal decision, your TSP account balance continues to accrue investment earnings. You continue to be able to reallocate your account among the three funds up to four times each year. But you cannot make new contributions to the account after you leave the government.

There are three distinct limits on how long you can defer your TSP withdrawal decision. First, if you leave government service with an account balance of $3,500 or less, you must either elect a withdrawal option or receive an automatic cashout of your account. A cashout will be subject to 20 percent mandatory withholding and, if you are younger than age 59 1/2, a 10 percent early withdrawal penalty. To avoid the cashout and tax liabilities, you may transfer all or a portion of your account to an IRA. Any amount you do not transfer to an IRA will be paid as an automatic cashout. These requirements do not apply if you return to government service before 31 full days have elapsed.

Second, you must begin withdrawing your TSP account on February 1 of the year after the year in which the latest of the following three events occurs: you become age 65; you have been eligible to participate in the TSP for 10 years, and you leave or retire from government service. Check how these three dates interact for you. Except for employees who join the government late in their careers and/or stay working beyond age 65, the date for required withdrawal will be February 1 of the year you turn age 66.

Third, under the rules governing tax-deferred retirement accounts, you must make certain minimum withdrawals when you reach age 70 1/2. At and after that age, you must withdraw income from the TSP—and from IRAs—at or above levels determined by IRS life expectancy tables.

If you leave the government and select a specific withdrawal option, you can change that selection at any time before your annuity is purchased or your non-annuity payments begin. You can change your selection to receive payments from your TSP account sooner, later or in a different form. For example, if you originally designated payments to begin at age 60, you can later decide to delay payments until age 65. Or, you could have payments start sooner as long as you meet the eligibility requirements. You could shift from an annuity to another form of payment, or from one form of annuity to another. Remember, any change to your payment selection must be made before the purchase of an annuity or before non-annuity payments begin. Changing your previous withdrawal election may delay your withdrawal.

TRANSFERS TO AN IRA OR OTHER QUALIFIED RETIREMENT PLAN

This option enables you to continue tax-deferred growth of your retirement savings after you leave federal or postal service. The TSP transfers your account directly to an IRA or another qualified retirement plan. You pay no income taxes on the amount of the transfer until the future date when you receive a distribution from the IRA or other plan. For example, if you leave government at age 45 and transfer your TSP account to an IRA, then withdraw your funds from the IRA at age 65, you pay no income taxes on the accumulated savings until age 65.

Key Issues:

Selecting Where to Transfer Your TSP Account. If you leave the government for other employment, your new employer may administer a tax-deferred savings plan similar to the TSP. A variety of employer-sponsored plans are "qualified" plans under the tax code and eligible to receive your TSP transfer—contributory pension plans, profit-sharing and stock bonus plans, for example. Check with your new employer to identify your specific options.

Note, however, that another employer's plan may not necessarily accept a transfer of your TSP account balance. Because of eligibility requirements or reasons, there may be a delay before you are eligible to transfer your TSP account to another employer's plan, or you may not be eligible to execute the transfer at all. If you are thinking about transferring your TSP account to another employer's plan, check with the employer and the TSP to determine whether and when the transfer would take place.

A more likely option will be for you to transfer your TSP account to an Individual Retirement Account (IRA). Be sure to keep in mind one important distinction. If you want to transfer your TSP account to an IRA and then be able to transfer the IRA to an employer plan, you must establish a conduit IRA for this purpose. You cannot make regular contributions to a conduit IRA. The conduit IRA serves only as a "holding" account for a second transfer. If you transfer your TSP account into a regular, contributory IRA, you cannot transfer money from the regular IRA to an employer plan. Also be sure to arrange direct account-to-account transfers. If you take personal possession of the money, even though you then deposit it directly into an IRA, you will be subject to 20 percent federal income tax withholding.

If you are choosing from among several different IRA options, look at the investment choices they provide. If you want to maintain long-term growth potential, make sure the IRA offers the possibility of favorable returns. If you're focusing on short-term maintenance of the account value, look for an IRA that provides the best low-risk investment. Many institutions that administer IRAs provide a wide range of investment options, while others are more limited.

If you're choosing between an IRA and a plan administered by your new employer, finding the best investment "fit" may again be an important factor. You also will want to look at the rules for withdrawing funds from the employer plan. An IRA allows withdrawals after you reach age 59 1/2—disbursements before age 59 1/2 incur a 10 percent early withdrawal penalty on top of normal income taxes. Your new employer's plan may in some instances allow you earlier penalty-free access to your funds. But in many cases you won't be able to withdraw your funds from a new employer's plan until you stop working for that employer.

One additional note of caution. A qualified plan with a new employer may include—or in some cases require—purchase of the employer's stock. The stock purchase plan may even include options to buy the stock at discounted prices. If the company's prospects are favorable, this may represent a very attractive investment opportunity.

But keep in mind that your transferred funds may represent an important portion of your anticipated retirement income. Investing them entirely in the stock of one firm is an inherently risky proposition. If you decide to transfer your TSP account to a new employer's stock purchase plan, be sure to balance the risk of that investment with safer retirement investments elsewhere in your portfolio. And, of course, make sure you are fully aware of the terms and conditions of the plan.

Deciding Whether to Transfer All or Part of Your TSP Account. In certain situations you may be able to choose between transferring all or part of your TSP account to an IRA or an employer plan. There are two basic situations in which you may elect a partial transfer.

First, if your TSP account balance is less than $3,500 at separation the TSP will distribute it to you as an automatic cashout unless you elect a specific payment option. This cashout will be subject to the mandatory 20 percent federal income tax withholding and you will pay a 10 percent early withdrawal penalty if you receive the cashout before you are eligible to receive FERS or CSRS retirement benefits. Note: There is no automatic withholding for state income taxes, but you may still owe state income taxes on your TSP withdrawals.

You can avoid the withholding and the penalty by **TIP** *transferring the entire account to an IRA or employer plan. But you may also elect to split the cashout, receiving part as taxable cash and transferring the balance to an IRA or employer plan.* For example, if you leave government with a $3,000 TSP account, you may transfer $2,000 to another plan and receive $1,000 as a cashout. Don't underestimate the potential tax-deferred value of even a relatively small partial transfer. If you transfer $2,000 to an IRA at age 30, it could grow to $10,000 or $15,000 by the time you reach age 60.

Second, you can combine a partial transfer with a lump sum payment or a series of equal payments. You cannot receive a lump sum or series of equal payments until you're eligible to begin receiving FERS or CSRS retirement benefits. Note: Congress has been working on legislation that would expand eligibility for these payments regardless of retirement status. At that time you may want to receive some of your TSP account balance as one or more cash payments, but set aside another portion for continued tax-deferred investment.

Let's look at some situations where you might find this

part-payment/part-transfer option useful. You might, for example, retire from the government at age 60, before your spouse is eligible to receive a pension at age 65. You might use your TSP account to set up a five-year stream of equal payments to ensure an adequate joint income until your spouse's pension becomes available. You could transfer the rest of your TSP account to an IRA for continued growth, for use in later years. Important note: You can only combine a partial transfer with a stream of equal payments if the payments are expected to last fewer than 10 years. But even with this restriction, the use of a part-cash/part-transfer option can be useful to set up "bridge" income for a defined period.

A partial transfer may also blend well with a single lump sum payment. Let's say you leave the government at age 60 with a $100,000 TSP account balance. You might decide to receive $25,000 in an immediate lump sum, to pay for a vacation, start a business venture or for a variety of other purposes. You transfer the balance of $75,000 to an IRA for later use as retirement income.

The availability of partial transfers gives you a tremendous amount of flexibility in "packaging" your TSP account into a mix of current and future income that fits your needs. Look at all your projected financial needs and income sources as you approach retirement to decide if a total or partial transfer fits your situation.

RECEIVING YOUR BALANCE IN A LUMP SUM PAYMENT

You may receive your TSP account balance as a single lump sum payment at or after the point when you're eligible to begin receiving your CSRS or FERS retirement benefits. This may be an attractive choice if a large current cash amount would help you realize an important short-term financial or personal goal. These might include, for example, capital to establish your own business or a down payment on a retirement home.

If you are considering the possibility of a lump sum payment, there are two very important steps you should take. First, make sure you understand the tax consequences of a single large payment. The entire amount of your cash payment will be taxable in the year you receive it. If it's a large sum, you may face a higher marginal tax rate than you've been accustomed to paying on your salary. Protect yourself against unwelcome surprises. You should also double-check your long-term retirement income needs and benefits. If you're comfortable with your guaranteed retirement income from other sources, then you can consider a lump sum TSP payment without concern. But if you are in doubt about the adequacy of your retirement income, make sure the lump sum—and the potential tax bite that comes with it—aren't jeopardizing your long-term financial security.

IRA TRANSFERS — SUMMARY

Eligibility: You are always eligible to elect this option at the time you leave the government. If, when you leave, your TSP account is $3,500 or less, you must either transfer your account to an IRA, receive an automatic cashout of your account or combine a cashout with a partial IRA transfer. Employees with accounts larger than $3,500 are also eligible to transfer the entire account to an IRA or combine a partial transfer with a lump sum payment or series of equal payments.

If you leave the government and decide to keep your account balance in the TSP, you may elect a transfer of your TSP balance at a later date. If you leave the government and are not eligible for retirement benefits, you must transfer your TSP account to another plan, although Congress has been working on allowing other withdrawal options in such cases.

How You Transfer Your TSP Account Balance: You transfer your entire account to an IRA or a qualified employer plan by completing Form TSP-7 (Election of Benefits) and Form TSP-13 (Designation of an Eligible Retirement Plan). You can make a partial transfer of a single payment—an automatic cashout or a lump sum payment—by completing Form TSP 12-P (Request for Part of a Single Payment to be Transferred to an IRA of Other Eligible Plan). A partial transfer of a series of equal payments requires Form TSP-12-E (Request for Part of Each Equal Payment to be Transferred to an IRA or Other Eligible Plan).

Tax Treatment: All amounts transferred to an IRA or other qualified plan continue to be tax-deferred. This treatment continues until you receive income from the other plan. Payments that you combine with a partial transfer—automatic cashout of less than $3,500, lump sum payment, equal payments for less than 10 years—are subject to mandatory 20 percent federal withholding. Automatic cashouts before eligibility for FERS/CSRS retirement benefits also involve a 10 percent early withdrawal penalty.

Important reminder: Have the TSP transfer your account directly to an IRA to avoid the mandatory 20 percent withholding. If you receive the money and then roll it over to an IRA yourself, 20 percent will be withheld. You'll either reduce the amount you can roll over or you'll have to make up the difference from other sources.

Spousal Rights: If you are not eligible for retirement benefits or eligible for CSRS benefits, the TSP notifies your spouse before transferring your account to an IRA or another plan. If you are eligible for FERS benefits, you and your spouse must complete Form TSP-14 (Joint Waiver of Spouse's Annuity). These requirements do not apply if your account is $3,500 or less.

Of course, the larger your account balance, the more careful you have to be in comparing your current and future financial needs. If you're thinking about taking a $10,000 lump sum for current spending or a business venture, you're probably "giving up" only about $50-$100 a month of retirement income, depending on your age. But if you're thinking about a $50,000 lump sum payment, take a close look at the overall long-term picture.

If you elect a "delayed lump sum" your TSP account continues to accrue investment earnings and you retain the opportunity to allocate your account among the three TSP funds.

Key Issues:

Accurately Comparing Short-Term and Long-Term Financial Outcomes. You're about to retire from federal or postal service. Or, you left the government a while ago, but soon you'll be eligible to receive your deferred CSRS or FERS retirement benefits. In either case you're considering taking your TSP account balance as a single lump sum payment.

You should not take a lump sum until you've thoroughly reviewed your short-term and long-term financial prospects. If you have a clear and important purpose for the lump sum funds and your guaranteed retirement income is adequate, then a lump sum might be quite useful. *If you're simply excited by the idea of having a large amount of money in your bank account, or you're counting on "making a killing" through future investments, then the lump sum could be more mirage than miracle.*

Start by taking a stock of your future retirement income. If you're married, look at joint retirement incomes for you and your spouse. Include your CSRS and/or FERS benefits, Social Security and any other pensions and savings. Carefully check when each income source will be available. Figure out your guaranteed retirement income at various ages.

If you have any doubts about your retirement income security, you're probably better off forgetting about a TSP lump sum. Perhaps the worst thing you could do would be to take a lump sum for a speculative, high-risk business opportunity or financial investment. Better to use your TSP account to supplement your steady retirement income and build from that base through future income and investments.

But if your basic retirement income is already secure, you have the freedom to weigh the pros and cons of a lump sum TSP payment. A good place to start is a comparison of your basic short-term and long-term choices. Figure 8-2 compares a range of lump sum payments with their equivalent lifetime annuity values. The example assumes a joint life annuity with 50 percent income to the survivor and increasing payments for inflation protection. Choosing other annuity options would increase or decrease the exact annuity amount, as shown in Figure 8-9.

Taking a Lump Sum Compared to Purchasing an Annuity

Amount of Lump Sum Payment	Approximate Monthly Annuity Payment			
	At Age 55	At Age 60	At Age 62	At Age 65
$10,000	$62	$68	$71	$76
$25,000	$155	$170	$177	$190
$50,000	$309	$339	$354	$381
$100,000	$618	$678	$708	$761

Figure 8-2

These are only approximate lifetime annuity values under one scenario. Actual annuity amounts would vary somewhat with different annuity options and interest rates.

When you're considering the possibility of electing a lump sum TSP payment, compare the short-term benefits of the lump sum with the long-term benefits of additional retirement income. Try to develop clear answers to specific questions. For example, suppose you're age 60 with a TSP balance of about $25,000. You're trying to choose between a lump sum payment and a monthly annuity of about $170. What exactly are you going to do with the lump sum? How would an extra $170 a month change your retirement budget and lifestyle?

If your "ideal retirement" involves buying a boat, then the lump sum may be a good idea. If instead it includes more trips to the beach or golf course, then enhancing your regular income may be preferable.

Taxes and Timing. Let's suppose you've cleared the first hurdle. You're confident that your basic monthly retirement income will be adequate without your TSP savings. You then compared your short-term use of a lump sum payment with the longer-term "extra value" of a larger monthly budget in retirement. You decided the short-term goal is more valuable to you and your family. Now what?

You'll want to look very closely at the tax treatment of your lump sum payment. And, depending on what the tax picture looks like, you may want to wait a short time before receiving the lump sum. The income tax rate you owe on your lump sum payment will depend on the size of the payment and your other income in the year you receive the lump sum. Estimate the taxes on your lump sum before applying for the payment. Your entire lump sum, or a large portion of it, may be subject to the highest marginal income tax rate. If you want to reduce the "tax bite" on your lump sum payment, there are three places to look for possible relief.

First, you may be able to reduce the taxes on your lump sum payment by using income averaging when you file your tax return. Under five-year averaging your lump sum will be taxed as if you received it in equal amounts over five years. Ten-year averaging taxes the payment as if you received it over 10 years.

Under either averaging technique you still pay the taxes on your lump sum at one time. But you compute the taxes on your lump sum based on five or 10 smaller payments rather than the total actual payment. For example, a $50,000 lump sum would be treated as five $10,000 payments (five-year averaging) or 10 $5,000 payments (10-year averaging). Income averaging can lower the tax rate on the lump sum because the smaller amounts may prevent the lump sum from pushing you into a higher tax bracket.

There are several restrictions that may determine whether you are eligible to use income averaging or whether it is worthwhile for you. If you are thinking about taking a TSP lump sum payment and using income averaging, check your tax options carefully. The most important restrictions are:

◇ You cannot use income averaging if you take part of your TSP account as a lump sum and part as a transfer to an IRA. Income averaging only applies when you take a taxable distribution of your entire account in one tax year.

◇ You must have had contributions—by you or your agency—to your TSP account for at least five years prior to the year you receive the lump sum payment.

◇ If you reached age 50 before January 1, 1986, you can use either five-year or 10-year averaging. Otherwise five-year averaging is your only option and you generally must be at least age 59 1/2 at the time of the lump sum payment.

◇ Five-year averaging uses the tax rates for single taxpayers for the year you receive your lump sum. Ten-year averaging uses the 1986 single taxpayer rates.

◇ You can only use income averaging once in your lifetime. If you have already used income averaging, you cannot use it for a TSP lump sum payment. If you use it for your TSP lump sum payment, you cannot use it for some other source of income in a later year.

◇ If you use income averaging you must use it for all lump sum distributions you receive from the TSP or any other employer plans in that year—for example, an outstanding TSP loan balance that was declared a taxable distribution, or a cashout of a savings or profit-sharing plan from another employer.

Income averaging may be a very effective method for you to enjoy the benefits of a lump sum payment while minimizing your tax liability. But if you are thinking about using income averaging, check in advance to verify your eligibility and to be sure that the tax savings make the restrictions worth accepting.

A second way to reduce taxes on your lump sum—if income averaging is not an available or attractive option—is by delaying the payment. For example, if you retire late

---

LUMP SUM PAYMENTS — SUMMARY

Eligibility: If you leave government eligible for immediate retirement benefits, you can elect to receive a lump sum payment immediately or at a specified later date. If you leave government eligible for deferred retirement benefits, you cannot receive an immediate lump sum payment. You can elect to receive a lump sum payment at or after the point when you are eligible to begin receiving your deferred retirement benefit. For example, if you leave the government with five or more years of service, you can instruct the TSP to pay you a lump sum at age 62 or later. Under FERS you may also begin receiving deferred benefits at the "minimum retirement age" with 10 years of service. If you qualify under this rule, you can receive a TSP lump sum at that age or later. Differences among various eligibility requirements that depend on retirement status likely will be eliminated eventually. Contact your TSP office to check the status.

How You Receive Your TSP Account as a Lump Sum Payment: You obtain a lump sum payment of your TSP account by requesting equal payments and specifying that you want one payment. If you are eligible for immediate retirement benefits, complete Form TSP-7 (Election of Benefits) and Form TSP-12 (Application for Equal Payments). To combine a lump sum and a transfer to an IRA, complete Form TSP-12-P (Request for Part of a Single Payment to be Transferred to an IRA or other Eligible Plan).

If you are eligible for deferred retirement benefits, you also file Forms TSP-7 and TSP-12. But on Form TSP-12 you must specify a future date for the payment, at or after the point when you can actually receive your deferred retirement benefits. The TSP will provide you with additional information about a full or partial transfer to an IRA as you approach your specified payment date.

Tax Treatment: There is an automatic 20 percent federal income tax withholding on the amount of your lump sum payment. There is no automatic withholding for state income taxes. Of course, your actual tax liability will depend on your total income, exemptions and deductions in the year you receive the lump sum. Income averaging, the timing of your payment or transferring part of your balance to an IRA may reduce your actual tax liability. Remember that you cannot combine income averaging for a lump sum amount and an IRA transfer for the balance of your account.

Spousal Rights: If you are eligible for CSRS benefits, TSP notifies your spouse before transferring your account to another plan. If you are eligible for FERS benefits, you and your spouse complete Form TSP-14 (Joint Waiver of Spouse's Annuity).

in the year and receive a TSP lump sum that same year, you'll pay taxes on the combination of your salary, pension and lump sum and any other incomes in that year. Delaying the TSP lump sum until the next year may spread out your taxable incomes to your advantage.

A third way to reduce the lump sum tax bite is to combine a lump sum payment and a transfer to an IRA. You don't have to view a TSP lump sum payment as an "all or nothing" proposition. For example, let's say you have a $50,000 TSP account balance. You've decided you want to obtain a large single payment, but you're also concerned about losing too much of that payment to income taxes. Look closely at your intended uses for the lump sum payment. If your short-term focus actually only requires $30,000, perhaps you should think about limiting your lump sum to $30,000 and setting aside $20,000 for future use by transferring it to an IRA. You'll realize your short-term goal and reduce your current tax liability.

RECEIVING YOUR BALANCE IN EQUAL MONTHLY PAYMENTS _____

This option enables you to use your TSP account to design a personalized schedule of retirement income payments. You must use monthly payments. But otherwise you have virtually complete freedom to design a payment schedule that fits your personal circumstances.

For example, you can use equal monthly payments to "frontload" your TSP income in the years before other retirement income becomes available. Or you can specify a monthly dollar amount that combines with other income to build a "target" retirement budget. Finally, you can have the TSP pay you minimum monthly payments based on IRS life expectancy tables. This lets you hold most of your balance "in reserve" for later use, giving you some flexibility to adapt to changing circumstances after retirement.

Whatever payment schedule you select, the TSP will invest your entire account in the G Fund at the time your payments begin. This protects against potential losses in the C Fund or F Fund, which might reduce your account below the level needed to meet your selected payment schedule.

Keep in mind the basic difference between equal monthly payments and an annuity. In an annuity you—or you and your spouse—receive guaranteed lifetime payments based on your account balance and average life expectancy. Regardless of how many years you—or you and your spouse—actually live, payments continue at a specified level.

Under equal monthly payments you define a specific payment schedule. If you select monthly payments for a designated period, the exact amount will vary slightly based on G Fund earnings after your payments begin. If you designate a specific dollar level, the exact duration of the payments may vary based on G Fund earnings. Either

way, the money funding the equal monthly payments will run out someday and you will no longer receive payments.

If you leave government eligible for deferred retirement benefits, you can start receiving equal monthly payments any time at or after the point when you can begin receiving your deferred retirement benefits. For example, if you leave the government with five or more years of service, you can start receiving equal payments at age 62 or later. Under FERS you may also begin receiving deferred benefits at the "minimum retirement age" with 10 years of service. If you qualify under this rule, you can receive equal monthly payments at that age or later.

If you elect "delayed equal payments" your TSP account continues to accrue investment earnings and you retain the opportunity to allocate your account among the three TSP funds. The TSP will invest your entire account in the G Fund when you begin to receive your monthly payments.

Key Issues:

Everyone's retirement reflects a unique mix of circumstances and choices. Some seek to retire as early as possible, others prefer to keep working as long as possible. Still others progress from full-time work to complete retirement gradually. Your health, your spouse's career and retirement options, shifting economic conditions and employment opportunities, your parents' and children's situations—these are but a few of the factors that may affect how you plan and adjust your retirement.

You may build your retirement around a relatively steady income level from one year to the next. But you might just as sensibly decide to plan on fluctuations in your retirement budget, reflecting variations in your expected activities and consumption choices. There are countless ways in which you might use equal monthly payments from your TSP account to fit your personal retirement strategy. Following are a few situations where monthly payments might make sense:

Extra Income Between Retirement and when You Start Receiving Social Security Benefits. The average retirement age for federal and postal employees is 62. That's also the earliest point you can start receiving Social Security retirement benefits. But many federal and postal employees retire before age 62, at ages 55-59 with at least 30 years of service, or at ages 60-61 with 20 years. FERS employees also may elect to retire with reduced benefits at age 55 with 10 years. Members of law enforcement, firefighter and other special employment categories may retire as early as age 50. And employees subject to reductions in force and other discontinued service retirement situations sometimes may retire at age 50 with 20 years or at any age with 25 years.

If you're thinking about retiring on a CSRS or FERS pension before age 62, look closely at your total retirement income opportunities. Suppose you're eligible to retire—or soon will be—and you're ready to do so.

There's one problem, however. While your long-term retirement income looks comfortable, the short-term picture isn't quite so rosy. Once you start receiving Social Security your retirement budget will be solid. But between your government retirement and age 62 your money looks a little tight. What to do?

You might decide to continue working a few more years. Or you might decide to retire anyway, and either scale back your budget or supplement your income with part-time employment. But you may want to consider a third option—using your TSP account to set up a "bridge" income that will let you retire comfortably while you wait for your Social Security benefits to become available.

As you approach retirement eligibility under either CSRS or FERS, take the time to check the approximate value of your government pension benefits and your projected Social Security benefits. If you're a CSRS employee you may have earned Social Security benefits through non-government employment. If you spent most of your career in CSRS your Social Security benefits may not be very large. But it will be worthwhile to know your approximate Social Security benefits—if any—as you begin to plan your retirement income and budget. Social Security benefits for CSRS employees may be subject to the "windfall benefit" and "government pension offset" reductions. Be sure to check with SSA and, if necessary, with additional advisers to project your Social Security benefits accurately.

If you're a FERS employee you'll be eligible at age 62 for Social Security benefits based on all your employment, both in FERS and outside the government. If you retire "early" under FERS with unreduced benefits—at ages 55-59 with 30 or more years of service, or at ages 60-61 with 20 or more years—you'll receive an extra "annuity supplement" until you reach age 62. This supplement is the part of your total Social Security benefit that you earned under FERS. The supplement will almost always be less than your actual Social Security benefits at age 62. For example, in simple terms, if you spend half your career working outside the government, your FERS "supplement" will be about one-half of your total Social Security benefit.

O꜀TIP *If you want to retire "early" and have a fairly level stream of retirement income, consider using equal monthly payments from your TSP account to "fill in" your Social Security benefit until age 62. The larger your Social Security benefit, the more important a temporary additional income might be in your overall retirement planning.*

How much of your TSP account will you need to finance a "bridge" to Social Security? The arithmetic is fairly simple. For every $100 of expected monthly Social Security benefits, you'll need $1,200 times the number of years between your retirement and age 62. Remember, if you're a CSRS employee your retirement income "gap" before age 62 is equal to your total Social Security benefit. If you're a FERS employee your gap is your Social Security benefit minus the value of your "annuity supplement."

Using Your TSP Account to Fill a Social Security Gap Before Age 62

Age of Your CSRS/FERS Retirement	Amount of TSP Account You Need to Fill a Monthly Social Security Gap of:			
	$200	$400	$600	$800
55	$16,800	$33,600	$50,400	$67,000
56	$14,400	$28,800	$43,200	$57,600
57	$12,000	$24,000	$36,000	$48,000
58	$9,600	$19,200	$28,800	$38,400
59	$7,200	$14,400	$21,600	$28,800
60	$4,800	$9,600	$14,400	$19,200
61	$2,400	$4,800	$7,200	$9,600

Figure 8-3

Technically, these estimates are a little on the high side. We're not counting the continued G Fund earnings on your account balance during the years you receive the payments. But we've done that for a reason. Keep in mind inflation during the years you receive the payments. As you receive payments between your CSRS/FERS retirement and age 62, G Fund earnings should stay ahead of inflation. Your equal payments will have built-in inflation protection.

If you decide to use your TSP account in this way, any additional funds in your TSP account can be transferred to an IRA. For example, suppose your TSP account balance when you retire is $60,000 and you want to receive about $20,000 worth of payments between your retirement and age 62. You can instruct the TSP to pay you equal monthly payments from your account balance, with one-third of the payment made directly to you and two-thirds of the payment transferred to an IRA.

You can use equal payments to set up a fairly smooth baseline retirement income that stretches from your CSRS/FERS retirement up to and beyond your start of Social Security benefits. And you may have an additional IRA reserve fund that continues to earn tax-deferred savings.

Maintaining a Level Income Between Your Retirement and Your Spouse's Retirement. Retirement planning can be a particularly complicated and sensitive challenge for married couples. One common problem arises when one partner is eligible to retire and the other is not. Retire now and reduce total household income for a few years? Or, keep working until you're both eligible for your pensions?

Your TSP account may enable you to retire when you TIP꜀ *want to without disrupting your family's income and consumption patterns.* Figure 8-4 shows how a married employee might use equal monthly payments from the TSP to maintain total household income during the transition to joint retirement.

Using Equal Payments to
Maintain Total Household Income

	You	Spouse	Total
Current Age	57	55	
Eligible for Pension	57	62	
Salary	$40,000	$35,000	$75,000
Income If You Retire	$25,000	$35,000	$60,000
Add $750/Month from TSP	+ $9,000		
Total Income with TSP	$34,000	$35,000	$69,000

Figure 8-4

This $750 monthly income will provide you with $63,000 total income over the seven years. Because your account continues to earn G Fund interest while you receive your payments, you can buy the $750 per month for less than $63,000.

In this example, your retirement income during the transition period is 85 percent of your pre-retirement salary—$34,000 instead of $40,000. Combined household income for you and your spouse drops by only 8 percent, from $75,000 to $69,000. Without the $750 monthly payment from your TSP account, household income would decline 20 percent, from $75,000 to $60,000.

If you use your TSP account to receive monthly payments until your spouse retires, you can split your payments—part paid directly to you, the rest transferred to an IRA. For example, if you need extra income equal to about half your total account, you can instruct the TSP to pay you each month for a designated period—half the payment directly to you, the other half to an IRA which you can draw on later.

Using TSP Monthly Payments to Avoid the Social Security "Earnings Test." You might make a clean break at retirement, shifting entirely from employment income to retirement income. But you might retire in stages—perhaps carefully planned in advance, perhaps depending on what opportunities arise as you meander into your golden years.

You may go through a period in which you combine retirement income with continued work and earnings. If so, beware of a potentially dangerous beast—the Social Security "earnings test." The "normal" or "full benefit" retirement age for Social Security retirement benefits is age 65. You can begin receiving Social Security as early as age 62, but with a reduction depending on your exact age when your benefits start. Currently the benefit reduction at age 62 is 20 percent.

In many cases you may decide to receive Social Security as soon as you're eligible, even with the resulting reduction in your benefits. But that is not likely to be a wise decision if you're planning a gradual transition to retirement. If you expect a period of continued work and earnings after you retire on your CSRS or FERS pension,

it's important for you to understand the Social Security "earnings test," how it might affect you and how your TSP account may be a useful tool during your retirement transition.

Figure 8-5 shows how the Social Security earnings test works. Under the formula for 1994, if you earn more than designated exempt amounts, your earnings reduce your Social Security benefits. The exact formula depends on your age. Also, the earnings limits are adjusted each year.

The Social Security Earnings Test

Your Age	Every $1 You Earn above	Reduces Your Benefits by	Examples: You Earn	Reduction
62-65	$8,040	$0.50	$18,040	$5,000
65-69	$11,160	$0.33	$20,160	$3,000

Figure 8-5

During 1994, if you were between age 62 and age 65, for every $2 you earn above $8,040 you lost $1 in Social Security benefits. From age 65 to age 69, you lost $1 for every $3 of earnings above $11,160. There is no earnings test from age 70 on.

See the problem? If you're making a gradual transition to complete retirement—combining a CSRS or FERS pension with some continued work and earnings—you may stumble into a "double booby trap." You could end up getting hit by both the age-based Social Security benefit reduction and the earnings test.

As you consider your retirement income choices, think about your Social Security eligibility and your work and earnings possibilities. If you expect to continue working beyond age 62, remember to take the Social Security earnings test into account. If you need extra income beyond your CSRS or FERS pension and your earnings, you may be better off using your TSP account as a supplement, and receiving higher Social Security benefits later on.

Some 'Brilliant' Ideas
That May Not Be So Smart

In the preceding section we looked at how TSP equal payments might help you fill temporary gaps in your retirement income. In these examples—and other situations you might face—you might decide to use some or all of your TSP account as a temporary supplement until another source of retirement income becomes available. If you only need some of your TSP account to finance these temporary "bridge payments," then you can transfer the rest of your account to an IRA and keep building additional future retirement income.

But be careful about "outsmarting" yourself. Temporary TSP payments may make sense to take the place of other retirement income until the other income becomes available. It will generally not be a good idea to use your TSP account in place of other retirement income that is available. Some pitfalls to avoid:

◇ *It does not make sense for you to use TSP money as a temporary substitute for Social Security just to avoid the effect of the age reduction. If you are not working and therefore are not going to be affected by the earnings test, you generally should begin receiving Social Security as soon as you are eligible.*

Let's suppose that you first become eligible for Social Security at age 62 and your benefits if you apply immediately will be $800 per month, or $9,600 annually. Yes, if you wait to apply for Social Security benefits, your monthly benefit will increase. Under the current reduction schedule, for example, if you turned 62 in 1994 your $800 monthly benefit would increase to $1,000 if you waited until age 65, and to $1,250 if you waited until age 70.

But it's a better value for you to take the Social Security benefits immediately at age 62, even with the reduction. The amount that your Social Security benefits go up when you wait does not make up for the money you would have to spend to replace those benefits.

In our example, you could get a monthly Social Security benefit of $1,250 by waiting until age 70. But you could accomplish the same total income by taking an $800 Social Security benefit at age 62 and purchasing a $450 monthly annuity with inflation protection at a cost of about $60,000. The alternative—waiting until age 70 for Social Security and using your own money from age 62 to age 69—would be much more expensive. Here's the math: You'd have to finance a $1,250 monthly benefit for eight years—total benefits of $120,000 that would cost you more than $100,000 to purchase!

Delaying your application for Social Security only makes sense if you are working or expecting to work. Then, because of the double effect of age reductions and the Social Security earnings test, you may be better off by waiting to apply for Social Security.

◇ If you're a FERS employee, generally it will not be wise to use TSP money to avoid FERS benefit reductions. For example, FERS employees are eligible for reduced benefits after reaching the minimum retirement age with at least 10 years of service. The minimum retirement age (MRA) is currently age 55 and is scheduled to increase gradually to age 57.

If you don't meet the age and service requirements for full FERS benefits—minimum retirement age and 30 years,

---

EQUAL MONTHLY PAYMENTS — SUMMARY

Eligibility: If you leave government eligible for immediate retirement benefits, you can elect a series of equal payments to begin immediately or at a specified later date. For example, if you leave at age 57 with 30 years of service, you can start your monthly payments then or instruct the TSP to start the payments at a later time.

How You Receive Equal Monthly Payments: You can receive a series of equal payments from your TSP account when you are eligible to begin receiving CSRS or FERS benefits. You obtain a series of equal payments from your TSP account by completing Form TSP-7 (Election of Benefits) and Form TSP-12 (Application for Equal Payments). On Form TSP-12 you may specify either the number of monthly payments you want to receive or the monthly payment amount you want to receive.

You may receive a series of equal payments and have the payments—or a portion of each payment—transferred to an IRA or other eligible retirement plan. To transfer the payments in full, complete Form TSP-12-T. To transfer a portion of each payment, complete Form TSP-12-E. In either case, you can combine equal payments with a transfer to an IRA or other plan only if your payments are expected to last less than 10 years.

Tax Treatment: If your equal payments are expected to last less than 10 years, there is an automatic 20 percent federal income tax withholding on the payments. There is no withholding on any portion of the payment transferred to an IRA or an employer-sponsored plan. There is no automatic withholding for state income taxes. Of course, your actual tax liability will depend on your total income, exemptions and deductions.

If your equal payments are expected to last 10 years or longer, federal income taxes will be withheld on the assumption that you are married and claiming three withholding allowances. You can adjust this withholding by sending the TSP Service Office a completed Form W-4P (Withholding Certificate for Pension or Annuity Payments). There is no withholding on any portion of the payment transferred to an IRA or an employer-sponsored plan. There is no automatic withholding for state income taxes. Again, your actual tax liability will depend on your total income, exemptions and deductions.

Income averaging can be used for equal payments only if your payments exhaust your entire TSP account balance in a single tax year and no portion of the payments is transferred to an IRA. (See the previous section on lump sum payments to learn more about your income averaging options.)

Spousal Rights: If you are eligible for CSRS benefits the TSP notifies your spouse before beginning to disburse a series of equal payments. If you're eligible for FERS benefits, you and your spouse complete Form TSP-14 (Joint Waiver of Spouse's Annuity).

age 60 and 20 years or age 62 and five years—you still can collect a FERS pension. But there is a permanent 5 percent benefit reduction for every year you're under age 62. For example, if you start receiving a FERS pension at age 60 with less than 20 years of service, there is a permanent 10 percent benefit reduction. If you start receiving a FERS pension at age 55 with less than 30 years of service, there is a permanent 35 percent reduction.

Should you delay applying for the FERS pension to avoid or reduce the reduction? Not if you're going to use TSP money or other savings to try to make up for the pension in the meantime. Let's suppose you leave federal or postal service at or before age 55 with 25 years of service and a high-three average salary of $40,000. If you wait until age 62 to receive your FERS pension, it will be $10,000 annually—25 years times 1 percent per year times $40,000. If you start receiving it at age 55 the pension will be reduced 35 percent—5 percent times seven years—and will be $6,500 at age 55 instead of $10,000 at age 62.

Compare two scenarios. If you retire at age 55 and receive a $6,500 FERS pension, you can add a $3,500 annuity with inflation protection at a cost of about $40,000. This will give you a combined FERS and annuity income of $10,000 from age 55 on. If you wait until age 62 to receive the unreduced $10,000 pension, it will cost you much more than that $40,000 to fill in the $10,000 per year for seven years.

If you're deciding whether or not to leave the government, then continuing to work will add to your pension value by increasing your years of service and your high-three salary. That's a different issue. But if you've decided to leave—or already have left—your choice is simply about whether or not the reduction is worth accepting. If you've decided you can afford to retire early, you're probably better off taking the reduced pension and making up for the reduction with a lifetime annuity. That will be a more cost-effective use of your TSP money—or any other resources—than waiting for unreduced benefits and financing your own retirement income until then.

RECEIVING YOUR TSP ACCOUNT AS A LIFETIME ANNUITY

You can use your TSP account balance to purchase a lifetime annuity. The TSP currently administers annuities through Metropolitan Life Insurance Company. When you instruct the TSP to purchase an annuity, the ownership of your account balance transfers to Metropolitan and you receive in return a guaranteed monthly income for the rest of your life.

This assurance of monthly payments for the rest of your lifetime is the essential feature and primary advantage of an annuity. If you use your TSP account to purchase an annuity, you enjoy a predictable income flow.

You also no longer have either the anxieties (or the opportunities) associated with management of your TSP assets. The annuity is "locked in" at the time of purchase.

One element of risk does remain, however. That is the possibility—however unlikely—that an annuity provider under contract to the TSP might encounter serious financial difficulties and be unable to fulfill its obligations. When selecting a TSP annuity provider, the Thrift Savings Board pays close attention to the financial security of the institution. Nonetheless, if the TSP annuity provider did encounter severe financial difficulties, the timeliness and full value of your annuity payments could be placed in jeopardy.

You have a wide range of specific annuity options. A single life annuity without any special features gives you monthly payments until you die.

Married retirees may elect a joint life annuity that will continue payments to the surviving partner after either partner dies. You may choose either a 50 percent option in which the surviving partner continues to receive one-half of the basic annuity amount, or a 100 percent option that continues the basic annuity in full. You also may use a joint life annuity to guarantee payments to someone who has an "insurable interest" in you—for example, a former spouse, a close relative or a common-law partner.

You can elect an annuity providing level payments or increasing payments. With level payments you receive the same dollar amount every month. With increasing payments your initial annuity amount is adjusted each year to help keep up with inflation during retirement, up to a maximum increase of 3 percent in any year.

Two additional options can provide payments to a designated beneficiary in certain circumstances. A cash refund option guarantees that if you—or you and your spouse—die before receiving annuity payments equal to the TSP account balance you used to buy the annuity, your beneficiary will receive the difference in a lump sum. For example, if you used a $60,000 TSP account balance to purchase an annuity and died after receiving only $45,000 in payments, your designated beneficiary would receive a $15,000 lump sum payment. This payment will be taxable in the year received unless rolled over into an IRA. Surviving spouses and/or former spouses under a court order may request the TSP to transfer the payment to an IRA, deferring taxes until the money is withdrawn.

The 10-year certain option guarantees monthly annuity payments for at least 10 years. If you die before 10 years of payments have been made, your beneficiary will receive continued payments until the 10 years are complete. For example, if you buy an annuity at age 65 and die at age 73, your beneficiary receives payments for two more years. This feature can only be combined with a single life annuity, however.

There is no particular annuity package that is intrinsically a "better deal" than others. When you're thinking about buying a TSP annuity, always remember that the options are actuarially equivalent. That is, they represent equal expected total financial values based on the amount of the payments and the expected duration of the payments.

🗝 *Think of the single life annuity with level payments as the "bare bones" model.* At whatever age you buy your annuity and whatever your account balance, an "unloaded" single life annuity will result in the highest starting annuity payment compared to other options. But it could leave you, your spouse or your beneficiary without valuable protection.

Any features you elect—a joint annuity, increasing payments, a cash refund or guaranteed 10-year payments—represent additional future financial value. To pay for the value of those future protections, you start off with lower annuity payments. When you add extra features to your annuity, you "pay" in the form of a lower initial annuity payment. The more protection you want, the more you pay.

Your TSP account balance must be at least $3,500 to purchase an annuity. You may, however, request an annuity to begin at a later date if you expect your account to reach the $3,500 minimum by that date. For example, if you leave the government at age 45 with a $2,500 TSP balance, you may request an annuity to begin at age 62 under the expectation that your account will gain at least $1,000 in investment earnings before you reach age 62.

Unlike the lump sum payment and equal payment options, you cannot split your annuity into two portions—part paid directly to you and part transferred to an IRA. If you elect an annuity your entire TSP account will be used to purchase the annuity and you will receive the entire annuity amount on a monthly basis.

If you leave government and elect to receive an annuity at a later date, you may continue to allocate your account among the three TSP investment funds, although you may not make new contributions. The TSP will send you an Annuity Request Package a few months before your requested annuity date. You complete this package to confirm the form of annuity you wish to receive. The TSP will transfer your entire account to the G Fund at the end of the month before your annuity purchase, to avoid the possibility of any investment losses that would reduce your annuity amount. (There has never been a negative G Fund return.)

Note: Throughout this section our examples and discussion reflect annuities based on an 8 percent annuity interest rate index. This enables you to consider and compare your annuities within a consistent framework. The actual interest rates in effect at the time you buy your annuity will affect the size of your annuity payments and how various options compare under close inspection. This section ends with a discussion of interest rate changes and how they might affect your annuity planning. Additional details about annuities and various interest rates are found in Appendix 4.

Key Issues:

Deciding Whether an Annuity Is Right for You. The first place to start in weighing the merits of a TSP annuity purchase is your guaranteed monthly retirement income. Take stock of all your potential retirement income sources and when they will become available. If you are married, be sure to assess your family's total needs and resources.

In general, if you have any doubt about the adequacy of your monthly retirement income, then using your TSP account to purchase an annuity is probably your most sensible choice. If your retirement income outlook is already comfortable, you still may choose the security and predictability of an annuity purchase. But you also enjoy the luxury of comparing the advantages of an annuity relative to other payment options and investment opportunities.

When you're thinking about whether an annuity purchase is right for you, there are two common pitfalls to avoid. First, be careful not to underestimate your life expectancy and its financial implications. At whatever age you retire, your life expectancy may be longer than you think. At age 55 average life expectancy is about 25 years. At age 65 average life expectancy is more than 17 years. And, of course, there is a chance that you will live longer than the average—perhaps substantially longer.

Using your TSP balance to purchase an annuity guarantees you a predictable income regardless of whether you ultimately live longer or shorter than the average for someone your age. Avoid the trap of undervaluing a small monthly annuity compared to a large lump sum payment or short-term income.

For example, let's suppose you are married and age 62, with a TSP account balance of $25,000. You're thinking about buying a joint life annuity with 100 percent continued payments to the survivor and increasing payments to help keep up with inflation during retirement. Your starting annuity at age 62 might only be about $150 a month, with increases each year if inflation rises. You may view that $150 monthly payment as a pittance compared to a $25,000 lump sum or $5,000 a year for five years. Think carefully before reaching this conclusion. You'll probably receive that $150 a month—plus inflation adjustments—for a longer period than you realize, and the value of the annuity is probably much higher than you appreciate. The same general principle holds true whatever your account balance is and whatever exact form of annuity you're considering. Avoid overvaluing short-term income possibilities and undervaluing long-term income guarantees. And don't forget the tax benefits of spreading out payments rather than taking them in large chunks.

Second, you may be tempted to think that you can "outperform" an annuity by investing on your own. You're considering receiving your TSP account as a lump sum payment—perhaps with income averaging to lessen the tax bite—or as equal monthly payments over a few years. You'll build a stockpile of retirement capital and live off your investment gains.

When you purchase an annuity, the calculation of your monthly payments reflects market interest rates at the time of purchase. The annuity reflects the average 10-year Treasury interest rate during the three months preceding your annuity purchase.

Purchasing an annuity does not mean you forfeit future investment gains. For example, let's say that your annuity purchase and resulting monthly payments include a 6 percent annuity interest rate index. You may be able to accomplish a superior retirement income by collecting your TSP account and managing your own investments. But you will be assuming the risk of future losses, as well as the time commitment and anxiety levels involved in managing your own funds.

⚷ *Before you pass up an annuity because you think you can do better through your own investing, ask yourself at least two basic questions. How much better will you have to do to make the risk, time demands and worry worthwhile? And how will you cope in the face of periods of poor investment performance?* When you purchase an annuity you are buying a certain amount of additional retirement income and eliminating the downside risks involved in trying to realize that income through your own investments.

Third, don't let the presence of a third-party provider convince you that you're not getting "full value" when you purchase an annuity. Annuity providers operate in a highly competitive environment and are subject to rigorous scrutiny by the Thrift Savings Board.

Yes, annuity providers make a profit on their transactions. But so do banks, brokers and accountants for their investment services. It is the Thrift Savings Board's job and legal responsibility to make sure you can purchase an annuity under fair and competitive terms. Your time and attention will be better spent focusing on whether an annuity purchase fits your retirement income needs, and if so, what particular form of annuity will work best for you and your family.

You always have the option of buying an annuity with your own funds, such as money you have in an IRA account or other savings. Remember, though, that the TSP contracts with an annuity provider—currently Metropolitan Life Insurance Company—under very competitive terms. If you buy an annuity on your own, you may not obtain rates as favorable as those secured when you purchase an annuity directly with your TSP account.

Choosing the Best Form of Annuity. Think of your TSP payment options as tools to perform a given task. Your first concern is to define the task you want to complete. Then you can pick the most suitable tool to accomplish the desired result. You wouldn't say that a saw is better or worse than a wrench—each is suited to particular tasks. Likewise, no particular form of annuity is better or worse than any other. Each is designed to achieve certain objectives and fit differing personal situations.

The essential characteristics of all annuities are that they provide a secure and predictable retirement income with an elimination of investment risk. You lock in a monthly income and the risk of future investment gains and losses is assumed by the annuity provider.

Now let's look at the particular types of annuities you can purchase with your TSP account balance. If you elect to receive a TSP annuity you can choose from among 18 different annuity forms. Don't panic—it's not as bewildering as it sounds. Your choice of an annuity that best fits your personal situation boils down to three key decisions.

➤ **Key Annuity Decision #1:** Do You Want to Guarantee that a Surviving Spouse or Dependent Continues to Receive a Lifetime Monthly Income?

If you are single and have no financial dependents you'll probably elect a single life annuity. This will provide you with a monthly income until you die. We'll discuss under the next two annuity decisions certain features you can build into your single life annuity.

But if you are married or single with financial dependents, you may decide to elect a joint life annuity. This choice will ensure that you and your joint annuitant—your spouse, child, former spouse, or any other dependent with an "insurable interest" in you—will continue to receive a monthly income for life. Upon the death of either you or your designated joint annuitant, monthly payments continue to the survivor.

Retirement Income Inventory for You and Your Spouse

	Annual Income While Both Alive	
	Your Income	Spouse's Income
CSRS/FERS Pension	$20,000	$0
Other Pensions	$0	$0
Social Security	$5,000	$9,000
Total Annual Income	$25,000 +	$9,000 = $34,000
+ Single Life ($4,400)		$38,400
+ 50% Joint Life ($4,200)		$38,200
+ 100% Joint Life ($3,600)		$37,600

	Annual Income For Survivor	
	Your Income	Spouse's Income
CSRS/FERS Pension	$20,000	$11,000
Other Pensions	$0	$0
Social Security	$9,000	$9,000
Total Annual Income	$29,000	$20,000
+ Single Life ($4,400)	$33,400	$20,000
+ 50% Joint Life ($2,100)	$31,100	$22,100
+ 100% Joint Life ($3,600)	$32,600	$23,600

Figure 8-6

You can select either a 100 percent payment or a 50 percent payment for the survivor. For example, if your monthly annuity is $250, the survivor would continue to receive the full $250 payment for life under the 100 percent option. Under the 50 percent option the survivor would receive a $125 monthly payment for life. Of course, buying the extra protection for your survivor costs you more in the form of reductions to your annuity.

Should you select a joint life annuity? If so, does the 100 percent option or the 50 percent option make more sense? Define the task. Then pick the best tool.

You can define the task by carefully reviewing expected future income for you and your spouse or dependents. Look at all known sources of income and when they will be available. Then consider the two worst-case scenarios—you die relatively early and your spouse (or insurable interest) lives considerably longer, or you survive for a lengthy period after the death of your spouse or insurable interest.

Figure 8-6 illustrates how you might develop a joint retirement income inventory. You can supplement it with any additional assets or income that apply in your individual situation.

This example provides a simplified version the kind of "what if" scenarios you should be considering as you and your spouse weigh the merits of your TSP annuity options. Each individual circumstance will vary widely. But there are some basic facts you should keep in mind as you and your spouse or dependents assess your TSP annuity options:

☞ TIP ◇ *The larger the difference between your retirement income and your spouse's retirement income, the more important a joint life annuity becomes. If there is a large difference in individual retirement incomes, there will be a significant decline in income for the surviving spouse if the higher-income spouse dies first.* Look at your retirement income as a share of your joint retirement income. If your income dominates your joint retirement finances, then survivor protection for your spouse becomes all the more important.

◇ The larger your TSP account, the more important your TSP annuity decisions. For many CSRS employees, TSP account balances will be only a small portion of total retirement income. In these cases, survivor benefits based on your CSRS pension may be the most important factor in your spouse's long-term financial security. But for most FERS employees and some CSRS employees, a TSP account will represent a more substantial portion of total retirement income potential. Shape your annuity decision-making accordingly.

◇ Buying survivor annuity protection is generally not expensive. If your spouse is the same age as you are, 50 percent survivor payments will reduce your monthly annuity by about 3 percent. For example, if your single life annuity would be $300 per month, your joint life annuity would be about $290 per month with $145 payments continued to the survivor at your death.

Buying 100 percent survivor payments reduces your

annuity by 15 percent if you start receiving the annuity at age 55, by 17 percent at age 60 and by 19 percent at age 65. But if your survivor would face a significant drop in income at your death, the cost of 100 percent survivor payments could be worthwhile to eliminate anxiety about future prospects.

The cost of survivor coverage increases if your spouse or insurable interest is younger than you are. Conversely, the cost is lower if your joint annuitant is older than you are. A few years difference in age does not have a large impact on your annuity amounts. But if your spouse or dependent is substantially younger than you are, examine your annuity options carefully to make sure the protection you're buying is worth the cost.

◇ If you want survivor coverage, first elect survivor benefits based on your CSRS or FERS pension, then look at your TSP options if you need more survivor protection. Both CSRS and FERS provide substantial survivor income protection at a reasonable cost. CSRS will pay your surviving spouse 55 percent of your pension if you die, with your pension reduced by 9 percent or less. The combination of FERS and Social Security survivor benefits is also advantageous. Your surviving spouse will receive 50 percent of your FERS pension with a 10 percent reduction of your benefit. Social Security pays a surviving spouse the larger of the survivor's or the deceased's benefits.

As you consider your survivor income options, look first at your CSRS or FERS pension benefits. Then you and your spouse can make a basic decision. Do you want maximum protection for the survivor to be on the safe side? Or do you want to have more income to enjoy while you're both alive? Remember that 50 percent annuity payments for the survivor are inexpensive. Chances are you'll barely notice the reduction in your TSP annuity.

➤ **Key Annuity Decision #2:** Do You Want to Guarantee Inflation Protection in Your TSP Annuity Payments?

In the preceding discussion about survivor benefits we considered five different options—single life annuity, joint life annuities with your spouse with 50 percent or 100 percent survivor payments, and joint life annuities with an "insurable interest" with 50 percent or 100 percent survivor payments. Now let's focus on the uncertainty of inflation during your retirement years.

Under either a single life annuity or any of the joint life annuity options, you can select level payments or increasing payments. Let's make sure we understand the difference. Level payments give you a fixed monthly amount for life. That fixed payment either stops (single life annuity), continues in full (100 percent survivor option) or is reduced by one-half (50 percent survivor option) when you or your joint annuitant dies.

Increasing payments provide for an annual adjustment of your annuity to reflect changes in the cost of living.

Each year the annuity increases by the rise in the Consumer Price Index, up to a maximum annual increase of 3 percent. If inflation in a given year is between 0.1 percent and 3.0 percent, your TSP annuity keeps pace with rising prices. If inflation exceeds 3 percent in a given year, your annuity increases 3 percent, but it still retains much more of its purchasing power than under the level payment option.

Under a joint life annuity, 50 percent or 100 percent survivor payments are calculated on the basis of the adjusted payment amount when the first annuitant dies. Depending on your age—and therefore, the expected length of your annuity payments—buying this inflation protection will reduce your starting payment by between 15 and 25 percent. See Figure 8-9 for exact amounts.

Again, this is not a question of one choice being a "better deal" than the other. It's a question of risk and cost. Level payments represents the higher-risk, lower-cost route. Increasing payments is the lower-risk, higher-cost route.

To see this tradeoff in tangible terms, Figure 8-7 shows a situation in which you begin receiving a TSP annuity at age 62 and the cost of living rises 3 percent per year during your retirement. We'll compare the actual payments you would receive and the purchasing power of those payments.

Comparison of TSP Annuity with Level and Increasing Payments

Assumes Inflation of 3% Per Year
Monthly Annuity
Payments Beginning at Age 62

Actual Payment Amounts			Real Purchasing Power	
Level	Increasing		Level	Increasing
$500	$394	At Age 62	$500	$394
$500	$431	At Age 65	$456	$394
$500	$500	At Age 70	$394	$394
$500	$579	At Age 75	$337	$394
$500	$671	At Age 80	$289	$394

Figure 8-7

As Figure 8-7 shows, even an inflation rate of 3 percent can substantially erode the purchasing power of your annuity payments. Selecting increasing payments to buy inflation protection will reduce your initial annuity payments. In our example, your choice at age 62 is between a $500 level payment and a $394 increasing payment.

The higher initial payment may be tempting, but look closely at the long-term results. You may be receiving your annuity payments for 20 years or longer. If prices are rising by 3 percent a year or more, increasing payments will gradually catch up with level payments during your first eight retirement years. After about eight years increasing payments will exceed the level payments and the purchasing power of level payments will continue to decline.

When you elect a TSP annuity there's no way to know in advance how long you'll receive your payments and how much prices will rise during that period. But if your TSP annuity is an important part of your basic retirement budget, increasing payments will reduce the risk that you'll have to adjust your budget and lifestyle in your later retirement years.

Level payments may make sense if your TSP annuity is 🔑 *"extra" income that you don't need to maintain a comfortable retirement budget. If so, you may decide you want to have higher annuity payments during your early, more active retirement years.* Your level payments will lose purchasing power over time, but you'll be scaling back your activities and expenses at the same time.

➤ **Key Annuity Decision #3:** Do You Want to Guarantee that You or Your Survivors Receive at Least a Minimum Value from Your Annuity, Regardless of How Long You Live?

When you elect a TSP annuity, your monthly payment will depend in part on the average life expectancy for someone your age. Your individual longevity is, of course, uncertain. When you purchase an annuity you buy the security of knowing that you will receive monthly payments regardless of how long you and your spouse live.

At the time you purchase the annuity, you don't know whether you—or you and your joint annuitant—will ultimately experience longer, shorter or roughly average longevity. As a result, you don't know whether you'll end up receiving more or less than the "full value" of the money you spent to buy the annuity.

There are two special annuity features that you can use to guarantee definite minimum payments regardless of your longevity. Selecting a cash refund feature guarantees that the total payments made under your annuity will at least equal the amount of TSP account balance you spent to buy the annuity. For example, suppose that you have a $50,000 TSP account and at age 62 buy a single life annuity with level payments. Your monthly payment is $464. If you die at age 67 after receiving 60 monthly payments totaling $27,840, then your designated beneficiary would receive a lump sum payment of $12,160. A cash refund can be combined with either a single life annuity or a joint life annuity.

Selecting a 10-year certain feature guarantees that either you or a designated beneficiary will receive payments for at least 10 years. Continuing our example, suppose you start receiving a $464 monthly annuity at age 62. If you die at age 67 your designated beneficiary will receive the $464 payment for five more years. This feature can only be used in combination with a single life annuity.

Figure 8-8 shows what you would pay for the extra protection of a cash refund or ten-year certain option. The cost of the protection is the reduction of your TSP annuity to finance the assurance of the guaranteed payments.

Reduction of Annuity for Cash Refund or 10-Year Certain Features

Approximate Reduction of Your Annuity

Age You Purchase Annuity	55	60	62	65	70
Cash Refund					
With Single Life	5-6%	7-8%	7-8%	9-10%	9-10%
With Joint 50% Life	2-3%	3-4%	3-4%	4- 5%	4- 5%
With Joint 100% Life	1-2%	1-2%	1-2%	2- 3%	2- 3%
Ten-Year Certain					
With Single Life	3%	4%	5%	6%	10%

Figure 8-8

Both features become more expensive as your starting annuity age increases. This is because your average life expectancy becomes shorter as you become older. As a result, the chance of a refund or continued payments to your beneficiary becomes greater.

This same logic explains why a cash refund combined with a single life annuity is more expensive than a cash refund with a joint life annuity. A refund will only be payable to your beneficiary after both you and your joint annuitant die. Under a joint life annuity, the chance of a refund and the average size of the refund become lower because your combined life expectancy is longer.

In combination with a single life annuity, the cash refund is more expensive than the 10-year certain feature—assuming you are younger than age 70 when you start receiving your TSP annuity. This does not mean that the cash refund is always going to be more valuable to your beneficiary than the continuation of payments through 10 years. When you buy an annuity, the annuity provider expects to earn investment returns on your TSP account balance over a long period. If your death results in a cash refund to your beneficiary, the annuity provider loses the expected future investment returns on your TSP account balance. This is factored into the cost of the cash refund feature and makes it more expensive than the 10-year certain feature.

When you're considering a cash refund or 10-year certain option, base your decision on a realistic look at your situation and needs. There are basically two reasons to consider one of these special features:

◇ You—or you and your joint annuitant—may have health conditions or hereditary patterns that might shorten your life expectancy. You want the security of an annuity if you do enjoy a lengthy retirement, but you also want to get "higher value" from your annuity if your payment period is brief.

◇ You may have a beneficiary who depends on you for income protection. Even a very slight risk of your dying fairly soon is unacceptable. If you need to use your TSP annuity as a supplement to life insurance and other

potential sources of money for your beneficiary, look closely at your beneficiary's needs over time and the costs of the cash refund and 10-year features. Choose the feature that works best for you and your beneficiary.

Remember, however, that the *cash refund and 10-year certain features are not substitutes for joint lifetime income for you and your spouse. The refund and 10-year provisions provide extra protection in special circumstances.*

➤ **Key Annuity Decision #4:** Should You Time Your Annuity Purchase According to Movements in the Annuity Interest Rate Index?

The exact size of your annuity payments will depend on four factors—how much money is in your TSP account; the specific annuity option you select; your age (and, if applicable, the age of a joint annuitant); and, last but not least, the annuity interest rate index in effect at the time you purchase the annuity. It's important that you have a basic understanding of how interest rate movements can affect your lifetime annuity payments. This will help you make sound financial judgments as you approach your TSP withdrawal.

The TSP annuity interest rate index is a three-month moving average of the interest rate for 10-year U.S. Treasury securities. By using a three-month moving average, the TSP smoothes out the effects of short-term fluctuations in interest rates. Generally speaking, the 10-year rates used to calculate the annuity interest rate index will correspond fairly closely with G Fund interest rates. You can obtain the current interest rate index by calling 1-800-447-8777.

The critical point is that the level of the interest rate index when you purchase your annuity affects your annuity payments for the rest of your life. When you're investing money, as inflation and interest rates move up and down over time, your investment earnings increase and decrease accordingly. But when you buy an annuity, the interest index at that moment gets locked in permanently.

How much does the interest rate index level affect your annuity payments? That depends on your age and the type of annuity you select. The younger you are, the more significant the effect of interest rate variations. Interest rates affect annuities with increasing payments to a larger extent than annuities with level payments. And, joint life annuities vary more widely than single life annuities.

As you approach the point when you might use your TSP account to buy an annuity, start to consider the interest rate situation more closely. Historically, 10-year Treasury interest rates—and interest rates generally—typically move up or down fairly gradually. There have, however, been some periods in which rates are more volatile and average rates move quite sharply from one year to the next, or even over the course of a few months. For example, during the late 1970s and early 1980s, 10-year Treasury rates rose substantially, from an average of 7.42 percent during 1977 to an average of 13.91 percent during 1981. Then, as inflation and anxieties about future inflation began to subside, interest rates began declining, reaching an average of 7.68 percent in 1986.

How any interest rate movements will affect your annuity depends on the specific interest rate levels in effect as you approach your purchase. As a rough measure, consider a situation in which you're examining your annuity options and the interest rate index is 8 percent. If, by the time you actually buy the annuity, the index has increased to 9 percent, your annuity payments will increase by anywhere from 6 to 12 percent, depending on your age and the annuity option you select. On the other hand, if the index has dropped from 8 to 7 percent, your payments will increase by 6 to 12 percent. See Appendix 4 for a specific breakdown of how interest rate changes affect different types of annuities at varying ages.

What should you do about possible interest rate movements as you're thinking about buying a TSP annuity? In most cases, absolutely nothing. Go about your business and focus on the important questions at hand. Is now a good time to begin receiving retirement income from your TSP account? Does an annuity fit your personal needs better than other withdrawal options? If so, what type of annuity best suits your needs and preferences?

After all, you don't know how interest rates are going to shift if you wait a month, three months, six months or a year. If you had the crystal ball that correctly predicted future interest rate movements, you could not worry about your TSP account and make a considerable fortune selling your knowledge. You don't, so don't try to act on knowledge that you don't have.

However, if you're thinking about buying an annuity and you face a very extreme interest rate environment, you may want to respond accordingly. If interest rates are at historically very high levels—such as during the late 1970s and early 1980s—you may want to lock in these very high rates by buying your annuity before rates have dropped significantly. On the other hand, if interest rates are at historically very low levels, and you don't absolutely need to buy the annuity right now, you may want to wait awhile to see if the very low rates begin to rise.

Remember, though, we're talking about situations in which interest rates are at extremely high or low levels and have the potential to begin dropping or rising significantly. In more normal circumstances, trying to be cute about guessing future interest rate movements and timing your annuity purchase will probably not be worth the trouble and may in fact backfire on you. For example, during the period from 1986 to 1994, when 10-year Treasury rates moved up and down within a range from 6 to 9 percent, you would have been hard pressed to anticipate whether rates would be higher or lower a few months or a year down the road.

SUMMARY OF YOUR ANNUITY OPTIONS

Let's recap your choices by summarizing the financial tradeoffs involved in picking a particular type of annuity.

We have characterized the single life annuity with level payments and no additional features as the "stripped down" annuity model. Just as when you buy a car, every feature that you add to your annuity increases the base price. In the case of an annuity, you pay for the additional features by receiving a lower initial monthly payment. By accepting the lower initial payment, you buy the right to additional protections in the future—cost of living adjustments (increasing payments), continued payments to your survivors (50% and 100% joint life annuities), guaranteed payments for a minimum number of years (the 10-year certain feature), or guaranteed payments at least equal to the value of your account (the cash refund feature).

Amount of Initial Payments For Various Annuity Options

| | If You Purchase Your Annuity at Age: | | | | |
	55	60	62	65	70
Single Life Annuity					
No Options	100%	100%	100%	100%	100%
with Cash Refund	95%	93%	93%	91%	91%
with 10-Year Certain	97%	96%	95%	94%	90%
with Increasing Payments	76%	78%	79%	80%	83%
with Cash Refund and Increasing Payments	71%	72%	73%	72%	75%
with 10-Year Certain and Increasing Payments	74%	75%	75%	76%	75%
Joint Life Annuity, 100% to Survivor					
with Level Payments	89%	87%	86%	84%	81%
with Level Payments and Cash Refund	88%	86%	85%	82%	80%
with Increasing Payments	65%	65%	65%	65%	65%
with Increasing Payments and Cash Refund	63%	64%	64%	63%	63%
Joint Life Annuity, 50% to Survivor					
with Level Payments	98%	98%	97%	97%	97%
with Level Payments and Cash Refund	96%	95%	95%	93%	93%
with Increasing Payments	74%	76%	76%	77%	80%
with Increasing Payments and Cash Refund	71%	72%	73%	74%	76%

Figure 8-9

Figure 8-9 summarizes your choices by showing the value of your initial payments under various options. The value of the "stripped down model"—a single life annuity with no additional features—is shown as 100 percent. Then the tradeoffs involved in other annuity options are shown by comparing your initial annuity payments to the 100 percent figure. Thus, if a particular option is listed as 95 percent, it means that your initial payments under this option would be 5 percent lower than the simple single life annuity.

Remember, these figures capture the "price" you pay for the added benefits of the extra features you might build into your annuity. The figures do not suggest in any way that any particular annuity option is a "better deal" than another. On the contrary, your choices among annuity options are neutral in terms of their total expected financial value. The different options reflect different ways of receiving that value.

As these figures illustrate, the two "expensive" annuity features are (1) 100 percent survivor protection, which reduces your initial annuity by 11 percent or more, and (2) increasing payments, which reduces your initial annuity by 20 percent or more. The cash refund, 10-year certain and 50 percent survivor features are less expensive. Remember, though, that full survivor protection and/or having your payments adjusted for inflation after you retire may be very important in your circumstances. Weigh your choices and tradeoffs carefully before making your decision

DISTRIBUTION OF YOUR TSP BALANCE AT DEATH

If you die while still employed, after separating from service but before you elect a withdrawal option, or after electing a lump sum payment but before receiving it, the TSP will pay the full amount of your vested account balance to your designated beneficiaries. If you elect a series of equal payments and die before receiving your entire account balance, your beneficiaries receive the remainder in a single payment.

If you use your TSP account to purchase an annuity, payments after your death are determined by the specific annuity you select. Once the TSP purchases your annuity, the features you elect are in effect. Be sure you understand your annuity options and their implications for your survivors.

You may designate one or more TSP beneficiaries by filing Form TSP-3, Designation of Beneficiary. If your marital status or other family circumstances change, review your Form 3 and, if appropriate, file a new designation. You may change your beneficiaries at any time and without notice to the existing beneficiaries of record. If you die without a Form 3 on file, any payments to your survivors will be made in order of legal precedence, as follows: (1) to your widow or widower; (2) to a child or children; (3) to your parents; (4) to the executor or administrator of your estate; (5) to your next of kin as defined by law in the state where you reside. To

---

PURCHASING AN ANNUITY — SUMMARY

Eligibility: If you leave government eligible for retirement benefits—either immediate or deferred—you can elect to receive your entire TSP account balance as a life annuity. You may begin receiving the annuity immediately or you may instruct the TSP to purchase the annuity at a specified later date.

How You Purchase an Annuity: If you leave the government and are eligible for CSRS or FERS retirement benefits, you can use your TSP account to purchase an annuity beginning immediately or at a later date. Your account balance must be at least $3,500 to purchase an annuity.

You request an annuity by completing Form TSP-7 (Election of Benefits) and Form TSP-11 (TSP Annuity Benefits). If you indicate a later date for your annuity purchase, the TSP will send you an Annuity Request Package a few months before you want the annuity to begin.

All annuity purchases are based on your entire TSP account balance at the time of purchase. You cannot divide your account balance between an annuity and an IRA transfer.

Tax Treatment: All annuity payments are taxable as ordinary income in the tax years you or your joint annuitant receive the payments. There are no early withdrawal penalties on annuity payments. When you purchase an annuity the annuity provider will provide you with information about your withholding options. Cash refunds and 10-year certain payments are taxable as ordinary income in the year they are received by the designated beneficiary. However, spouses or former spouses can request that the TSP transfer these payments to an IRA, deferring taxes until withdrawn.

Spousal Rights: If you are eligible for CSRS benefits, TSP notifies your spouse that you have elected to receive an annuity. If you are eligible for FERS benefits, should you elect any annuity form other than a joint life annuity with 50 percent to the survivor, level payments and no cash refund, then you and your spouse must complete Form TSP-11-C (Consent to Annuity Request).

obtain any applicable payments upon your death, your beneficiaries must file Form TSP-17, Application for Account Balance of Deceased Participant.

TSP WITHDRAWALS UNDER A REDUCTION IN FORCE _____

If you lose your job due to a reduction in force (RIF) at your agency, you are entitled to the full array of TSP withdrawal options, whether or not you are eligible to receive an immediate CSRS or FERS benefit. Because of the uncertainties associated with RIF situations, you should review your TSP account and your withdrawal options carefully if there is any chance of an imminent RIF at your agency. By doing so, you'll improve your ability to assess your career choices and financial needs. This will help you cope with both the financial and emotional strains of a RIF environment.

If you are a younger employee who would go to work elsewhere, you probably want to retain as much as possible of your TSP account for long-term growth and future retirement income. But there may be situations in which you need to tap all or a portion of your TSP account for transitional income after the RIF. Review the previous sections on equal payments, lump sum payments and combining these payments with a partial transfer of your account to an IRA, particularly the discussions of the tax implications.

If you are an older employee who leaves federal or postal service under a RIF, your choice of TSP withdrawal options will depend on your specific circumstances. If you are eligible for a CSRS or FERS pension immediately, look at whether you need to use all or part of your TSP account to supplement your retirement benefit. If you will not be eligible for your CSRS or FERS benefits until several years down the road, your TSP account may combine with your severance pay to ensure a reasonable post-RIF income. Your choice may depend on your likely employment and income prospects following the RIF. Above all, assess your situation thoroughly and realistically. Your TSP account may play a crucial part in your financial planning.

You may encounter a situation in which you are offered a special "buyout" with a lump sum incentive payment if you retire or resign. In such cases, the issues you face about what to do with your TSP account are the same as in a RIF situation. Review your personal financial needs, whether you're going to need retirement income or are planning to go to work somewhere else. If you're going to take the buyout and actually retire, look at how your TSP account fits into your retirement income needs now and in the future. Review the specific options described in this chapter. Before deciding how to use your TSP money, take stock of the other income you might receive when you leave—the buyout payment, severance pay and a lump sum payment for unused annual leave.

If you're going to take the buyout and go to work elsewhere, remember the long-term focus of the TSP. You'll probably want to either leave the money in the TSP or transfer it to an IRA. If you do withdraw the money, you may face a 10 percent early withdrawal penalty. Again, remember to check on the other income you'll receive when you resign. A final reminder: Under no circumstances can the buyout payment or any other lump sum payments be rolled over into your TSP account or into an IRA.

A REMINDER ABOUT PAPERWORK ____

The TSP withdrawal process is fairly simple. By being aware of procedures and requirements you can help the process be as smooth and quick as possible. In our discussion of each withdrawal option, we identified the pertinent TSP forms you have to file. Let's review the paperwork involved in a TSP withdrawal:

◇ TSP Form 18. Your employing agency files this form with the TSP at your retirement or separation. This informs the TSP that you are leaving federal or postal service and confirms your retirement eligibility status. This status—eligible for immediate retirement benefits, eligible for deferred retirement benefits, or not eligible for retirement benefits—determines the range of withdrawal options available to you. When you separate or retire, check with your personnel office to be sure Form 18 is complete and accurate. Retain a copy for your records.

◇ TSP Form 7. This is the form through which you indicate your basic withdrawal selection. A specimen form appears in Appendix 5. You should mail Form 7 directly to the Thrift Service Office. Remember, you are not required to file Form 7 at the time you separate. Take the time to make the withdrawal decision that makes sense for you and your family.

◇ Depending on the withdrawal option you select, you file an additional form that pertains to your choice. Specimens of these forms also appear in Appendix 5. File this form with the Thrift Service Office at the same time you file Form 7.

When the Thrift Service Office has received all three forms, your withdrawal selection will be processed within two months. Take this time lag into account when planning your transitional finances. If you are retiring, there will also be an interval of usually one, but up to three months before you receive your first retirement check from the government. Before you separate, check the amount of your lump sum payment for unused annual leave. This will normally be the first payment you receive after you separate.

5 THINGS TO DO

1. Periodically take the time to think about your withdrawal options and what you would do with your TSP account if you left your federal or postal job next month, next year or in 10 years. Know your career options and how the TSP fits into your financial planning. It's an uncertain world, but staying abreast of your options can help you deal with that uncertainty.

2. If you are thinking about leaving federal or postal employment, or if you're coming up on retirement eligibility, take a thorough look at your financial prospects. While there's no rush to make a TSP withdrawal decision, there's every reason to make the best possible decision when the time comes. If you're married, be sure to review how your TSP withdrawal options fit into your combined career and retirement planning.

3. Keep an eye on current economic conditions and future economic forecasts. They may play a large part in the TSP withdrawal option you select and the timing of your withdrawal. For example, in economically uncertain periods, the guaranteed payments under a TSP annuity may take on added value compared to the risks of managing your own assets. Current and future inflation rates may affect how you want to structure your withdrawal for immediate income and long-term protection. Interest rates may increase or decrease the value of the annuity if you purchase it now rather than a year, three years or five years from now. The more you know about the broader economic environment, the more informed and effective your choices can be.

4. Pay attention to the tax treatment of your TSP withdrawal options. If you stay up to date on how your withdrawal will be taxed, you can obtain the maximum possible value from your accumulated TSP savings.

5. Always frame your planning in terms of what makes sense for you and your family. The TSP provides a wide range of withdrawal options that can accommodate a variety of financial circumstances and personal preferences. Just as in the case of your investment strategy, there is no one best withdrawal option. And, most definitely, what makes sense for your neighbor or carpool companion does not necessarily make sense for you. Gather the information you need to make a withdrawal decision with confidence, and don't feel rushed to make that decision until you've gained that confidence. It's your money—use it wisely.

◆9◆ A REVIEW OF TSP ESSENTIALS

Throughout this book we've identified and analyzed the issues and choices you'll face as you save for retirement during your federal or postal career. Your Thrift Savings Plan offers a framework for evaluating the TSP as an investment opportunity, building a strategy that fits your financial situation and withdrawing your TSP savings to meet your retirement income needs.

Let's pull it all together.

Tax-deferred savings plans can be a particularly effective mechanism for developing and expanding your long-term, retirement-focused savings. All federal and postal employees enjoy the tax-deferred treatment of contributions and investment earnings under the TSP. Employees covered under FERS also benefit from agency matching contributions.

Your TSP savings decisions must fit your current household budget and your medium-term and long-term financial goals. The initial and overriding goal for FERS employees is to build up TSP contributions to at least the level of 5 percent of pay. This ensures maximum agency matching contributions, an opportunity that should not be forfeited or delayed except in emergency situations. The top priority for CSRS employees—and for FERS employees once they reach the 5 percent contribution level—is to weigh additional investments in the TSP against other savings goals and investment vehicles.

The TSP has a decidedly long-term focus. That has advantages as you seek to ensure an adequate retirement income for you and for your family. But the TSP's long-term focus includes some restrictions—prominently, limits on interim withdrawals—that you should think about carefully as you consider whether putting additional contributions into the TSP makes sense within your overall financial strategy.

Bear in mind the notion of a three-part financial portfolio—an emergency fund for short-term needs, a retirement and estate fund for long-term goals, and a buffer fund in which you save money for the future but retain some flexibility for the interim. The TSP can be a significant part of your retirement and estate fund, while other investments are generally better suited for your emergency and buffer funds. The availability of TSP loans gives you some flexibility to use your TSP account for short-term and medium-term financial needs.

The bottom line? If you're a FERS employee, you probably want to establish the TSP as the anchor for your overall financial planning, and adjust your other savings to fit with your basic commitment to the TSP. CSRS employees should consider the TSP and other financial opportunities in terms of several key variables—liquidity, convenience, investment options, potential returns and tax treatment. Some CSRS employees will make the TSP a key part of their financial planning. Others will choose to emphasize other investment opportunities. Both choices are sensible in different circumstances.

For most FERS employees, developing a substantial TSP account is important in ensuring an adequate or superior retirement income. For many long-term CSRS employees, basic government retirement benefits will provide a substantial guaranteed retirement income. However, the TSP can provide an important income supplement. And, for FERS and CSRS employees alike, the TSP offers the advantage of enhanced career flexibility. By building up a pool of savings that is yours and that you can take with you at any time during your career, the TSP helps you take a broader and more balanced approach to all your financial and career opportunities.

A few important principles when weighing the TSP against other investment opportunities:

◇ If you're a FERS employee, take maximum advantage of TSP matching contributions. Other investments would have to earn consistently superior returns to generate the value you get from the first 5 percent of pay you invest in the TSP. Take the known return from matched TSP contributions before you go searching for other investment opportunities.

◇ If you're a CSRS employee, look closely at your retirement income prospects. *While CSRS offers substantial* **TIP** *benefits for long-term employees, it may not be enough by itself.* You would need to work 40 years under CSRS to approach the 80 percent "salary replacement" that many financial advisers view as an adequate retirement income. *The TSP and other investments can provide the extra cushion you need to ensure a financially comfortable retirement.*

⊘ TIP ◇ *When you're comparing unmatched TSP contributions to other investment opportunities, choose investments that meet your needs and preferences. If you want to be able to tap into your assets without restrictions or penalties, don't lock all your savings into the TSP or an IRA.* On the other hand, keep in mind how sales loads, fees and taxes can erode your actual returns from stocks, bonds, mutual funds and other investment vehicles. There are thousands of mutual funds and other investments opportunities, but only a fraction can legitimately claim greater long-term growth potential than the TSP. And few cost less to invest in than the TSP.

The TSP offers three investment options—the G Fund (government securities), the C Fund (a stock market index fund) and the F Fund (government and corporate bonds and mortgage-backed securities). Each fund has its distinct characteristics. Taken together, the three investment options give you a range of choices—although certainly not as wide a range as is available through other forms of investing—tracking the movements of certain financial markets.

The G Fund is a relatively stable and consistent fund that provides a modest but dependable rate of return. You can generally expect your G Fund investments to grow about 3 percent a year in real terms, over and above inflation. Historically, there have been periods in which the interest on long-term government bonds has been higher or lower than the 3 percent real return benchmark. In periods of high inflation, the G Fund can pay below-inflation rates. So, while the G Fund presents no risk of actual loss, there is some possibility of your G Fund assets lagging behind the cost of living.

The C Fund, by comparison, is not stable or consistent. It will experience sharp fluctuations from one month to the next. Over time those fluctuations tend to balance out. And, overall, the balance is on the positive side. Since 1926 the stock market as a whole has achieved average yearly real gains, above inflation, in the neighborhood of 7 percent. From 1984-1993, the S&P 500 averaged an 11 percent annual real return, one of the strongest growth periods in market history.

⊘ TIP Future investment results are inherently uncertain. *But if you invest in the C Fund steadily over 10 years or longer, the chance of loss over the entire period is low. The potential for gain—at or above 5 percent real growth per year—is high.*

The F Fund represents a middle ground between the G and C Funds. It reflects the market prices of long-term bonds, with the fluctuations that result as investors buy and sell bonds in response to changing interest rates and economic conditions. The F Fund is not as stable as the G Fund, but over time may have a slightly higher growth potential. It's not as volatile as the C Fund, but likely won't match the C Fund's performance in the long-term.

Investment returns are uncertain, but they are not entirely unpredictable. You can develop your own invest-

ment plan based on reasonable expectations about how the various funds will perform, given sufficient time. The best place to start is by understanding the relationship among the three TSP funds and the broad financial markets they reflect. You have no guarantee that any or all of the funds will perform in the future as they have in the past. But understanding how they operate, and learning when and why they move the way they do, will put you in a position to build a TSP strategy that can fulfill your long-term savings goals.

A key strategic starting point is a realistic assessment of your financial goals and your TSP savings potential. There is no one correct strategy that fits all circumstances. Your long-term investment strategy should be a road map between two points—where you are now and where you want to go.

Only you can define your desired financial targets and how much uncertainty you're willing to endure in order to achieve those results. Some TSP participants will emphasize the stability of the G Fund, others the higher growth potential of the C Fund, yet others the "hybrid" nature of the F Fund, which in terms of both potential risk and return generally falls between the two others. Many employees will build a diversified TSP portfolio that includes investment in all three funds.

Remember one technical tip that may serve you well. The G Fund and the F Fund both reflect long-term interest rates, but in different ways. The G Fund pays the average rate on a mix of government securities. The F Fund is a portfolio of long-term bonds and pays the interest on that portfolio plus the shifting market value of bonds as they are bought and sold. When interest rates are rising or expected to rise, the market value of bonds generally declines. On the other hand, when rates are dropping or expected to drop, the market value of bonds generally goes up.

You may want to "hedge" your bets on future interest rate movements by combining G Fund and F Fund investments. Within the "safer" portion of your TSP portfolio, a mix of G Fund and F Fund investments will smooth out fluctuations in response to interest rate changes and—over time—may give you somewhat higher earnings potential.

Among current FERS employees who contribute to the TSP, the typical portfolio is 60 percent G Fund, 30 percent C Fund and 10 percent F Fund; for CSRS people, it is 50 percent G Fund, 39 percent C Fund and 11 percent F Fund. However, TSP account balances are steadily being reallocated away from the G Fund and into the C Fund and, to a lesser extent, the F Fund. It's likely that within a few years the "average" TSP investment portfolio will be widely diversified and fairly balanced among the three investment funds.

There are some practical steps you can take to manage your long-term investment strategy in response to medium-term and short-term developments. Periodically assess the status of your TSP account and measure how well you're progressing toward your retirement savings goals. Make TSP "checkpoints"—at least every year and when you face important career and financial decisions—a regular part of your financial planning. Use them to measure and, if needed, revise your TSP goals and strategies.

There are also some day-to-day and month-to-month techniques valuable for managing your TSP portfolio. There is no substitute for a sound, general financial self-education. Over time you'll build an understanding of how the TSP funds work and why they might or might not meet your preferences. Don't just follow the lead of the office TSP "expert." You are in different situations—besides, he probably knows less than he lets on. Build your own base of knowledge and the confidence that comes with it.

In general, the TSP is suited to longer-term "buy and hold" investment strategies. It is less well suited to time-sensitive, fine-tuned adjustments in response to rapid changes in market conditions. You should be very cautious about focusing on aggressive "market-timing" approaches in your TSP investment strategy. The monthly TSP investment cycle means you're 15 to 45 days behind the market. The information you're responding to has very likely already been taken into account by the financial markets.

This doesn't mean that you should be completely passive, establishing a single investment mix and sticking with it forever, regardless of developments. If you judge that a particular TSP fund should reasonably be expected to do particularly well or poorly in the coming months or years, by all means move your money accordingly. The longer you participate in the TSP and the more informed you become, the more confident you'll be in assessing and acting on expected market performance.

Avoid, as much as you can, "hot tips" that either have no factual foundation or have already been discounted by other investors. Train yourself not to overreact to short-term fluctuations. If you are shifting out of funds when they have a poor month or two, history suggests that you'll lose out on a substantial amount of market upswings before you get back in. Act on the basis of long-term market trends that are supported by underlying economic indicators, not short-term market corrections that have little or no bearing on future performance.

If you believe something and know logically why you believe it, behave accordingly. Act, don't react. Here's how:

◇ Take the long-term view. The TSP encourages tax-deferred retirement savings, but limits access to your funds in the interim. Invest accordingly. When you define your basic TSP investment strategy, try to avoid focusing on what you'll gain or lose next month, or even next year. Look at extended periods to draw informed conclusions about risks and returns. If $1,000 goes into your TSP this year and it earns a 4 percent annual real return for 30 years, you'll end up with $3,200 from the original invest-

ment. If the original $1,000 earns a 7 percent real return each year it will be worth $7,600 after 30 years. The added benefits of higher rates of return are substantial, but to get them, you'll have to endure higher risk. Time reduces risk in the long-run, but not necessarily in the short-run.

◇ Fit the TSP within your total savings portfolio. Look at the purposes of your investments and how those goals match up with your overall mix of risks and returns. If your other savings are primarily in money market accounts or short-term CDs, you may want to emphasize maximum growth potential from your TSP account. If you're heavily invested in growth-oriented mutual funds, you may want minimal risks in your TSP account. Build a total portfolio that can achieve your savings goals, and design your TSP investment strategy with the entire portfolio in mind.

◇ TSP tax-deferred investments help you maximize gains from long-term market trends. More flexible investment mechanisms, such as mutual funds, enable you to respond quickly—when necessary—to short-term market developments. Whatever your overall mix of "risky" and "safe" investments, think about how you balance them within the TSP and in other investments. As you draw closer to retirement, you might want to reconfigure your portfolio to reduce the risk of short-term loss in your less flexible TSP account.

◇ As you draw closer to withdrawing your TSP savings, think about shifting your investments to reduce the risk of short-term loss. This is particularly important if you're planning to buy an annuity at a specific date. Any short-term losses would permanently reduce your lifetime income. If, on the other hand, you're continuing to manage TSP or IRA funds after you retire, you could pay a price in lost potential growth by moving all your money to lower-return investments.

You can use the TSP loan program to help meet interim financial needs during your federal or postal career. The TSP offers the advantage of "borrowing" your own money—you face minimal qualification requirements and the interest you pay on your TSP loan goes back into your TSP account. *In general, the TSP loan program compares* **TIP** *favorably with other financing sources. The one financing source that can compete with TSP loans is a home equity loan, because the interest payments are tax-deductible.*

It's important to remember, though, that the TSP loan program has certain restrictions that you should consider carefully. First, there are strict limits on how much you can borrow, the length of the repayment period and what financial needs qualify. Plan carefully well in advance of when you need the money. And don't assume that the TSP is going to be able to be a complete and sufficient source of financing to meet your interim needs.

Second, and very important, the TSP loan program requires full repayment of your loan balance within 90 days after you leave federal or postal employment. If you don't have the cash available to repay your loan in its entirety, then you may end up paying a tax penalty on the outstanding amount of your account that you've, in effect, taken as income through the loan program. If you're thinking about applying for a TSP loan, but there's a possibility that you might leave government service during the loan period, be extra careful to consider how you'll manage your finances as these events unfold.

You have a wide range of options for turning your TSP account into retirement income. You can tailor your account withdrawal to fit your particular circumstances. Some employees will want to use their TSP account to purchase lifetime annuities that will supplement their CSRS or FERS retirement checks every month. Others may want to focus their TSP retirement income on a particular time period—perhaps to build a bridge income before other retirement income becomes available, perhaps to finance particular activities or opportunities after retirement from the government. Yet others will determine that they don't need income from the TSP immediately.

Some considerations for withdrawing your TSP account:

◇ *If you don't need your TSP savings for current income, you'll probably want to continue tax-deferred investing through the TSP or transfer your funds to an IRA. An IRA will offer a wider range of investment options—although possibly a narrower range of withdrawal options—than the TSP.*

If you choose this route, remember to arrange for a direct transfer from the TSP to the IRA. If you take possession of your account balance and then "roll it over" to an IRA, you'll be subject to mandatory tax withholding. You'll get the withholding back eventually, after you complete the roll over. But in the meantime you'll either have a lower amount to put into the IRA and you'll have to reach into your own pocket to make up the difference. Also remember that once you roll TSP money into an IRA, you can't roll it back the other way.

◇ You may be comfortable with your TSP investment options and decide it's not worth the bother to move your money from the TSP to an IRA. Even though you cannot add new money to your TSP account in retirement, you can continue managing your TSP balance through interfund transfers. Remember that whether your money is in the TSP or an IRA, you'll have to begin withdrawing it no later than age 70 1/2. If you have large TSP and/or IRA balances, you may want to consult with a financial adviser to design a withdrawal schedule that minimizes your tax liability.

◇ An annuity can serve several purposes. Buying an annuity eliminates any risks and anxieties involved in managing your money. You hand over your account balance to an insurance company and they pay you a monthly payment for the rest of your life. You can tailor your annuity to fit your preferences—with or without inflation protection, with or without continued payments to sur-

vivors, with or without guaranteed minimum payments if you die fairly soon after you start receiving your annuity.

No particular type of annuity is the "best buy." You can compare different annuity options and decide which additional protections and guarantees make sense for you and your family. The insurance company—under a clear and specific contract with the TSP—adjusts your annuity payments to pay for any "extras" you want to have. Use the tables in Appendix 4 to consider your choices.

◇ A lump sum payment or series of equal payments may make sense if you have a specific short-term financial need that's more important than raising your permanent, lifetime retirement income. Starting a business, enjoying travel or other leisure activities during your "more active" retirement years, coordinating your and your spouse's incomes—these and other goals may lead you to concentrate your TSP income during a defined period.

Be sure to check how your payment schedule will affect your total taxable income and resulting tax rates. Take the time to review all your assets and income sources, with a financial adviser if necessary, to make sure you coordinate your TSP withdrawal with other financial resources as effectively as possible.

◇ Don't forget that you can split your withdrawal, receiving a portion as a lump sum or series of payments and transferring the remainder to an IRA. This lets you combine current income for a near-term financial goal and a reserve fund that keeps earning for your later retirement years.

◇ Planning your withdrawal carefully will help you tailor your TSP retirement income to your individual circumstances. There's no reason to rush your decision. Be sure you're comfortable with your choice before filing your withdrawal paperwork. While you're making your decision, your funds will continue to earn monthly investment returns. Once you submit your paperwork to the Thrift Service Office, allow two months for execution of your withdrawal request.

From the moment you begin your federal or postal career, throughout your working years and on into retirement, the TSP can be an important and profitable part of your lifetime financial planning. You can take advantage of the opportunities it offers, and build a complete financial portfolio with the TSP as a long-term foundation.

As you consider the TSP and what it might do for you, always remember to take a realistic and practical approach to your needs and savings potential. Become as informed as you can or want to be about the details of financial markets and investment strategies. But always stay focused on the essentials from a long-term perspective.

Never underestimate the results you can achieve through the simple, rigorous application of common sense.

APPENDIX
TSP INFORMATION DIRECTORY

<diagram: number 1 in a diamond shape>

This appendix lists the major sources of information you may need to consult at various stages of your participation in the TSP.

TSP TELEPHONE NUMBERS

TSP Inquiry Line (504) 255-8777
  Current account balance in each fund
  Most recent monthly rates of return for each fund
  Amount you may be eligible to borrow from your account
  Current interest rate for TSP loans
  Request a Form TSP-30 for Interfund Transfer
  Status of your account withdrawal request

Hardship Loan Application (504) 255-6050
  To request Form TSP-20-H, Hardship Loan Application
  Note: This telephone number is for hardship loans only

Interest Rate Index (annuities) 1-800-447-8777
  The current interest rate index for annuity purchases
  Use this if you are considering withdrawing you TSP account balance and want to estimate what your annuity payments might be

Telecommunications
Device for the Deaf (TDD) (504) 255-5113

TSP ADDRESSES

TSP Service Office National Finance Center P.O. Box 61500 New Orleans, LA 70161-1500	Loans Account maintenance after you leave federal/ postal service
TSP Service Office National Finance Center P.O. Box 60012 New Orleans, LA 70161-0012	Interfund Transfers

TSP BOOKLETS

(obtain from your employing agency, or from TSP Service Office after you leave federal/postal service)

Summary of the Thrift Savings Plan for Federal Employees

Open Season Update (new issue every six months)

Thrift Savings Plan Loan Program

Withdrawing Your TSP Account Balance

Thrift Savings Plan Annuities

TSP FACT SHEETS

(obtain from your employing agency, or from TSP Service Office after you leave federal/postal service)

The Thrift Savings Plan and IRAs

C, F and G Fund Monthly Returns (new issue every month)

Calculating Participant Earnings on Thrift Savings Plan Investments

⟨2⟩ APPENDIX
ACCOUNT TABLES FOR FERS EMPLOYEES

This appendix contains tables enabling FERS employees to estimate the future growth of their TSP accounts under varying circumstances. Use Table 2-1 to estimate the future growth of your current account balance, regardless of any future contributions you will make to the TSP. Use Table 2-2 to estimate the additional growth of your account from all new contributions you will make in the future. To obtain a total estimate of your future account growth—combining what you've saved so far the additional savings you'll accumulate in the future—add the results from Tables 2-1 and 2-2.

If you are considering leaving the government and want to see how your account will grow if you continue to invest it in the TSP, use Tables 2-1 and 2-2 to estimate how much TSP account will grow up to the time you leave the government. Then, based on that "separation" account balance, use Table 2-1 again to estimate how much that balance will grow based on how many years you leave it in the TSP after you separate or retire.

TABLE 2-1 _____

Estimating How Much Your Current TSP Account Balance Will Grow

1. Determine your current balance from your semi-annual account statement or by calling the TSP Inquiry Line—(504) 255-8777.

2. Locate the row in the following table for the number of years you will continue to invest your current balance in the TSP. Then locate the column that matches the average real annual return you expect to achieve on your TSP investments. For example, if you expect to earn about 10 percent per year, with inflation of about 3 percent, use the column for 7 percent growth.

3. Find the multiplier where the row and the column intersect. Multiply your current TSP account balance by that factor. The result is the estimated value of your current account balance after the number of years you specified, based on the purchasing power of today's dollars.

Example: Current Account Balance $20,000
Number of Future Years you Expect in TSP   15

Expectation for Real Annual Return	7%
Resulting Account Growth	2.85
Multiply $20,000 X 2.85	$57,000

__ Annual Real Growth in Future Years __

Years	Conservative			Moderate		Optimistic		
	3%	4%	5%	6%	7%	8%	9%	10%
5	1.16	1.22	1.28	1.35	1.42	1.49	1.57	1.65
10	1.35	1.49	1.65	1.82	2.01	2.22	2.45	2.71
15	1.57	1.82	2.11	2.45	2.85	3.31	3.84	4.45
20	1.82	2.22	2.71	3.31	4.04	4.93	6.01	7.33
25	2.12	2.71	3.48	4.46	5.73	7.34	9.41	12.06
30	2.46	3.31	4.47	6.02	8.12	10.94	14.73	19.84
35	2.85	4.05	5.73	8.12	11.51	16.29	23.06	32.64
40	3.32	4.94	7.36	10.96	16.31	24.27	36.11	53.70

TABLE 2-2 _____

Estimating How Much Your Future Contributions Will Add to Your TSP Account Balance

1. Find the table below that matches the average annual real investment returns you expect to achieve. For example, if you expect to earn about 10 percent per year, with inflation of about 3 percent, use the table for 7 percent growth.

2. Locate the row in the table for the number of years you will make new contributions to the TSP. Then locate the column that matches the percentage of pay you expect to contribute to the TSP during those years.

3. Find the multiplier where the row and the column intersect. Multiply your current annual salary by that factor. The result is the estimated amount of additional account balance you will generate from future TSP contributions, expressed in terms of the purchasing power of today's dollars.

Example: Expectation for Real Annual Return	7%
Number of Future Years in TSP	15
Expected Contribution to TSP	5% of pay
Resulting Salary Multiple	2.65
Current Salary	$30,000
Multiply $30,000 X 2.65	$79,500

4. To estimate the total amount of your ending TSP balance, add your results from Table 2-1 and Table 2-2.

Example: Growth of Current Balance $57,000
    Estimated Value of New Contributions $79,500
    Total Projected TSP Account Balance $136,500

Percentage of Pay You Contribute to the TSP

3% Annual Real Growth

Years	0%	1%	2%	3%	4%	5%	6%	7%	8%	9%	10%
5	0.06	0.17	0.28	0.38	0.46	0.54	0.60	0.64	0.70	0.75	0.81
10	0.11	0.36	0.59	0.83	1.00	1.18	1.29	1.40	1.52	1.63	1.74
15	0.19	0.58	0.97	1.36	1.64	1.93	2.12	2.30	2.48	2.65	2.83
20	0.28	0.85	1.42	1.99	2.41	2.82	3.08	3.33	3.59	3.84	4.10
25	0.37	1.15	1.92	2.70	3.27	3.83	4.18	4.53	4.87	5.22	7.57
30	0.49	1.52	2.54	3.57	4.31	5.05	5.50	5.95	6.42	6.84	7.28
35	0.62	1.95	3.27	4.59	5.54	6.48	7.04	7.61	8.17	8.72	9.27
40	0.78	2.45	4.12	5.79	6.97	8.15	8.83	9.52	10.2	10.9	11.6

4% Annual Real Growth

Years	0%	1%	2%	3%	4%	5%	6%	7%	8%	9%	10%
5	0.06	0.17	0.28	0.39	0.47	0.55	0.61	0.66	0.72	0.77	0.83
10	0.12	0.37	0.61	0.86	1.04	1.23	1.35	1.47	1.60	1.72	1.84
15	0.21	0.62	1.03	1.44	1.74	2.05	2.26	2.46	2.67	2.87	3.08
20	0.31	0.92	1.53	2.14	2.60	3.06	3.37	3.67	3.98	4.28	4.59
25	0.43	1.29	2.14	3.00	3.65	4.29	4.72	5.15	5.57	6.00	6.43
30	0.58	1.74	2.89	4.05	4.92	5.79	6.37	6.95	7.53	8.10	8.68
35	0.76	2.29	3.81	5.33	6.48	7.62	8.38	9.15	9.91	10.7	11.4
40	0.99	2.96	4.93	6.90	8.38	9.86	10.8	11.8	12.8	13.8	14.8

5% Annual Real Growth

Years	0%	1%	2%	3%	4%	5%	6%	7%	8%	9%	10%
5	0.06	0.17	0.29	0.40	0.48	0.56	0.63	0.68	0.74	0.79	0.85
10	0.13	0.39	0.64	0.91	1.10	1.30	1.42	1.55	1.69	1.82	1.94
15	0.23	0.67	1.12	1.57	1.89	2.23	2.46	2.67	2.90	3.12	3.35
20	0.35	1.03	1.72	2.40	2.92	3.43	3.78	4.12	4.46	4.80	5.15
25	0.50	1.50	2.48	3.48	4.23	4.97	5.47	5.97	6.46	6.96	7.45
30	0.70	2.09	3.47	4.86	5.90	6.95	7.64	8.34	9.04	9.72	10.4
35	0.95	2.85	4.74	6.63	8.06	9.48	10.4	11.4	12.3	13.3	14.2
40	1.28	3.82	6.37	8.92	10.8	12.7	14.0	15.2	16.5	17.8	19.1

6% Annual Real Growth

Years	0%	1%	2%	3%	4%	5%	6%	7%	8%	9%	10%
5	0.06	0.17	0.30	0.41	0.49	0.58	0.65	0.70	0.76	0.81	0.87
10	0.14	0.41	0.68	0.96	1.16	1.37	1.50	1.64	1.78	1.92	2.05
15	0.25	0.73	1.22	1.71	2.06	2.43	2.68	2.91	3.16	3.40	3.65
20	0.39	1.16	1.94	2.70	3.29	3.86	4.25	4.64	5.02	5.40	5.79
25	0.58	1.75	2.89	4.05	4.93	5.79	6.37	6.95	7.52	8.11	8.68
30	0.85	2.52	4.19	5.87	7.13	8.40	9.23	10.1	10.9	11.7	12.6
35	1.19	3.58	5.95	8.32	10.1	11.9	13.1	14.3	15.4	16.7	17.8
40	1.67	4.99	8.32	11.7	14.1	16.6	18.3	19.9	21.6	23.2	24.9

7% Annual Real Growth

Years	0%	1%	2%	3%	4%	5%	6%	7%	8%	9%	10%
5	0.06	0.18	0.30	0.42	0.51	0.60	0.66	0.72	0.78	0.84	0.90
10	0.14	0.43	0.72	1.01	1.23	1.44	1.59	1.73	1.88	2.02	2.17
15	0.26	0.79	1.32	1.85	2.25	2.65	2.91	3.17	3.44	3.70	3.97
20	0.43	1.30	2.17	3.04	3.70	4.35	4.78	5.22	5.65	6.09	6.52
25	0.68	2.03	3.38	4.73	5.75	6.76	7.44	8.11	8.79	9.47	10.1
30	1.02	3.05	5.09	7.13	8.66	10.2	11.2	12.2	13.2	14.3	15.3
35	1.50	4.51	7.52	10.5	12.8	15.0	16.5	18.0	19.5	21.1	22.6
40	2.19	6.57	11.0	15.3	18.6	21.9	24.1	26.3	28.5	30.7	32.9

8% Annual Real Growth

Years	0%	1%	2%	3%	4%	5%	6%	7%	8%	9%	10%
5	0.06	0.18	0.31	0.43	0.52	0.62	0.68	0.74	0.80	0.86	0.92
10	0.15	0.45	0.76	1.07	1.30	1.52	1.68	1.83	1.99	2.14	2.30
15	0.28	0.86	1.44	2.02	2.46	2.90	3.18	3.46	3.76	4.04	4.34
20	0.49	1.47	2.46	3.44	4.19	4.92	5.41	5.91	6.39	6.89	7.38
25	0.80	2.39	3.97	5.56	6.76	7.94	8.74	9.53	10.3	11.1	11.9
30	1.25	3.73	6.22	8.72	10.6	12.5	13.7	14.9	16.1	17.5	18.7
35	1.91	5.75	9.59	13.4	16.3	19.1	21.0	22.9	24.9	26.9	28.8
40	2.92	8.75	14.6	20.4	24.8	29.2	32.1	35.0	37.9	40.9	43.8

9% Annual Real Growth

Years	0%	1%	2%	3%	4%	5%	6%	7%	8%	9%	10%
5	0.06	0.18	0.32	0.44	0.53	0.64	0.70	0.76	0.82	0.88	0.95
10	0.16	0.48	0.80	1.13	1.38	1.61	1.78	1.94	2.11	2.27	2.43
15	0.31	0.94	1.58	2.21	2.69	3.17	3.48	3.79	4.11	4.42	4.75
20	0.56	1.68	2.80	3.92	4.77	5.61	6.17	6.74	7.28	7.85	8.41
25	0.94	2.81	4.66	6.53	7.94	9.33	10.3	11.2	12.1	13.0	14.0
30	1.54	4.59	7.65	10.7	13.0	15.4	16.8	18.3	19.8	21.5	23.0
35	2.45	7.38	12.3	17.2	20.9	24.5	27.0	29.4	32.0	34.5	37.0
40	3.92	11.7	19.6	27.4	33.3	39.2	43.1	47.0	50.9	54.9	58.8

10% Annual Real Growth

Years	0%	1%	2%	3%	4%	5%	6%	7%	8%	9%	10%
5	0.06	0.19	0.32	0.45	0.55	0.65	0.71	0.78	0.84	0.91	0.97
10	0.17	0.51	0.86	1.20	1.45	1.71	1.88	2.05	2.22	2.40	2.57
15	0.35	1.04	1.73	2.42	2.94	3.46	3.81	4.15	4.50	4.85	5.19
20	0.63	1.90	3.17	4.44	5.39	6.34	6.98	7.61	8.24	8.88	9.51
25	1.11	3.32	5.54	7.76	9.42	11.1	12.2	13.3	14.4	15.5	16.6
30	1.89	5.66	9.44	13.2	16.1	18.9	20.8	22.7	24.5	26.4	28.3
35	3.17	9.51	15.9	22.2	27.0	31.7	34.9	38.1	41.2	44.4	47.6
40	5.28	15.9	26.4	37.0	44.9	52.8	58.1	63.4	68.7	74.0	79.2

APPENDIX ACCOUNT TABLES FOR CSRS EMPLOYEES

⟨3⟩

This appendix contains tables enabling CSRS employees to estimate the future growth of their TSP accounts under varying circumstances. Use Table 3-1 to estimate the future growth of your current account balance, regardless of any future contributions you will make to the TSP. Use Table 3-2 to estimate the additional growth of your account from all new contributions you will make in the future. To obtain a total estimate of your future account growth—combining what you've saved so far the additional savings you'll accumulate in the future—add the results from Tables 3-1 and 3-2.

If you are considering leaving the government and want to see how your account will grow if you continue to invest it in the TSP, use Tables 3-1 and 3-2 to estimate how much TSP account will grow up to the time you leave the government. Then, based on that "separation" account balance, use Table 3-1 again to estimate how much that balance will grow based on how many years you leave it in the TSP after you separate or retire.

TABLE 3-1 _____

Estimating How Much Your Current TSP Account Balance Will Grow

1. Determine your current balance from your semi-annual account statement or by calling the TSP Inquiry Line—(504) 255-8777.

2. Locate the row in the following table for the number of years you will continue to invest your current balance in the TSP. Then locate the column that matches the average real annual return you expect to achieve on your TSP investments. For example, if you expect to earn about 10 percent per year, with inflation of about 3 percent, use the column for 7 percent growth.

3. Find the multiplier where the row and the column intersect. Multiply your current TSP account balance by that factor. The result is the estimated value of your current account balance after the number of years you specified, based on the purchasing power of today's dollars.

Example: Current Account Balance	$20,000
Number of Future Years you Expect in TSP	15
Expectation for Real Annual Return	7%
Resulting Account Growth	2.85
Multiply $20,000 X 2.85	$57,000

__ Annual Real Growth in Future Years __

	Conservative			Moderate		Optimistic		
Years	3%	4%	5%	6%	7%	8%	9%	10%
5	1.16	1.22	1.28	1.35	1.42	1.49	1.57	1.65
10	1.35	1.49	1.65	1.82	2.01	2.22	2.45	2.71
15	1.57	1.82	2.11	2.45	2.85	3.31	3.84	4.45
20	1.82	2.22	2.71	3.31	4.04	4.93	6.01	7.33
25	2.12	2.71	3.48	4.46	5.73	7.34	9.41	12.06
30	2.46	3.31	4.47	6.02	8.12	10.94	14.73	19.84
35	2.85	4.05	5.73	8.12	11.51	16.29	23.06	32.64
40	3.32	4.94	7.36	10.96	16.31	24.27	36.11	53.70

TABLE 3-2 _____

Estimating How Much Your Future Contributions Will Add to Your TSP Account Balance

1. Find the table below that matches the average annual real investment returns you expect to achieve. For example, if you expect to earn about 10 percent per year, with inflation of about 3 percent, use the table for 7 percent growth.

2. Locate the row in the table for the number of years you will make new contributions to the TSP. Then locate the column that matches the percentage of pay you expect to contribute to the TSP during those years.

3. Find the multiplier where the row and the column intersect. Multiply your current annual salary by that factor. The result is the estimated amount of additional account balance you will generate from future TSP contributions, expressed in terms of the purchasing power of today's dollars.

Example: Expectation for Real Annual Return	7%
Number of Future Years in TSP	15

Expected Contribution to TSP | 5% of pay
Resulting Salary Multiple | 1.32
Current Salary | $30,000
Multiply $30,000 X 1.32 | $39,600

4. To estimate the total amount of your ending TSP balance, add your results from Table 3-1 and Table 3-2.

Example: Growth of Current Balance	$57,000
Estimated Value of New Contributions	$39,600
Total Projected TSP Account Balance	$96,500

Percentage of Pay
＿＿＿＿ You Contribute to the TSP ＿＿＿＿

3% Annual Real Growth

Years	1%	2%	3%	4%	5%
5	0.06	0.11	0.17	0.22	0.28
10	0.11	0.23	0.36	0.47	0.59
15	0.19	0.38	0.58	0.77	0.97
20	0.28	0.56	0.85	1.13	1.42
25	0.37	0.76	1.15	1.53	1.92
30	0.49	1.00	1.52	2.03	2.54
35	0.62	1.28	1.95	2.61	3.27
40	0.78	1.61	2.45	3.28	4.12

4% Annual Real Growth

Years	1%	2%	3%	4%	5%
5	0.06	0.11	0.17	0.22	0.28
10	0.12	0.24	0.37	0.49	0.61
15	0.21	0.41	0.62	0.82	1.03
20	0.31	0.61	0.92	1.22	1.53
25	0.43	0.86	1.29	1.71	2.14
30	0.58	1.16	1.74	2.31	2.89
35	0.76	1.52	2.29	3.05	3.81
40	0.99	1.97	2.96	3.94	4.93

5% Annual Real Growth

Years	1%	2%	3%	4%	5%
5	0.06	0.11	0.17	0.23	0.29
10	0.13	0.26	0.39	0.51	0.64
15	0.23	0.45	0.67	0.89	1.12
20	0.35	0.69	1.03	1.37	1.72
25	0.50	1.00	1.50	1.99	2.48
30	0.70	1.39	2.09	2.78	3.47
35	0.95	1.90	2.85	3.79	4.74
40	1.28	2.55	3.82	5.09	6.37

6% Annual Real Growth

Years	1%	2%	3%	4%	5%
5	0.06	0.11	0.17	0.23	0.30
10	0.14	0.27	0.41	0.54	0.68
15	0.25	0.49	0.73	0.97	1.22
20	0.39	0.77	1.16	1.55	1.94
25	0.58	1.16	1.75	2.32	2.89
30	0.85	1.68	2.52	3.35	4.19
35	1.19	2.38	3.58	4.76	5.95
40	1.67	3.33	4.99	6.65	8.32

7% Annual Real Growth

Years	1%	2%	3%	4%	5%
5	0.06	0.12	0.18	0.24	0.30
10	0.14	0.28	0.43	0.57	0.72
15	0.26	0.52	0.79	1.05	1.32
20	0.43	0.86	1.30	1.73	2.17
25	0.68	1.35	2.03	2.70	3.38
30	1.02	2.03	3.05	4.07	5.09
35	1.50	3.00	4.51	6.01	7.52
40	2.19	4.38	6.57	8.76	11.00

8% Annual Real Growth

Years	1%	2%	3%	4%	5%
5	0.06	0.12	0.18	0.24	0.31
10	0.15	0.30	0.45	0.60	0.76
15	0.28	0.57	0.86	1.15	1.44
20	0.49	0.98	1.47	1.96	2.46
25	0.80	1.59	2.39	3.18	3.97
30	1.25	2.49	3.73	4.97	6.22
35	1.91	3.83	5.75	7.67	9.59
40	2.92	5.83	8.75	11.70	14.60

9% Annual Real Growth

Years	1%	2%	3%	4%	5%
5	0.06	0.12	0.18	0.25	0.32
10	0.16	0.32	0.48	0.64	0.80
15	0.31	0.62	0.94	1.26	1.58
20	0.56	1.12	1.68	2.24	2.80
25	0.94	1.87	2.81	3.73	4.66
30	1.54	3.06	4.59	6.12	7.65
35	2.45	4.91	7.38	9.84	12.30
40	3.92	7.81	11.70	15.60	19.60

10% Annual Real Growth

Years	1%	2%	3%	4%	5%
5	0.06	0.12	0.19	0.25	0.32
10	0.17	0.34	0.51	0.68	0.86
15	0.35	0.69	1.04	1.38	1.73
20	0.63	1.26	1.90	2.53	3.17
25	1.11	2.21	3.32	4.43	5.54
30	1.89	3.77	5.66	7.55	9.44
35	3.17	6.34	9.51	12.70	15.90
40	5.28	10.60	15.90	21.10	26.40

APPENDIX — ESTIMATING APPROXIMATE ANNUITY PAYMENTS

Use the following tables from the Thrift Savings Board to estimate your approximate annuity payments under various annuity options. Annuities purchased in 1994 will be paid at the indicated rates multiplied by a factor of .996. For example, a single life annuity with increasing payments and no other features, purchased at age 60, would be paid at the rate of $6.97 per $1,000 of account balance ($7.000 x .996). See the explanation and worksheet following the tables.

TABLE 1

Single Life Annuities

Monthly Annuity Factors per $1,000 Account Balance

Instructions: Find your age (at the expected annuity purchase date) in the left-hand column marked "Annuitant's Age." Find the column that describes the annuity option you are estimating.

Then find the number where the row for your age intersects with the column for your annuity option. Enter that number on the worksheet on line (7).

Annuitant's Age	Level Payment			Increasing Payment		
	No Added Features	Cash Refund	10-Year Certain	No Added Features	Cash Refund	10-Year Certain
55	$8.39	$7.97	$8.17	$6.36	$5.97	$6.20
56	8.49	8.07	8.25	6.47	6.08	6.30
57	8.60	8.17	8.34	6.59	6.20	6.40
58	8.72	8.29	8.43	6.72	6.32	6.51
59	8.85	8.41	8.52	6.85	6.44	6.62
60	8.98	8.35	8.63	7.00	6.44	6.74
61	9.13	8.49	8.73	7.15	6.58	6.86
62	9.28	8.63	8.85	7.32	6.73	6.99
63	9.45	8.79	8.97	7.49	6.89	7.13
64	9.63	8.95	9.09	7.68	7.06	7.27
65	9.82	8.94	9.22	7.88	7.09	7.42
66	10.03	9.13	9.36	8.10	7.29	7.58
67	10.26	9.34	9.51	8.34	7.50	7.74
68	10.51	9.56	9.65	8.59	7.73	7.91
69	10.77	9.80	9.81	8.86	7.98	8.08
70	11.06	10.07	9.97	9.16	8.24	8.26

TABLE 2

Joint Life Annuities

Monthly Annuity Factors per $1,000 Account Balance

Instructions: Table 2 contains eight sections. The four sections on page 11 include the monthly annuity factors for the joint life *level payment* options (with 100 percent or 50 percent to the survivor, and with or without the cash refund feature). The four sections on page 12 contain the annuity factors for the *increasing payment* options. Be sure you use the section of the table that matches your annuity choice.

When you have found the correct section of this table, find your age (at the expected annuity purchase date) in the left-hand column marked "Primary Annuitant's Age." Then find the column that describes the **age difference** between you and your joint annuitant, which you calculated on line (4) of the worksheet. The table includes joint annuitant age differences from four years younger than you to three years older. Find the number where the row for your age intersects with the column for the age difference. Enter that number on the worksheet on line (7).

TABLE 2

Level Payment – No Cash Refund: 100 Percent to Survivor
Joint Annuitant's Age

Primary Annuitant's Age	Younger				Same Age	Older		
	4 Years	3 Years	2 Years	1 Year		1 Year	2 Years	3 Years
55	$7.31	$7.34	$7.37	$7.40	$7.43	$7.46	$7.49	$7.53
56	7.36	7.39	7.42	7.46	7.49	7.52	7.56	7.59
57	7.41	7.45	7.48	7.52	7.55	7.59	7.62	7.66
58	7.47	7.50	7.54	7.58	7.62	7.66	7.69	7.73
59	7.53	7.57	7.61	7.65	7.69	7.73	7.77	7.81
60	7.59	7.63	7.68	7.72	7.77	7.81	7.86	7.90
61	7.66	7.71	7.75	7.80	7.85	7.90	7.95	8.00
62	7.74	7.79	7.84	7.89	7.94	7.99	8.04	8.10
63	7.82	7.87	7.92	7.98	8.04	8.09	8.15	8.21
64	7.91	7.96	8.02	8.08	8.14	8.20	8.27	8.33
65	8.00	8.06	8.13	8.19	8.26	8.32	8.39	8.46
66	8.10	8.17	8.24	8.31	8.38	8.46	8.53	8.61
67	8.21	8.29	8.36	8.44	8.52	8.60	8.68	8.77
68	8.34	8.42	8.50	8.58	8.67	8.76	8.85	8.94
69	8.47	8.55	8.64	8.74	8.83	8.93	9.03	9.12
70	8.61	8.71	8.81	8.91	9.01	9.11	9.22	9.33

Level Payment - With Cash Refund: 100 Percent to Survivor
Joint Annuitant's Age

Primary Annuitant's Age	Younger				Same Age	Older		
	4 Years	3 Years	2 Years	1 Year		1 Year	2 Years	3 Years
55	$7.24	$7.27	$7.30	$7.33	$7.36	$7.39	$7.42	$7.45
56	7.29	7.32	7.35	7.38	7.41	7.45	7.48	7.51
57	7.34	7.37	7.41	7.44	7.47	7.51	7.55	7.58
58	7.39	7.43	7.47	7.50	7.54	7.58	7.62	7.66
59	7.45	7.49	7.53	7.57	7.61	7.65	7.69	7.74
60	7.52	7.56	7.60	7.64	7.69	7.73	7.78	7.82
61	7.59	7.63	7.68	7.72	7.77	7.82	7.87	7.92
62	7.66	7.71	7.76	7.81	7.86	7.91	7.96	8.02
63	7.74	7.79	7.85	7.90	7.96	8.01	8.07	8.13
64	7.83	7.88	7.94	8.00	8.06	8.12	8.18	8.25
65	7.84	7.90	7.96	8.03	8.09	8.16	8.23	8.29
66	7.94	8.01	8.07	8.14	8.21	8.29	8.36	8.44
67	8.05	8.12	8.20	8.27	8.35	8.43	8.51	8.59
68	8.17	8.25	8.33	8.41	8.50	8.58	8.67	8.76
69	8.30	8.38	8.47	8.56	8.66	8.75	8.84	8.94
70	8.44	8.53	8.63	8.73	8.83	8.93	9.04	9.14

Level Payment – No Cash Refund: 50 Percent to Survivor
Joint Annuitant's Age

Primary Annuitant's Age	Younger				Same Age	Older		
	4 Years	3 Years	2 Years	1 Year		1 Year	2 Years	3 Years
55	$8.04	$8.08	$8.12	$8.17	$8.21	$8.26	$8.31	$8.36
56	8.13	8.17	8.22	8.26	8.31	8.36	8.41	8.47
57	8.22	8.27	8.31	8.36	8.41	8.47	8.52	8.58
58	8.32	8.37	8.42	8.47	8.52	8.58	8.64	8.70
59	8.43	8.48	8.53	8.58	8.64	8.70	8.76	8.83
60	8.54	8.59	8.65	8.70	8.77	8.83	8.90	8.97
61	8.66	8.71	8.77	8.83	8.90	8.97	9.04	9.12
62	8.78	8.84	8.91	8.97	9.04	9.12	9.20	9.28
63	8.92	8.98	9.05	9.12	9.20	9.28	9.36	9.46
64	9.06	9.13	9.20	9.28	9.36	9.45	9.55	9.65
65	9.22	9.29	9.37	9.45	9.54	9.64	9.75	9.86
66	9.38	9.46	9.55	9.64	9.74	9.85	9.96	10.08
67	9.56	9.65	9.75	9.85	9.96	10.07	10.20	10.33
68	9.76	9.86	9.96	10.07	10.19	10.32	10.46	10.60
69	9.97	10.08	10.19	10.32	10.45	10.59	10.74	10.89
70	10.20	10.32	10.45	10.58	10.72	10.88	11.04	11.21

Level Payment - With Cash Refund: 50 Percent to Survivor
Joint Annuitant's Age

Primary Annuitant's Age	Younger				Same Age	Older		
	4 Years	3 Years	2 Years	1 Year		1 Year	2 Years	3 Years
55	$7.88	$7.92	$7.96	$8.00	$8.05	$8.09	$8.14	$8.19
56	7.97	8.01	8.05	8.10	8.14	8.19	8.24	8.30
57	8.06	8.10	8.15	8.20	8.25	8.30	8.35	8.41
58	8.16	8.20	8.25	8.30	8.35	8.41	8.47	8.53
59	8.26	8.31	8.36	8.41	8.47	8.53	8.59	8.66
60	8.28	8.33	8.39	8.44	8.50	8.57	8.63	8.70
61	8.40	8.45	8.51	8.57	8.63	8.70	8.77	8.85
62	8.52	8.58	8.64	8.70	8.77	8.84	8.92	9.00
63	8.65	8.71	8.78	8.85	8.92	9.00	9.08	9.17
64	8.79	8.86	8.93	9.00	9.08	9.17	9.26	9.36
65	8.85	8.92	8.99	9.08	9.16	9.26	9.36	9.46
66	9.01	9.09	9.17	9.26	9.35	9.45	9.56	9.68
67	9.18	9.27	9.36	9.45	9.56	9.67	9.79	9.92
68	9.37	9.46	9.56	9.67	9.78	9.91	10.04	10.18
69	9.57	9.68	9.79	9.90	10.03	10.16	10.31	10.46
70	9.80	9.91	10.03	10.16	10.30	10.44	10.60	10.76

TABLE 2 (continued)

Increasing Payment - No Cash Refund: 100 Percent to Survivor

Joint Annuitant's Age

Primary Annuitant's Age	Younger				Same Age	Older		
	4 Years	3 Years	2 Years	1 Year		1 Year	2 Years	3 Years
55	$5.27	$5.30	$5.34	$5.38	$5.42	$5.46	$5.50	$5.54
56	5.33	5.37	5.41	5.45	5.49	5.53	5.58	5.62
57	5.39	5.44	5.48	5.52	5.57	5.61	5.66	5.70
58	5.46	5.51	5.56	5.60	5.65	5.70	5.74	5.79
59	5.54	5.59	5.64	5.68	5.73	5.78	5.83	5.88
60	5.62	5.67	5.72	5.77	5.83	5.88	5.93	5.99
61	5.70	5.76	5.81	5.87	5.92	5.98	6.04	6.10
62	5.79	5.85	5.91	5.97	6.03	6.09	6.15	6.21
63	5.88	5.95	6.01	6.08	6.14	6.21	6.27	6.34
64	5.99	6.05	6.12	6.19	6.26	6.33	6.40	6.47
65	6.10	6.17	6.24	6.32	6.39	6.47	6.54	6.62
66	6.21	6.29	6.37	6.45	6.53	6.61	6.70	6.78
67	6.34	6.42	6.51	6.60	6.68	6.77	6.86	6.95
68	6.47	6.57	6.66	6.75	6.85	6.94	7.04	7.14
69	6.62	6.72	6.82	6.92	7.03	7.13	7.23	7.34
70	6.78	6.89	6.99	7.11	7.22	7.33	7.44	7.55

Increasing Payment - With Cash Refund: 100 Percent to Survivor

Joint Annuitant's Age

Primary Annuitant's Age	Younger				Same Age	Older		
	4 Years	3 Years	2 Years	1 Year		1 Year	2 Years	3 Years
55	$5.16	$5.20	$5.24	$5.27	$5.31	$5.35	$5.39	$5.43
56	5.22	5.26	5.30	5.34	5.38	5.42	5.46	5.50
57	5.29	5.33	5.37	5.41	5.46	5.50	5.54	5.59
58	5.35	5.40	5.44	5.49	5.54	5.58	5.63	5.67
59	5.43	5.47	5.52	5.57	5.62	5.67	5.72	5.77
60	5.50	5.55	5.61	5.66	5.71	5.76	5.81	5.87
61	5.59	5.64	5.69	5.75	5.81	5.86	5.92	5.97
62	5.67	5.73	5.79	5.85	5.91	5.97	6.03	6.09
63	5.77	5.83	5.89	5.95	6.02	6.08	6.15	6.21
64	5.87	5.93	6.00	6.07	6.14	6.21	6.28	6.35
65	5.91	5.98	6.05	6.13	6.20	6.27	6.35	6.42
66	6.03	6.10	6.18	6.26	6.34	6.42	6.50	6.58
67	6.15	6.23	6.31	6.40	6.48	6.57	6.66	6.74
68	6.28	6.37	6.46	6.55	6.64	6.74	6.83	6.92
69	6.42	6.52	6.62	6.71	6.81	6.91	7.02	7.12
70	6.58	6.68	6.78	6.89	7.00	7.11	7.22	7.33

Increasing Payment - No Cash Refund: 50 Percent to Survivor

Joint Annuitant's Age

Primary Annuitant's Age	Younger				Same Age	Older		
	4 Years	3 Years	2 Years	1 Year	Same Age	1 Year	2 Years	3 Years
55	$5.99	$6.03	$6.08	$6.13	$6.18	$6.23	6.29	6.35
56	6.08	6.13	6.18	6.23	6.29	6.34	6.40	6.46
57	6.19	6.24	6.29	6.34	6.40	6.46	6.52	6.59
58	6.29	6.35	6.40	6.46	6.52	6.58	6.65	6.72
59	6.41	6.46	6.52	6.58	6.65	6.72	6.78	6.86
60	6.53	6.59	6.65	6.72	6.78	6.85	6.93	7.01
61	6.65	6.72	6.79	6.85	6.93	7.00	7.08	7.17
62	6.79	6.86	6.93	7.00	7.08	7.16	7.25	7.34
63	6.93	7.01	7.08	7.16	7.24	7.33	7.42	7.52
64	7.09	7.17	7.25	7.33	7.42	7.52	7.62	7.72
65	7.25	7.34	7.42	7.51	7.61	7.72	7.82	7.94
66	7.43	7.52	7.61	7.71	7.82	7.93	8.05	8.18
67	7.62	7.71	7.82	7.93	8.04	8.16	8.29	8.43
68	7.82	7.93	8.04	8.16	8.28	8.42	8.56	8.71
69	8.04	8.16	8.28	8.41	8.55	8.69	8.84	9.00
70	8.28	8.41	8.54	8.68	8.83	8.99	9.16	9.33

Increasing Payment - With Cash Refund: 50 Percent to Survivor

Joint Annuitant's Age

Primary Annuitant's Age	Younger				Same Age	Older		
	4 Years	3 Years	2 Years	1 Year	Same Age	1 Year	2 Years	3 Years
55	$5.81	$5.85	$5.90	$5.95	$5.99	$6.05	$6.10	$6.16
56	5.90	5.95	6.00	6.05	6.10	6.15	6.21	6.27
57	6.00	6.05	6.10	6.15	6.21	6.27	6.33	6.39
58	6.10	6.16	6.21	6.27	6.33	6.39	6.45	6.52
59	6.21	6.27	6.33	6.39	6.45	6.51	6.58	6.65
60	6.27	6.32	6.38	6.45	6.51	6.58	6.65	6.73
61	6.39	6.45	6.51	6.58	6.65	6.72	6.80	6.88
62	6.52	6.58	6.65	6.72	6.80	6.87	6.96	7.04
63	6.66	6.73	6.80	6.87	6.95	7.04	7.13	7.22
64	6.80	6.88	6.96	7.04	7.12	7.22	7.31	7.41
65	6.89	6.97	7.05	7.14	7.23	7.33	7.43	7.54
66	7.06	7.14	7.23	7.33	7.43	7.53	7.65	7.77
67	7.24	7.33	7.43	7.53	7.64	7.76	7.88	8.01
68	7.43	7.53	7.64	7.75	7.87	8.00	8.13	8.27
69	7.64	7.75	7.87	7.99	8.12	8.26	8.40	8.55
70	7.87	7.99	8.11	8.25	8.39	8.54	8.70	8.86

TABLE 3

Single Life Annuities

Interest Adjustment Factors

Instructions: Find your age (at the expected annuity purchase date) in the left-hand column marked "Annuitant's Age Bracket." Find the column that describes the annuity option you are estimating. Then find the number where the row for your age intersects with the column for your annuity option. Enter that number on the worksheet on line (12).

Annuitant's Age Bracket	Level Payment			Increasing Payment		
	No Added Features	Cash Refund	10-Year Certain	No Added Features	Cash Refund	10-Year Certain
55-59	0.081	0.081	0.080	0.098	0.098	0.096
60-64	0.073	0.073	0.072	0.087	0.087	0.085
65-70	0.064	0.064	0.065	0.075	0.075	0.075

TABLE 4

Joint Life Annuities

Interest Adjustment Factors

Instructions: Find your age (at the expected annuity purchase date) in the left-hand column marked "Primary Annuitant's Age Bracket." Find the column that describes the annuity option you are estimating. (Note: This table applies whether you elect a joint life annuity with or without a cash refund.) Then find the number where the row for your age intersects with the column for your annuity option. Enter that number on the worksheet on line (12).

Primary Annuitant's Age Bracket	Level Payment		Increasing Payment	
	100 percent to survivor	50 percent to survivor	100 percent to survivor	50 percent to survivor
55-59	0.094	0.084	0.117	0.104
60-64	0.087	0.078	0.105	0.093
65-70	0.078	0.069	0.092	0.081

Appendix

Estimating a Monthly Annuity Payment

Use the following worksheet to estimate the amount of the monthly annuity payment that you will receive when your annuity is purchased. The particular annuity option you want to estimate will determine which tables you use.

Annuity choice. Before you begin the worksheet, be sure you can answer the following questions:

❑ Are you estimating a single or a joint life annuity?

❑ If you are estimating a joint life annuity, is it a 100% or a 50% survivor annuity?

❑ Are you estimating a level payment or an increasing payment annuity?

❑ Are you adding either the cash refund or the ten-year certain feature?

Other basic information. In addition to your annuity choice, you will need to know:

❑ Your approximate TSP account balance at the expected annuity purchase date

❑ Your age (and the age of your spouse or other eligible person, if you are estimating a joint life annuity) at the expected annuity purchase date

Estimating an immediate annuity. Use your current age and account balance. Call the TSP Inquiry Line at (504) 255-8777 to find out your account balance, or estimate your balance using your most recent TSP Participant Statement (plus contributions and estimated earnings since the date of that statement).

Estimating an annuity for a later purchase date. Choose an expected annuity purchase date (e.g., five years from now), and determine how old you (and your joint annuitant, if applicable) will be at that date. Also estimate the amount of money that will be in your TSP account at that time (see "Projecting Your Account Balance" in the *Summary of the Thrift Savings Plan for Federal Employees*).

Completing the worksheet. The worksheet has three sections:

Part A — Participant information

Part B — Preliminary estimate of monthly annuity payment. This estimate is not adjusted

for current interest rate levels. It is based on monthly annuity payment factors using an 8% interest rate index. You may want to stop at the end of Part B if the preliminary estimate meets your need to compare several types of annuities, or to have a rough idea of what your annuity income will be.

Part C — Estimate adjusted to current interest rate levels. The current interest rate index used in TSP annuity calculations is based on a three-month moving average of the 10-year U.S. Treasury rate. If the current interest rate index is 8%, there is no adjustment to your preliminary monthly payment estimate. If the current interest rate index is higher than 8%, the adjustment will increase your estimate. If the current interest rate index is lower than 8%, the adjustment will decrease your estimate.

To obtain the current interest rate index to adjust your estimate, call 1-800-447-8777. (Once your annuity is purchased, the monthly payment you receive will not change when interest rates change.)

Using the tables. To estimate one of the single life annuity options, use Tables 1 and 3.

To estimate one of the joint life annuity options, use Tables 2 and 4. These tables are used for estimating either the joint life with spouse annuity or the joint life with other survivor annuity. (You must know both your age and the difference in age between you and your joint annuitant.)

All of the tables are based on your age at the time your annuity is purchased. Joint life annuity tables also take into account the age of the joint annuitant. (Neither the sex of the annuitants nor status as head-of-household affects the amount of the monthly annuity payment.)

The tables include the age ranges that cover most Federal employees (and their joint annuitants) who are at or near retirement age. If your age or your joint annuitant's age is not covered by these tables, you may consult the *Thrift Savings Plan Comprehensive Tables of Annuity Rates.** This volume is available in your agency personnel office.

---

*Tables 1 and 2 of the Comprehensive Tables are based on the 1988 annuity contract rates. The current contract rates may increase your monthly benefit by a few cents. The current annuity factors may be estimated by multiplying the factors in these tables by 1.00096. The interest rate adjustment factors (Tables 3 and 4) are unchanged.

Worksheet for Estimating a Monthly Annuity Payment

This worksheet can be used to estimate the monthly annuity payment that you will receive when your annuity is purchased. Enter information in Part A that is appropriate for your expected annuity purchase date.

		Example	Your estimate

A. Participant information

(1) Annuity option — *Joint with spouse—50%, level payments, no cash refund*

(2) Your age — **62**

(3) Your joint annuitant's age (if a joint life annuity) — **59**

(4) Age difference (if a joint life annuity):
line (2) − line (3)
Joint annuitant is — **3** (younger)/older years; years younger/older

(5) Estimated TSP account balance — $ **19,962.08** $ ____

B. Preliminary estimate of monthly annuity payment

(6) Estimated amount available for annuity in thousands of dollars: line (5) ÷ $1,000 — $ **19.96208** $ ____

(7) Monthly annuity factor per $1,000 account balance:
For single life annuity, use Table 1.
For joint life annuity, use Table 2. — $ **8.84** $ ____

(8) Preliminary estimate of monthly annuity payment: line (6) × line (7) — $ **176.46** $ ____

C. Estimate adjusted to current interest rate levels

(9) Current interest rate index (call 1-800-447-8777) — **8.625**

(10) Interest rate index used in monthly annuity factor tables — **8.000** — **8.000**

(11) Index increase (decrease): line (9) − line (10) — **.625**

(12) Interest adjustment factor:
For single life annuity, use Table 3.
For joint life annuity, use Table 4. — **.078**

(13) Adjustment multiplier: line (11) × line (12) — **.049**

(14) Increase (decrease) to estimate: line (8) × line (13) — $ **8.65** $ ____

(15) Estimated monthly annuity payment adjusted for current interest rate: line (8) + line (14) — $ **185.11** $ ____

THRIFT SAVINGS PLAN
ELECTION FORM

TSP-1

Use this form to:
- Start or change your contributions to the Thrift Savings Plan (TSP)
- Stop your contributions to the TSP
- Indicate how you want your future contributions to be invested in the three TSP Funds

Before completing this form, please read the *Summary of the Thrift Savings Plan for Federal Employees* and the instructions on the back of this form. Type or print all information. **Return the completed form to your agency employing office.** Do not remove your copy. Your agency will return it to you after completing Section VII.

I.
INFORMATION ABOUT YOU

1. _____
   Name *(Last)*   *(First)*   *(Middle)*

2. _____
   Street Address   City   State   Zip Code

3. _____
   Social Security Number

4. (___) _____
   Daytime Phone *(Area Code and Number)*

5. _____
   Date of Birth *(Month/Day/Year)*

6. _____
   Office Identification *(Agency and Organization)*

II.
AMOUNT OF YOUR CONTRIBUTIONS
If you complete this section, you must also complete Section IV

Complete either Part A or Part B of this section.

Part A. To contribute to your TSP account, enter **either** a whole percentage of your basic pay per pay period (Item 7) **or** a whole dollar amount per pay period (Item 8).

Part B. If you are a FERS employee who is not, and will not be, contributing to your TSP account at this time, but you are allocating your Agency Automatic (1%) Contributions, check Item 9.

7. _____.0%   **OR**   8. $ _____.00

9. ☐ (Noncontributing FERS)

III.
STOPPING YOUR CONTRIBUTIONS
Do not complete Section II. FERS employees must also complete Section IV.

To stop your contributions to the TSP, check Item 10 and sign and date Items 15 and 16. If you are a FERS employee, your Agency Automatic (1%) Contributions will continue. You must complete Section IV to show how you want these contributions to be divided among the three TSP Funds.

10. ☐ I want to stop contributing to my TSP account. I understand that my payroll deductions will stop at the end of the pay period in which my agency employing office accepts this form.

IV.
ALLOCATING CONTRIBUTIONS
You must also complete Section II or III.

Show how you want future contributions to your account to be divided among the G, F, and C Funds. Enter the percentage (in multiples of 5%) that you want invested in each Fund. Do not use dollar amounts. The total of Items 11, 12, and 13 must equal 100%. If you are a FERS employee, the percentages that you choose will be applied to all contributions to your account, including Agency Automatic (1%) Contributions and Agency Matching Contributions.

If you invest in either the F or C Fund, you must sign Item 14; otherwise, your form will be returned to you unprocessed.

11. **G Fund** Government Securities Investment Fund	_____.0%
12. **F Fund** Fixed Income Index Investment Fund	_____.0%
13. **C Fund** Common Stock Index Investment Fund	_____.0%
	Total	100.0%

V.
ACKNOWLEDGEMENT OF RISK
Also sign Section VI.

I have chosen to invest in the F and/or C Fund. I understand that I am making this investment at my own risk. I also understand that I am not protected by either the U.S. Government or the Federal Retirement Thrift Investment Board against investment loss in the F or C Fund, and that neither the U.S. Government nor the Federal Retirement Thrift Investment Board guarantees a return on my investment.

14. _____
    Participant's Signature

VI.
SIGNATURE

You must sign Item 15 and date Item 16; otherwise, your form will be returned to you unprocessed.

15. _____
    Participant's Signature

16. _____
    Date Signed

VII.
FOR EMPLOYING OFFICE USE ONLY

17. _____ Payroll Office Number

18. _____ Agency Code

19. _____ Effective Date

20. _____ TSP SCD (Optional)

21. _____
    Signature of Employing Office Official

22. _____ Acceptance Date

23. _____ New Eligibility Date if Item 10 Is Checked

24. _____ Remarks

Form TSP-1 Revised 2/91

GENERAL INFORMATION

You can start, change, or allocate your contributions only during the TSP open seasons (May 15 - July 31 and November 15 - January 31). **However**, you may submit the form at any time to **stop** your contributions (see Section III). Your Form TSP-1 will stay in effect until you submit another one or leave Federal service. You may not withdraw your TSP account balance while you are still employed by the Federal Government.

If you change your address, notify your agency employing office immediately so that they can correct your records for your TSP account.

INSTRUCTIONS FOR SECTION I

Complete all items in this section.

INSTRUCTIONS FOR SECTION II

Complete Part A to start, continue, or change your TSP contributions.

> **Item 7, Percentage of Basic Pay Per Pay Period.** If you are covered by FERS or an equivalent retirement plan, you may contribute up to 10% of your basic pay each pay period. If you are covered by CSRS or an equivalent retirement plan, you may contribute up to 5% of your basic pay each pay period.

> **Item 8, Dollar Amount Per Pay Period.** The dollar amount you contribute cannot exceed the percentages shown above. You can contribute as little as $1 per pay period.

Complete Part B only if you are covered by FERS **and** you choose not to contribute or are not eligible to contribute to your account at this time (that is, if you are submitting this form only to allocate your Agency Automatic (1%) Contributions in Section IV).

INSTRUCTIONS FOR SECTION III

Complete this section to stop your contributions. If you stop contributing during an open season, you will not be able to start again until the next TSP open season. If you stop contributing outside of an open season, you will not be able to start again until the second open season after this form is accepted by your agency employing office.

If you are a FERS employee who is stopping your contributions, you must also complete Section IV to show how you want your Agency Automatic (1%) Contributions to be divided among the G, F, and C Funds. You may submit another Form TSP-1 to change your allocation in any subsequent open season, even if you are not contributing to your account.

INSTRUCTIONS FOR SECTION IV

Complete this section to indicate how you want future contributions to be invested in the three TSP Funds. All participants may invest all or any portion of the contributions to their accounts in any of the three Funds. If you do not complete this section, your form will be returned to you unprocessed (unless you are a CSRS employee and you are submitting this form to stop your contributions).

INSTRUCTIONS FOR SECTION V

Complete this section if you invest in the F or C Fund. There is a risk of investment loss in both the F and C Funds. Read the acknowledgement of risk carefully before you sign it.

INSTRUCTIONS FOR SECTION VI

You must complete this section (even if you completed Section V).

INSTRUCTIONS FOR SECTION VII

(to be completed by employing office)

Enter the effective date of the action in Item 19. If this form is accepted during the portion of the open season that precedes the election period, the form should be made effective as of the first pay period that begins on or after the first day of the election period. (The election period is the last month of the open season.) If the form is accepted during the election period, it should be made effective as soon as administratively feasible, but no later than the first day of the pay period following acceptance of the form.

If a participant chooses to stop contributing to the TSP (Section III), deductions should stop at the end of the pay period in which the form is accepted, and the allocations should begin at the start of the following period.

Enter the acceptance date in Item 22. This is the date that the form is accepted by the agency employing office and is certified for processing. Item 23 is the date on which a participant may resume contributing to the TSP after stopping his or her contributions.

PRIVACY ACT NOTICE

We are authorized to request this information under Title 5, U.S. Code Chapter 84, Federal Employees' Retirement System, Subchapter III, Thrift Savings Plan. Executive Order 9397 authorizes us to ask for your Social Security number, which will be used to identify your account. We will use the information you give us to process your Thrift Savings Plan Election Form (TSP-1). This information will be placed in your Official Personnel Folder. This information may be shared with other Federal agencies in order to administer your account or for statistical, auditing, or archiving purposes. It may also be shared with Federal, state, and local agencies to determine benefits under their programs, to obtain information necessary under this program, or to report income for tax purposes. In addition, we may share this information with the Parent Locator Service, Department of Health and Human Services, for the purpose of enforcing child support obligations against the TSP participant. We may share this information with law enforcement agencies when they are investigating a violation of civil or criminal law. We may give this information to financial institutions, private sector audit firms, annuity vendors, current spouses and, to a limited extent, former spouses and beneficiaries. Finally, this information may also be disclosed to others on your written request. While the law does not require you to give any of the information we are asking for on this form, it may not be possible to process the actions you request by this form if you do not give us this information.

THRIFT SAVINGS PLAN
DESIGNATION OF BENEFICIARY
INFORMATION AND INSTRUCTIONS

TSP-3

This Designation of Beneficiary Form is to be used only for the disposition of amounts that are due and payable from your Thrift Savings Plan (TSP) account upon your death. It is **not** the same as Standard Form 3102, Designation of Beneficiary for Federal Employees' Retirement System; Standard Form 2808, Designation of Beneficiary, Civil Service Retirement System; Standard Form 1152, Designation of Beneficiary, Unpaid Compensation of Deceased Civilian Employee; or Standard Form 2823, Designation of Beneficiary, Group Life Insurance Program. To be valid, a Form TSP-3, Designation of Beneficiary, must be received by the participant's agency employing office (or the National Finance Center, if separated) *before* the death of the participant.

It is only necessary to designate a beneficiary if you want payment to be made in a way other than the order of precedence shown below.

Keep your designation current. If your family status changes (e.g., marriage, divorce, death), you may want to change your designation.

Submit the completed form to your agency employing office. If you are no longer employed by the Government, mail the form to:

National Finance Center, Thrift Savings Plan Service Office, P.O. Box 61500, New Orleans, LA 70161-1500

You will receive a copy of the certified form for your records.

ORDER OF PRECEDENCE	If you die without designating a beneficiary, the amounts that are due and payable from your Thrift Savings Plan account (as described in Section 8433(g) of Title 5, USC) will be payable to the person or persons who are alive at the date of your death, in the following order of precedence:

1. To your widow or widower.
2. If none of the above, to your child or children and descendants of deceased children, by representation.
3. If none of the above, to your parents or the surviving parent.
4. If none of the above, to the duly appointed executor or administrator of your estate.
5. If none of the above, to any other of your next of kin who is entitled under the laws of your domicile on the date of your death.

In the order of precedence listed above, child includes a natural child and an adopted child, but does not include a stepchild; parent does not include a stepparent, unless you have been adopted by the stepparent.

GENERAL INSTRUCTIONS	Type or print all entries on this form in ink (typewriting preferred). **This form must not have any erasures or alterations.**

You may change your designation at any time and without the knowledge or consent of any beneficiary. This right cannot be waived or restricted. A change or cancellation of beneficiary in a last will or testament or any other document that has not been witnessed and filed as required by the Federal Retirement Thrift Investment Board regulations in 5 CFR 1650.2(a)(1) has no force for the disposition of your TSP account. It is not necessary to file a new Designation of Beneficiary when your name or address changes, although you may do so if you wish.

INSTRUCTIONS FOR SECTION II	You may name as a beneficiary any person, firm, corporation, trust, or legal entity (except an agency of the Federal or District of Columbia governments), or your estate. You may designate more than one beneficiary. If you need additional space use a separate Form TSP-3 or a blank sheet of paper with your name, address, and social security number on it. Number each page and use the same date on each page. The examples printed on the back of this page show you how to name a beneficiary or cancel a prior Designation of Beneficiary.

For each beneficiary, enter the last/first/middle name, address, social security number (SSN), date of birth, and relationship to you. If the beneficiary is a firm, corporation, or other legal entity, enter the name and address of the legal representative; leave date of birth blank and enter the employer identification number (EIN) on the SSN line. Enter the name of the firm on the relationship line. If the beneficiary is a trust, enter the name and address of the trustee; enter "trustee" and the name of the trust on the relationship line and the date the trust was established as the date of birth. Enter the EIN on the SSN line. If the beneficiary is an estate, enter the name and address of the executor; enter "executor" and the name of the estate on the relationship line and leave date of birth blank. Enter the EIN on the SSN line. You may also designate one or more contingent beneficiaries as shown in the examples.

Indicate the percentage or fractional share of your TSP account to be paid to each beneficiary. Do not mix percentages and fractions. Shares must add up to 100 percent if percentages are used; they must add up to 1 if fractions are used. If no shares are indicated, your TSP account will be distributed equally among all named beneficiaries.

You and two witnesses who are not named as beneficiaries must sign and date the form and any additional pages.

INSTRUCTIONS FOR SECTION III	The Designation of Beneficiary must be signed by you and two witnesses over the age of 21 who are not named as beneficiaries. The signature of any witness who is also a beneficiary is not valid.

INSTRUCTIONS FOR SECTION IV	The certifying official should review the form for completeness and to ensure that there are no erasures or alterations.

The employing agency (or, in the case of a separated employee, the TSP Service Office) will complete this section, and provide the employee with his or her certified form.

For a current employee, the employing agency should place the original in the employee's Official Personnel Folder.

PRIVACY ACT NOTICE. We are authorized to request this information under Title 5, U.S. Code Chapter 84, Federal Employees' Retirement System, Subchapter III, Thrift Savings Plan. Executive Order 9397 authorizes us to ask for your social security number, which will be used to identify your account. We will use the information you give us to determine who your beneficiary(ies) are for amounts due and payable from your Thrift Savings Plan account. This information may be placed in your Official Personnel Folder. This information may be shared with other Federal agencies in order to administer your account or for statistical, auditing or archiving purposes. It may also be shared with Federal, state, and local agencies to determine benefits under their programs, to obtain information necessary under this program, or to report income for tax purposes. In addition, we may share this information with the Parent Locator Service, Department of Health and Human Services, for the purpose of enforcing child support obligations against the TSP participant. We may share this information with law enforcement agencies when they are investigating a violation of civil or criminal law. We may give this information to financial institutions, private sector audit firms, annuity vendors, current spouses and, to a limited extent, former spouses and beneficiaries. Finally, this information may also be disclosed to others on your written request. While the law does not require you to give any of the information we are asking for on this form, it may not be possible to process the actions you request by this form if you do not give us this information.

FORM TSP-3 (Revised 8/88)

EXAMPLES OF DESIGNATION OF BENEFICIARY

I. DESIGNATING ONE BENEFICIARY

1. **Morgan** (Name *(Last)*)   **Katherine** (*First*)   **Anne** (*Middle*)   Share **100%**
   - **1279 Lake Avenue** (Street Address)   **New Orleans,** (City)   **LA** (State)   **70124** (Zip Code)
   - **6/22/42** (Date of Birth *(Month, Day, Year)*)   **000-00-0000** (Social Security Number)   **Sister** (Relationship)

> Do not write name as K.A. Morgan or as Mrs. Keith H. Morgan

II. DESIGNATING MORE THAN ONE BENEFICIARY

1. **Larson** (Name *(Last)*)   **Susan** (*First*)   **Maria** (*Middle*)   Share **¼**
   - **4231 Oregano Street** (Street Address)   **Cincinnati,** (City)   **OH** (State)   **45239** (Zip Code)
   - **9/07/50** (Date of Birth *(Month, Day, Year)*)   **000-00-0000** (Social Security Number)   **Sister** (Relationship)

2. **Larson** (Name *(Last)*)   **Elliott** (*First*)   **Harris** (*Middle*)   Share **¼**
   - **4231 Oregano Street** (Street Address)   **Cincinnati,** (City)   **OH** (State)   **45239** (Zip Code)
   - **4/20/52** (Date of Birth *(Month, Day, Year)*)   **000-00-0000** (Social Security Number)   **Brother** (Relationship)

3. **Steinway** (Name *(Last)*)   **Sarah** (*First*)   **Ruth** (*Middle*)   Share **½**
   - **P.O. Box 812** (Street Address)   **Covington,** (City)   **KY** (State)   **40117** (Zip Code)
   - **12/02/60** (Date of Birth *(Month, Day, Year)*)   **000-00-0000** (Social Security Number)   **Friend** (Relationship)

> Be sure that the shares to be paid to the beneficiaries add up to 100 percent if using percentages, or to 1 if using fractions.

III. DESIGNATING A CONTINGENT BENEFICIARY

If living:

1. **Kraus** (Name *(Last)*)   **Michael** (*First*)   **Thomas** (*Middle*)   Share **100%**
   - **6287 Laurel Post Drive** (Street Address)   **Stone Mountain,** (City)   **GA** (State)   **30058** (Zip Code)
   - **3/12/36** (Date of Birth *(Month, Day, Year)*)   **000-00-0000** (Social Security Number)   **Father** (Relationship)

Otherwise to:

2. **Richardson** (Name *(Last)*)   **Cecilia** (*First*)   **Jean** (*Middle*)   Share **100%**
   - **6287 Laurel Post Drive** (Street Address)   **Stone Mountain,** (City)   **GA** (State)   **30058** (Zip Code)
   - **8/16/70** (Date of Birth *(Month, Day, Year)*)   **000-00-0000** (Social Security Number)   **Sister** (Relationship)

IV. DESIGNATING A TRUST

1. **Manos** (Name *(Last)*)   **Eric** (*First*)   **Paul** (*Middle*)   Share **100%**
   - **1111 Delaware Lane** (Street Address)   **New York,** (City)   **NY** (State)   **14607** (Zip Code)
   - **7/22/86** (Date of Birth *(Month, Day, Year)*)   **00-0000000** (Social Security Number)   **Trustee-John P. Manos Trust** (Relationship)

V. DESIGNATING AN ESTATE

1. **McClain** (Name *(Last)*)   **Marilyn** (*First*)   **Diane** (*Middle*)   Share **100%**
   - **150 Rossmoyne Drive** (Street Address)   **Alameda,** (City)   **CA** (State)   **94510** (Zip Code)
   - (Date of Birth *(Month, Day, Year)*)   **00-0000000** (Social Security Number)   **Executor- Estate of Ruth R. Jones** (Relationship)

VI. CANCELING A DESIGNATION OF BENEFICIARY SO THAT THE AMOUNT DUE WILL BE PAID ACCORDING TO THE ORDER OF PRECEDENCE

1. **Cancel prior designations** (Name *(Last)*)   (*First*)   (*Middle*)   Share
   - (Street Address)   (City)   (State)   (Zip Code)
   - (Date of Birth *(Month, Day, Year)*)   (Social Security Number)   (Relationship)

FORM TSP-3 (Revised 8/88)

THRIFT SAVINGS PLAN
DESIGNATION OF BENEFICIARY

TSP-3

I. INFORMATION ABOUT YOU

1. _____
Name *(Last)* _____ *(First)* _____ *(Middle)*

2. _____
Street Address

_____
City _____ State _____ Zip Code

3. _____ 4. _____ 5. _____
Social Security Number _____ Date of Birth *(Month, Day, Year)* _____ Daytime Phone

II. DESIGNATING YOUR BENEFICIARIES

I designate the beneficiary(ies) named below to receive those amounts from my Thrift Savings Plan account that are due and payable after my death. I understand that this Designation of Beneficiary relates only to money due as defined in Section 8433 (g) of Title 5, USC, Chapter 84. It does not affect any other benefit that may apply to my Government service. I also understand that this Designation of Beneficiary will remain in effect until I replace or revoke it in writing as explained in the accompanying instructions. This signed Designation of Beneficiary cancels any previous Thrift Savings Plan Designation of Beneficiary.

1. _____ | Share |
Name *(Last)* _____ *(First)* _____ *(Middle)*

_____
Street Address _____ City _____ State _____ Zip Code

_____
Date of Birth *(Month, Day, Year)* _____ Social Security Number _____ Relationship

2. _____ | Share |
Name *(Last)* _____ *(First)* _____ *(Middle)*

_____
Street Address _____ City _____ State _____ Zip Code

_____
Date of Birth *(Month, Day, Year)* _____ Social Security Number _____ Relationship

3. _____ | Share |
Name *(Last)* _____ *(First)* _____ *(Middle)*

_____
Street Address _____ City _____ State _____ Zip Code

_____
Date of Birth *(Month, Day, Year)* _____ Social Security Number _____ Relationship

☐ Check here if additional pages are used to designate beneficiaries. All pages submitted must be completed, signed by you, and witnessed. This is page number _____ of _____ pages.

I understand that the share of any beneficiary who dies before I die will be distributed equally among the surviving beneficiaries or entirely to the surviving beneficiary. This Designation of Beneficiary will be void if none of the designated beneficiaries is alive at the time of my death. This Designation of Beneficiary will not be valid if it contains any erasures or alterations.

I have the right to cancel or change any designation of my Thrift Savings Plan beneficiary at any time, without the knowledge or consent of the beneficiary(ies).

_____ _____
Signature of Employee _____ Date Signed

III. WITNESSES TO SIGNATURE

_____ _____
Typed or Printed Name of Witness _____ Typed or Printed Name of Witness

_____ _____
Signature of Witness _____ Signature of Witness

IV. OFFICIAL USE ONLY

_____ _____
Typed or Printed Name of Agency Official _____ Phone Number

_____ _____
Certification of Receipt *(Agency Official's Signature)* _____ Date Signed

FORM TSP-3 (Revised 8/88)

OFFICIAL PERSONNEL FOLDER—ORIGINAL

THRIFT SAVINGS PLAN
STATEMENT REGARDING SPOUSES

TSP-6

Read the instructions on the back before you complete this form. **You must complete all sections of the form.** Legal documentation is not required. Please type or print all information. Make a copy for your records and return the signed original form to: Thrift Savings Plan Service Office, National Finance Center, P.O. Box 61500, New Orleans, LA 70161-1500.

I.
INFORMATION
ABOUT YOU

1. Name _____
            (Last)   (First)   (Middle)

2. ____ – ____ – _____   **3.** _____   **4.** (____) ____
Social Security Number   Date of Birth (Month/Day/Year)   Daytime Phone

5. Address _____
         Street address or box number

6. City _____ **7.** _____ **8.** _____
                                   State/Country   Zip Code

II.
INFORMATION
ABOUT YOUR
MARITAL STATUS

9. Are you married (even if separated from your spouse)? ☐ **Yes.** Complete Items 10-12.   ☐ **No.** Skip to Section III.

10. Spouse's Name _____
                  (Last)   (First)   (Middle)

11. ____ – ____ – _____   **12.** Is your spouse's address the same as yours?
Spouse's Social Security Number

                  ☐ **Yes.** Skip to Section III.   ☐ **No.** Complete Items 13-16 or Item 17.

13. Spouse's Address _____
                         Street address or box number

14. City _____ **15.** _____ **16.** _____
                                   State/Country   Zip Code

17. ☐ Check here if you do not know your spouse's address.

III.
ADDITIONAL
INFORMATION

18. Are you eligible for retirement benefits, either immediate or deferred? Generally, this means you have five or more years of creditable civilian service, or you are eligible for disability retirement or certain workers' compensation benefits. **(See back of form.)**

                  ☐ **Yes.** Skip to Section IV.   ☐ **No.** Go to Item 19.

19. Do you have a former spouse? (You have a former spouse for TSP purposes if **all three** of the following conditions are met: (a) you were formerly married for at least 9 months — regardless of whether you were employed by the Federal Government during your marriage, and (b) you have at least 18 months of creditable civilian service, and (c) your marriage ended in divorce or court-approved annulment. **(See back of form.)**

☐ **Yes. I have a former spouse as defined above.** Complete the rest of this section.   ☐ **No. I do not have a former spouse as defined above.** Skip to Section IV.

20. Former Spouse's Name _____
                           (Last)   (First)   (Middle)

21. Former Spouse's Address _____
                              Street address or box number

22. City _____ **23.** _____ **24.** _____
                                   State/Country   Zip Code

25. ☐ Check here if you do not know your former spouse's address.

Complete Items 26-32 ☞ if you have more than one former spouse.

26. Former Spouse's Name _____
                           (Last)   (First)   (Middle)

27. Former Spouse's Address _____
                              Street address or box number

28. City _____ **29.** _____ **30.** _____
                                   State/Country   Zip Code

31. ☐ Check here if you do not know this former spouse's address.

32. ☐ Check here if you have more than two former spouses. **(Attach separate sheet; see back of form.)**

IV.
CERTIFICATION

I certify under penalty of perjury that the information that I have provided is true to the best of my knowledge. **Warning:** Any intentional false statement in this information or willful misrepresentation concerning it is a violation of the law that is punishable by a fine of as much as $10,000 or imprisonment for as long as 5 years, or both (18 USC 1001).

33. _____   **34.** _____
     Participant's Signature   Date

Form TSP-6 (Revised 4/92)
PREVIOUS EDITION OBSOLETE

Make a Copy for Your Files

GENERAL INFORMATION	When you make a decision regarding the withdrawal of your TSP account, we must obtain certain information regarding your marital status in order to fulfill legal requirements to notify your spouse and former spouses or to obtain a waiver of your spouse's right to an annuity. Spouse notice and waiver requirements are shown in the chart below.

You must complete this form if your vested account balance is greater than $3,500. If your vested account balance is $3,500 or less at disbursement, notice and waiver requirements do not apply and this form is not required.

Retirement System and Eligibility for Retirement Benefits	Requirement*	Exceptions**
FERS — Not eligible for retirement benefits	Notify spouse and former spouse	Whereabouts unknown
FERS — Eligible for retirement benefits	Joint waiver of annuity benefit***	Whereabouts unknown Exceptional circumstances
CSRS — Not eligible for retirement benefits	Notify spouse and former spouse	Whereabouts unknown
CSRS — Eligible for retirement benefits	Notify spouse	Whereabouts unknown

* These requirements do not apply if your vested account balance is $3,500 or less at disbursement.

** If you believe that one of these exceptions applies to you, submit Form TSP-16, Request for Waiver, at the time you make your withdrawal election.

***Form TSP-14, Joint Waiver of Spouse's Annuity, is required for all withdrawal options except a joint life annuity with your spouse, with 50 percent survivor benefit, level payments, and no cash refund.

More information on spouse notice and waiver requirements is contained in the booklet, "Withdrawing Your TSP Account Balance," which your agency should have given you when you left Federal service. If you did not receive the booklet, you can request a copy from the TSP Service Office.

INSTRUCTIONS FOR SECTION I	**You must complete all items in this section.**

INSTRUCTIONS FOR SECTION II	**You must complete this section.** If you are not currently married or have never been married, complete only Item 9.

INSTRUCTIONS FOR SECTION III	**Item 18. You must complete this item.** If you are unsure of your retirement eligibility, contact your former agency employing office or review your copy of Form TSP-18, Validation of Retirement Information, which states whether you are eligible for retirement benefits, either immediate or deferred. Your agency should have given you a copy of Form TSP-18 when you left Federal service.

Item 19. You must complete this item if you are not eligible for retirement benefits. If you are not eligible for retirement benefits and your situation meets all three of the conditions listed in this item, answer yes; by law we must notify your former spouse(s) of your withdrawal election. If any one of the three conditions is not met, answer no; the TSP is not required to notify your former spouse(s). Also, if your former spouse is deceased, answer no.

Item 32. If you have more than two former spouses (according to the criteria listed in Item 19), for each additional former spouse you must provide the information requested in Items 20-24 (or Item 25, if appropriate). Provide this information on an additional sheet of paper along with your name and identifying information (Items 1-4). Please write "Form TSP-6 Attachment" at the top, in the event the attachment becomes separated from your form.

INSTRUCTIONS FOR SECTION IV	**You must sign and date this section.**

PRIVACY ACT NOTICE. We are authorized to request this information under Title 5, U.S. Code Chapter 84, Federal Employees' Retirement System, Subchapter III, Thrift Savings Plan. Executive Order 9397 authorizes us to ask for your Social Security number, which will be used to identify your account. We will use the information you give us to comply with spouse notice and waiver requirements of the TSP. This information may be shared with other Federal agencies in order to administer your account or for statistical, auditing or archiving purposes. It may also be shared with Federal, state, and local agencies to determine benefits under their programs, to obtain information necessary under this program, or to report income for tax purposes. In addition, we may share this information with the Parent Locator Service, Department of Health and Human Services, for the purpose of enforcing child support obligations against the TSP participant. We may share this information with law enforcement agencies when they are investigating a violation of civil or criminal law. We may give this information to financial institutions, private sector audit firms, annuity vendors, current spouses and, to a limited extent, former spouses and beneficiaries. Finally, this information may also be disclosed to others on your written request. While the law does not require you to give any of the information we are asking for on this form, it may not be possible to process the withdrawal of your TSP account if you do not give us this information.

THRIFT SAVINGS PLAN
ELECTION OF BENEFITS

Notice to Participant: If your vested account balance is $3,500 or less, you will be notified about automatic cashout procedures. **Do not submit this form if you want to receive an automatic cashout.**

If you are not eligible for immediate or deferred retirement benefits, you must transfer your vested account balance to an Individual Retirement Account (IRA) or other eligible retirement plan. You are not eligible for any other TSP withdrawal option (except an automatic cashout if your account is $3,500 or less at disbursement).

Note: If, when you separated, you were eligible for disability retirement or workers' compensation benefits, or if you were separated from service after June 30, 1993 as a result of a Reduction in Force (RIF), you have the same TSP withdrawal options as participants who are eligible for immediate retirement benefits.

General Instructions Regarding Spouses' Rights: 5 USC §8351 and §8435 and the regulations of the Federal Retirement Thrift Investment Board specify certain rights for spouses of participants whose accounts are more than $3,500 at disbursement. These rights must be considered before money can be paid out or transferred from a participant's account. These rights differ depending on whether the participant is covered under FERS or CSRS. If your vested account balance is more than $3,500 at disbursement, the following notice and waiver requirements apply, and you must submit a completed Form TSP-6, Statement Regarding Spouses, to the TSP Service Office.

If you are a FERS or CSRS participant who is not eligible for an immediate or deferred retirement, your transfer will be made effective only after the Board has sent to your current spouse and each former spouse a notice that you are transferring your funds.

If you are a married FERS participant who is eligible for an immediate or deferred retirement, your choice of benefits can only be effective when your spouse has either signed a Form TSP-14, Joint Waiver of Spouse's Annuity, or has been provided a survivor annuity.

If you are a married CSRS participant who is eligible for an immediate or deferred retirement, your choice of benefits can only be effective after the Board has sent a notice to your current spouse about your choice.

Note: If, when you separated, you were eligible for disability retirement or workers' compensation benefits, or if you were separated after June 30, 1993 as a result of a RIF, you are subject to the same spouse notice and waiver requirements as participants who are eligible for immediate retirement benefits.

Changing Your Benefit: If you have already chosen a benefit on a previous Form TSP-7, you may choose a different benefit by completing another Form TSP-7. You may only make such a change before the first payment has been made from your TSP account or before an annuity has been purchased. Any change you make must comply with the provisions regarding spouses' rights.

SECTION A - IDENTIFICATION.

1. NAME (Last)	(First)	(Middle)	2. DATE OF BIRTH			3. SOCIAL SECURITY NUMBER
			Month	Day	Year	

4. FIRST LINE ADDRESS	5. SECOND LINE ADDRESS

6. CITY	7. STATE/COUNTRY	8. ZIP CODE	9. DAYTIME PHONE (Area Code and Number)

SECTION B - TRANSFERRING ACCOUNT BALANCE.

Any participant who leaves Government service may choose to transfer the vested amount in his or her Thrift Savings Plan account into an Individual Retirement Account (IRA) or other eligible retirement plan. A participant who is not eligible for immediate or deferred retirement must transfer the vested amount in his or her TSP account into an IRA or other eligible retirement plan.

☐ I choose to transfer the money in my Thrift Savings Plan account to an eligible retirement plan. I understand that I must submit Form TSP-13, Designation of an Eligible Retirement Plan, before this transfer can be made.

10. PARTICIPANT'S SIGNATURE	11. DATE SIGNED

SECTION C - WITHDRAWING ACCOUNT BALANCE (Must be eligible for immediate or deferred retirement).

☐ I choose to withdraw the money in my Thrift Savings Plan account as a single payment or in substantially equal payments. I understand that I must send in Form TSP-12, Application for Equal Payments, indicating the date on which I want payments from my account to begin. I understand these payments will be made monthly and will begin no earlier than the date on which I become eligible for my basic retirement annuity.

12. PARTICIPANT'S SIGNATURE	13. DATE SIGNED

SECTION D - ANNUITY (Must be eligible for immediate or deferred retirement).

☐ I choose to receive an annuity from my Thrift Savings Plan account. I understand that I must send in Form TSP-11, TSP Annuity Benefits, indicating the type of annuity I want and the date I want my annuity payments to begin.

14. PARTICIPANT'S SIGNATURE	15. DATE SIGNED

SECTION E - DEFERRED ELECTION (Must be eligible for immediate or deferred retirement).

☐ I do not wish to make a choice at this time.

16. PARTICIPANT'S SIGNATURE	17. DATE SIGNED

FORM TSP - 7 (Revised 6/93)

MAKE A COPY FOR YOUR FILES

INSTRUCTIONS FOR COMPLETING
ELECTION OF BENEFITS

Please type or print the information on this form. Make a copy for your records, and send the original form to:

Thrift Savings Plan Service Office
National Finance Center
P.O. Box 61500
New Orleans, LA 70161-1500

SECTION A - IDENTIFICATION.

Block 1, Name. Enter your name.

Block 2, Date of Birth. Enter your date of birth.

Block 3, Social Security Number. Enter your 9-digit social security number.

Blocks 4 through 8. Enter your address.

Block 9, Daytime Phone (Area Code and Number). Enter your daytime area code and phone number.

SECTION B - TRANSFERRING ACCOUNT BALANCE.

If you choose to transfer your vested account balance into an IRA or other eligible retirement plan, you must sign and date Blocks 10 and 11. If you are separating from Government service and are not eligible for immediate or deferred retirement, you must choose this option (unless you are taking an automatic cashout of your vested account balance of $3,500 or less at disbursement). If you want to receive an automatic cashout, do not submit this form.

If you choose this option, you must send in a Form TSP-13, Designation of an Eligible Retirement Plan, before this transfer can be made.

SECTION C - WITHDRAWING ACCOUNT BALANCE.

If you are eligible for immediate or deferred retirement and choose to withdraw your account balance as a single payment or in a number of substantially equal payments, you must sign and date Blocks 12 and 13.

If you choose this option, you must send in a Form TSP-12, Application for Equal Payments. These payments will be made monthly and will begin no earlier than the date on which you become eligible for your basic retirement annuity.

SECTION D - ANNUITY.

If you are eligible for immediate or deferred retirement and choose to receive an annuity from your account, you must sign and date Blocks 14 and 15.

If you choose this option, you must send in a Form TSP-11, TSP Annuity Benefits, to indicate the type of annuity and the date you want your payments to begin.

SECTION E - DEFERRED ELECTION.

If you are eligible for immediate or deferred retirement and you do not wish to choose your benefits at the time you separate from Government service, you must sign and date Blocks 16 and 17.

You **must** make a withdrawal election before February 1 of the year following the year in which the **latest** of these events occurs:

(1) You become 65 years of age

(2) You have been eligible for 10 years to participate in the TSP

(3) You separate or retire from Government service.

If you do not make a withdrawal election by the latest of these dates, the Thrift Investment Board will purchase an annuity for you.

 **FEDERAL RETIREMENT THRIFT SAVINGS PLAN** **TSP-11**

TSP ANNUITY BENEFITS

Notice to Participant: You must fill out this form if you chose to receive an immediate or deferred annuity from your Thrift Savings Plan account on Form TSP-7, Election of Benefits. Please make sure that you have filled out this form completely. Incomplete forms will not be processed. You must sign and date this form and mail it to the Thrift Savings Plan Service Office. Because of the various options available for these three basic types of annuities, you may have to fill out additional forms before your annuity begins. See instructions on the back of this form.

SECTION A - IDENTIFICATION.

1. NAME (Last)	(First)	(Middle)	2. DATE OF BIRTH Month / Day / Year	3. SOCIAL SECURITY NUMBER

4. FIRST LINE ADDRESS		5. SECOND LINE ADDRESS	

6. CITY	7. STATE/COUNTRY	8. ZIP CODE	9. DAYTIME PHONE (Area Code and Number)

SECTION B - TYPE OF ANNUITY.

These are the three basic types of annuities that the Thrift Savings Plan offers. For each basic type, we will also be offering a number of options, such as fixed or increasing payments and various forms of death benefits. Before you choose an immediate annuity, you should review the options currently available to you. If you choose a deferred annuity, the options available at that time will be included in the information you will receive approximately 90 days before your annuity is purchased. (Choose one)

	10. *An annuity paid to me while my spouse and I are alive. When one of us dies, I want an annuity paid for the lifetime of whichever one of us survives.*
	11. *An annuity paid to me only during my lifetime.*
	12. *An annuity paid to me and a person having an insurable interest in me as prescribed in regulations issued by the Executive Director. When one of us dies, I want an annuity paid for the lifetime of whichever one of us survives.*

13. NAME OF PERSON WITH INSURABLE INTEREST	14. RELATIONSHIP TO PARTICIPANT

SECTION C - DATE ANNUITY BEGINS.

15. DATE I WANT MY ANNUITY PAYMENTS TO BEGIN Month / Year	I understand that I may delay the date my annuity payments begin. However, my payments must begin no later than April 1 of the year following the year in which I become 70½ years of age. I understand that I may change the date my annuity payments begin at any time before my annuity is purchased.

SECTION D - CERTIFICATION.

I hereby certify, under penalty of perjury, that all information stated on this form is true to the best of my knowledge. **Warning:** Any intentional false statement in this application or willful misrepresentation concerning it is a violation of the law that is punishable by a fine of not more than $10,000 or imprisonment of not more than 5 years or both (18 USC 1001).

16. PARTICIPANT'S SIGNATURE	17. DATE SIGNED

FORM TSP - 11 (8/87)

PRIVACY ACT NOTICE

We are authorized to request this information under Title 5, U.S. Code Chapter 84, Federal Employees' Retirement System, Subchapter III, Thrift Savings Plan. Executive Order 9397 authorizes us to ask for your social security number, which will be used to identify your account. We will use the information you give us in administering the Thrift Savings Plan. We may share this information with the Office of Personnel Management, and it may be placed in your Official Personnel Folder. The information may be shared with other Federal agencies or Congressional offices for certain official purposes. It may also be shared with national, state, and local agencies to determine benefits under their programs, to obtain information necessary under this program, or to report income for tax purposes. In addition, we may share this information with law enforcement agencies when they are investigating a violation of civil or criminal law. Finally, we may give this information to financial institutions, private sector audit firms, annuity vendors, beneficiaries, current spouses and, to a limited extent, former spouses. While the law does not require you to give any of the information we are asking for on this form, it may not be possible to process the form if you do not give us this information.

Make a Copy for Your Files

Additional information on annuity options may be found in the TSP annuity booklet.

Please type or print the information on this form. Send completed forms to:

Thrift Savings Plan Service Office
National Finance Center
P. O. Box 61135
New Orleans, LA 70161-1135

SECTION A - IDENTIFICATION.

Block 1, Name. Enter your name.

Block 2, Date of Birth. Enter your date of birth.

Block 3, Social Security Number. Enter your 9-digit social security number.

Blocks 4 through 8. Enter your address.

Block 9, Daytime Phone (Area Code and Number). Enter your daytime area code and phone number.

SECTION B - TYPE OF ANNUITY. (Choose One)

If you are a FERS participant and you are married at the time your annuity begins, you must choose a joint and survivor annuity or submit a waiver. A joint and survivor annuity is an annuity that provides for a surviving spouse (Block 10). If you do not choose this annuity, you must send in Form TSP-14, Joint Waiver of Spouse's Annuity, signed by both you and your spouse.

If you are a married CSRS participant, and you do not choose a joint and survivor annuity, the TSP Service Office will send a notice to your current spouse in accordance with the Board's regulations before your choice of annuity benefits will become effective.

If you choose Block 12, you must enter the name of the designated person in Block 13. You must also indicate his or her relationship to you in Block 14.

The following people are presumed to have an insurable interest in you:

● a blood or adopted relative closer than a first cousin; or
● your former spouse; or
● a person with whom you are living in a relationship that would constitute a common-law marriage in a jurisdiction that recognizes common-law marriages.

If the person you have chosen does not fit one of these categories, you must send affidavits from one or more people stating (1) that they know of the relationship between you and the person whom you have chosen; and (2) the extent to which the person you have chosen is dependent on you; and (3) why the person you have chosen could reasonably expect to benefit financially from you while you are alive. Affidavits should be sent to the TSP Service Office at the above address.

SECTION C - DATE ANNUITY BEGINS.

Block 15, Date I Want My Annuity Payments To Begin. Enter the month and year you want your annuity payments to begin.

Block 16, Participant's Signature. Sign your name.

Block 17, Date Signed. Enter the date you signed Block 16.

THRIFT SAVINGS PLAN
APPLICATION FOR EQUAL PAYMENTS

TSP-12

If you were eligible for immediate or deferred retirement when you separated from Government service, you have the option of withdrawing your Thrift Savings Plan account in one or more substantially equal payments. If you are a married FERS participant and your vested account balance is more than $3,500, you are required to submit Form TSP-14, Joint Waiver of Spouse's Annuity, before this application can be processed. The TSP Service Office will send a notice to spouses of married CSRS participants before any payments are made.

Note: If, when you separated, you were eligible for disability retirement or workers' compensation benefits, or if you were separated from service after June 30, 1993 as a result of a Reduction in Force (RIF), you are eligible to withdraw your account immediately in one or more equal payments. You are subject to the same spouse notice and waiver requirements as participants who are eligible for immediate retirement benefits.

See instructions on the back of this form.

SECTION A - IDENTIFICATION.

1. NAME (Last) (First) (Middle)	2. DATE OF BIRTH Month Day Year	3. SOCIAL SECURITY NUMBER

4. FIRST LINE ADDRESS	5. SECOND LINE ADDRESS	

6. CITY	7. STATE/COUNTRY	8. ZIP CODE	9. DAYTIME PHONE (Area Code and Number)

SECTION B - PAYMENT SCHEDULE.

I choose to withdraw the vested amount in my Thrift Savings Plan account in one or more substantially equal payments as indicated below. I understand that these payments will be made monthly, and will begin no earlier than the date on which I become eligible for my basic retirement annuity. My choice is indicated below:

10. A single payment					11. DATE I WANT TO RECEIVE MY PAYMENT Month Year
12. Equal monthly payments ▶	13. MAXIMUM NUMBER OF PAYMENTS **OR**	14. MINIMUM PAYMENT AMOUNT $ **OR**	15. ☐	COMPUTE MY MONTHLY PAYMENTS	16. DATE I WANT MY PAYMENTS TO BEGIN Month Year

SECTION C - CERTIFICATION.

I hereby certify, under penalty of perjury, that all statements made in this request are true to the best of my knowledge. **Warning:** Any intentional false statement in this application or willful misrepresentation concerning it is a violation of the law that is punishable by a fine of not more than $10,000 or imprisonment of not more than 5 years or both (18 USC 1001).

17. PARTICIPANT'S SIGNATURE	18. DATE SIGNED

FORM TSP-12 (Revised 6/93)

MAKE A COPY FOR YOUR FILES

INSTRUCTIONS FOR COMPLETING
APPLICATION FOR EQUAL PAYMENTS

Please type or print the information on this form. Make a copy for your records, and send the original form to:

Thrift Savings Plan Service Office
National Finance Center
P.O. Box 61500
New Orleans, LA 70161-1500

SECTION A - IDENTIFICATION.

Block 1, Name. Enter your name.

Block 2, Date of Birth. Enter your date of birth.

Block 3, Social Security Number. Enter your 9-digit social security number.

Blocks 4 through 8. Enter your address.

Block 9, Daytime Phone (Area Code and Number). Enter your daytime area code and phone number.

SECTION B - PAYMENT SCHEDULE.

You may choose to receive the vested amount in your TSP account in one or more substantially equal payments according to one of the payment schedules described in Blocks 10 or 12. The Internal Revenue Service (IRS) requires that monthly payments not be less than a certain amount depending on your age at the time your payments are to begin. These minimum amounts are computed using the IRS Expected Return Multiples Tables. You may choose to receive your funds in a single payment, or you may specify the maximum number of payments or the minimum dollar amount you want to receive. In order to meet the IRS minimum, it may be necessary to pay your funds in fewer payments or in a higher amount than you have requested.

When selecting a date for payments to begin, you should allow two months for processing. We will process your request as soon as possible after all forms have been received.

If you choose:

Block 10, A Single Payment—you will be issued one check for the vested amount in your account.

Block 11, Date I Want To Receive My Payment. Enter the month and year you wish to receive your payment.

If you choose:

Block 12, Equal Monthly Payments—You have three choices:

1. You may enter the maximum number of payments you wish to receive in **Block 13; or**

2. You may enter the minimum monthly payment amount in **Block 14; or**

3. You may check **Block 15** if you want the Thrift Savings Plan System to compute your monthly payments for you using the IRS Expected Return Multiples Tables.

Block 16, Date I Want My Payments To Begin (Month, Year). Enter the month and year you wish your monthly payments to begin. You will receive a check each month, after earnings have been posted to your account.

SECTION C - CERTIFICATION.

Block 17, Participant's Signature. Sign your name.

Block 18, Date Signed. Enter date you signed Block 17.

FPI-LOM

FORM TSP-12 (Revised 6/93)

THRIFT SAVINGS PLAN
DESIGNATION OF
AN ELIGIBLE RETIREMENT PLAN

TSP-13

Use this form to transfer your Thrift Savings Plan (TSP) account to an Individual Retirement Arrangement (IRA) or other eligible retirement plan. Please read the instructions on the back of this form and type or print your responses.

**I.
INFORMATION
ABOUT YOU**

1. Name _____
Last   First   Middle

2. Social Security No. _____ - ___ - _____ **3.** Date of Birth ___ / ___ / ___
Month   Day   Year

4. Address _____
Street address or box number

_____

5. City _____ **6.** _____ **7.** _____
State/Country   Zip Code

8. Daytime Phone (Area Code and Number) (_____) _____ - _____

9. Type of Account   ☐ IRA   ☐ Other Eligible Retirement Plan

10. _____ **11.** _____
Participant's Signature   Date Signed

**II.
INFORMATION
ABOUT THE
IRA OR OTHER
ELIGIBLE PLAN**

*To be completed
by financial
institution/plan
administrator*

The financial institution or the plan administrator must ensure that the plan described in this section is an eligible retirement plan as defined in the Internal Revenue Code. An eligible retirement plan is: an IRA (which is either an Individual Retirement Account or an Individual Retirement Annuity), a tax-qualified employee benefit plan, or an annuity plan described in section 403(a) of the Internal Revenue Code.

Do not submit transfer forms of financial institutions or plans. The institution/plan should retain a copy of this form in order to identify the account to which the check should be deposited when it is received.

12. Make check payable to (plan trustee): _____
Limit response to 25 characters.

13. Contact Person _____
For routing purposes, this name will appear on the check stub.

14. Address _____
Check will be sent to this address.

_____

15. City _____ **16.** _____ **17.** _____
State   Zip Code

18. Plan Name _____

19. Account Number _____

**III.
CERTIFICATION**

*To be completed
by financial
institution/plan
administrator*

I confirm the identity of the above-named TSP participant (Section I) and the accuracy of the information in Section II. As a representative of the financial institution or plan to which the participant's TSP account is being transferred, I certify that the financial institution or plan agrees to receive the funds directly from the TSP and deposit them in an IRA or other eligible retirement plan as indicated in Section II.

20. _____
Typed or Printed Name of Certifying Representative

21. _____
Signature of Certifying Representative

22. (_____) _____ - _____ **23.** _____
Daytime Phone (Area Code and Number)   Date

Form TSP-13 (Revised 11/92)

Make a Copy for Your Files

INSTRUCTIONS	Please be sure to type or print clearly the information requested on this form. You should complete Section I, Information About You. The financial institution or administrator of the plan to which you want to transfer your TSP account should complete Sections II and III. After all sections have been completed, please send the original to:

> Thrift Savings Plan Service Office
> National Finance Center
> P.O. Box 61500
> New Orleans, LA 70161-1500
> (504) 255-6000

Give the representative of the financial institution or plan a copy and keep one for yourself.

Note: The form may be submitted to the TSP Service Office by the financial institution or plan; however, the transfer may be processed more quickly if you submit this form with your other TSP withdrawal forms.

I. **INFORMATION** **ABOUT YOU**	**1-8:** Provide the requested information.

9: Type of Account. Check the box that indicates whether your account will be transferred to an Individual Retirement Arrangement (IRA) or another eligible retirement plan. An Individual Retirement Arrangement is an Individual Retirement Account or an Individual Retirement Annuity. A tax-deferred transfer cannot be made to a regular savings or checking account.

10: Signature. Check that all the information you have provided is accurate and sign your name.

11: Date. Enter the date you signed the form.

II. **INFORMATION** **ABOUT THE** **IRA OR OTHER** **ELIGIBLE** **PLAN**	This section must be completed by the financial institution or plan administrator; the TSP Service Office **cannot** accept the forms of financial institutions or plans. Type or print all information.

Note: If the transfer is to an IRA, the TSP will report this transfer on Form 1099-R. The institution accepting the transfer should submit Form 5498 to the IRS.

12: Make check payable to: This must be the name of the trustee of the plan identified in Item 18. If the plan does not have a trustee, provide the name of the custodian of the plan. Provide the exact name that should appear on the check.

13: Contact Person. Provide the name of the person at the financial institution or plan who is responsible for the account. The check for the TSP account balance will be directed to the attention of this person.

14-17: Address. Provide the address of the financial institution or plan. The IRA or plan must be a trust established inside the United States (i.e., the 50 states and the District of Columbia).

18: Plan Name. Enter the name of the IRA (e.g., Individual Retirement Account of John Doe) or other eligible retirement plan.

19: Account Number. Enter the account number (if available) of the IRA or plan to which the money is to be transferred.

III. **CERTIFICATION**	This section must be completed by the financial institution or plan administrator.

20: Certifying Representative. Type or print the name of the certifying representative.

21: Signature. The certifying representative must read the certification and sign his or her name.

22: Phone. Enter the daytime phone number of the certifying official.

23: Date. The certifying representative must enter the date he or she signed the form.

**TSP** FEDERAL RETIREMENT
THRIFT SAVINGS PLAN   **TSP-14**

JOINT WAIVER OF SPOUSE'S ANNUITY

SECTION A - IDENTIFICATION.

1. NAME (Last)	(First)	(Middle)	2. DATE OF BIRTH Month | Day | Year	3. SOCIAL SECURITY NUMBER
4. FIRST LINE ADDRESS				
5. SECOND LINE ADDRESS				

6. CITY	7. STATE/COUNTRY	8. ZIP CODE	9. DAYTIME PHONE (Area Code and Number)

SECTION B - BENEFIT ELECTION.

I have chosen to receive benefits from my Thrift Savings Plan account that do not provide for a joint and survivor annuity with my current spouse. My choice is indicated below. I understand that my choice cannot be processed unless my current spouse waives his or her rights to a joint and survivor annuity by signing Section C. In addition, I understand that if my current spouse refuses to waive his or her rights, the Executive Director will purchase, at the required time, a joint and survivor annuity with the vested amount in my Thrift Savings Plan account. I have chosen:

10. **To transfer** the money in my account to an IRA or other qualified plan.	11. EFFECTIVE DATE Month | Year
12. **To withdraw** the money in my account in one or more substantially equal payments.	13. EFFECTIVE DATE Month | Year
14. **To receive** an annuity paid to me only during my lifetime.	15. EFFECTIVE DATE Month | Year
16. **To receive** an annuity paid to me during my lifetime and the lifetime of a named person who has an insurable interest in me (other than my current spouse). When one of us dies, the survivor will receive an annuity for his or her lifetime.	17. NAME OF PERSON WITH INSURABLE INTEREST 18. RELATIONSHIP TO PARTICIPANT 19. EFFECTIVE DATE Month | Year

SECTION C - SPOUSE'S WAIVER. To be completed by participant's spouse.

I am aware of the choice of benefits my spouse has made. I understand that by signing below I am giving up my rights to the spouse's annuity benefits and that I am agreeing to the choice indicated in Section B above.

20. TYPED NAME OF SPOUSE	21. SPOUSE'S SIGNATURE	22. DATE SIGNED

SECTION D - CERTIFICATION AND PARTICIPANT'S WAIVER.

I hereby certify, under penalty of perjury, that the above information is correct and true to the best of my knowledge. **Warning:** Any intentional false statement in this application or willful misrepresentation concerning it is a violation of the law that is punishable by a fine of not more than $10,000 or imprisonment of not more than 5 years or both (18 USC 1001).

23. PARTICIPANT'S SIGNATURE	24. DATE SIGNED

FORM TSP - 14 (8/87)

PRIVACY ACT NOTICE

We are authorized to request this information under Title 5, U.S. Code Chapter 84, Federal Employees' Retirement System, Subchapter III, Thrift Savings Plan. Executive Order 9397 authorizes us to ask for your social security number, which will be used to identify your account. We will use the information you give us in administering the Thrift Savings Plan. We may share this information with the Office of Personnel Management, and it may be placed in your Official Personnel Folder. The information may be shared with other Federal agencies or Congressional offices for certain official purposes. It may also be shared with national, state, and local agencies to determine benefits under their programs, to obtain information necessary under this program, or to report income for tax purposes. In addition, we may share this information with law enforcement agencies when they are investigating a violation of civil or criminal law. Finally, we may give this information to financial institutions, private sector audit firms, annuity vendors, beneficiaries, current spouses and, to a limited extent, former spouses. While the law does not require you to give any of the information we are asking for on this form, it may not be possible to process the form if you do not give us this information.

Make a Copy for Your Files

INSTRUCTIONS FOR COMPLETING
JOINT WAIVER OF SPOUSE'S ANNUITY

This form applies to FERS participants only. If you are a CSRS participant, you are not required to complete this form.

Please type or print the information on this form. Send completed forms to:

Thrift Savings Plan Service Office
National Finance Center
P.O. Box 61135
New Orleans, LA 70161-1135

SECTION A - IDENTIFICATION

Block 1, Name. Enter your name.

Block 2, Date of Birth. Enter your date of birth.

Block 3, Social Security Number. Enter your 9-digit social security number.

Blocks 4 through 8. Enter your address.

Block 9, Daytime Phone (Area Code and Number). Enter your daytime area code and phone number.

SECTION B - BENEFIT ELECTION

If you have chosen to receive benefits from your Thrift Savings Plan account that do not provide for a joint and survivor annuity for you and your current spouse, you must check your choice in Block 10, 12, 14, or 16 (check one block only). A joint and survivor annuity with your spouse is one in which the annuity is paid to the participant while the participant and spouse are alive, and when one of them dies, an annuity is paid to the survivor.

If you checked Block 10, you must enter in Block 11, Effective Date, the date you entered in Block 11 of Form TSP - 7, Election of Benefits.

If you checked Block 12, you must enter in Block 13, Effective Date, the date you entered in Block 11 or Block 16, as appropriate, of Form TSP - 12, Application for Equal Payments.

If you checked Block 14, you must enter in Block 15, Effective Date, the date you entered in Block 15 of Form TSP - 11, TSP Annuity Benefits.

If you checked Block 16, you must enter the name of the designated person in Block 17 and that person's relationship to you in Block 18. You must also enter in Block 19, Effective Date, the date you entered in Block 15 of Form TSP - 11, TSP Annuity Benefits.

The following people are presumed to have an insurable interest in you:

- a blood or adopted relative closer than a first cousin; or
- your former spouse; or
- a person with whom you are living in a relationship that would constitute a common-law marriage in a jurisdiction that recognizes common-law marriages.

If the person you have chosen does not fit one of these categories, you must send affidavits from one or more people stating:

1. that they know of the relationship between you and the person whom you have chosen; and
2. the extent to which the person you have chosen is dependent on you; and
3. why the person you have chosen could reasonably expect to benefit financially from you while you are alive.

SECTION C - SPOUSE'S WAIVER. To be completed by participant's spouse.

By completing Blocks 20 through 22, a participant's spouse is indicating that he or she is aware of the benefit choice that the participant made in Section B, and understands that he or she is giving up all rights to the annuity benefits from the participant's Thrift Savings Plan account.

Notice to Participants: We will not accept this form unless it has your spouse's signature. If you cannot obtain your spouse's signature because his or her whereabouts are unknown or because exceptional circumstances make it inappropriate to obtain his or her signature, you may apply to the Executive Director for a waiver of the requirement for the spouse's signature. You must make this request on Form TSP-16, Request for a Waiver of Notice to Spouse or Waiver of Spouse's Consent, and attach the required supporting documentation.

If you are a FERS participant eligible for immediate or deferred retirement and if your current spouse refuses to waive his or her rights to a joint and survivor annuity, you must choose a joint and survivor annuity with your current spouse.

SECTION D - CERTIFICATION AND PARTICIPANT'S WAIVER

Block 23, Participant's Signature. Sign your name.

Block 24, Date Signed. Enter the date you signed Block 23.

THRIFT SAVINGS PLAN
REQUEST FOR WAIVER

TSP-16

See the instructions on the back of this form. Send the completed form to:

National Finance Center, Thrift Savings Plan Service Office, P.O. Box 61500, New Orleans, LA 70161-1500

I. INFORMATION ABOUT YOU

1. Name *(Last)* _____ *(First)* _____ *(Middle)* _____

2. Street Address _____

City _____ State _____ Zip Code _____

3. Social Security Number _____ **4.** Date of Birth *(Month, Day, Year)* _____ **5.** Daytime phone _____

6. I am applying for a Thrift Savings Plan loan *(Check One)* ☐ Yes ☐ No

---

II. REQUEST FOR WAIVER

7. Whereabouts Unknown.

☐ I am covered by the Federal Employees' Retirement System (FERS) and am asking for a waiver of the requirement to: (1) notify my current (or separated) and/or any former spouse or (2) obtain the signature of my current (or separated) spouse because I do not know where the individual is. Each individual is identified below and three notarized affidavits are attached to this form.

☐ I am covered by the Civil Service Retirement System (CSRS) and am asking for a waiver of the requirement to notify my current (or separated) and/or former spouse because I do not know where the individual is. Each individual is identified below and three notarized affidavits are attached to this form.

Name of current (or separated) spouse *(Last, First, Middle)* _____

Name of former spouse *(Last, First, Middle)* _____

Name of former spouse *(Last, First, Middle)* _____

8. Exceptional Circumstances.

☐ **For FERS Employees Only.** I am asking for a waiver of the requirement to obtain the signature of my current (or separated) spouse identified below, because exceptional circumstances make it impossible or inappropriate for me to obtain my spouse's signature. An explanation of these circumstances and a copy of an order or determination of a court or other governmental body which supports the claim of exceptional circumstances are attached.

Name of Spouse *(Last, First, Middle)* _____

III. CERTIFICATION

I certify, under penalty of perjury, that the information listed above is true to the best of my knowledge. **Warning:** Any intentional false statement on this request or willful misrepresentation concerning it is a violation of the law that is punishable by a fine of as much as $10,000 or imprisonment for as long as 5 years, or both (18 USC 1001).

9. _____ Signature of Participant

10. _____ Date Signed

IV. OFFICIAL USE ONLY

11. Retirement System ☐ FERS ☐ CSRS

12. Eligible for immediate or deferred retirement as indicated by the personnel office on the TSP-18 (for withdrawals only). ☐ Yes ☐ No **13.** ☐ Approved ☐ Disapproved

14. _____ Title of Approving Official

15. _____ Signature of Approving Official

16. _____ Date Signed

FORM TSP-16 (Revised 8/88)

INFORMATION AND INSTRUCTIONS

Type or print all entries on this form. Completed forms should be sent to the National Finance Center, Thrift Savings Plan (TSP) Service Office, P.O. Box 61500, New Orleans, LA 70161-1500. You will be notified of the decision of the Federal Retirement Thrift Investment Board.

By law, spouses and former spouses of TSP participants are given certain rights regarding the funds in a participant's TSP account. The Board must honor any qualifying court decree; or order of divorce, annulment, or legal separation; or any court-ordered or court-approved property settlement regarding you and any separated or former spouse which specifically relates to any money in your TSP account. A waiver would have no effect on a qualifying court order or decree.

If you were eligible for immediate or deferred retirement benefits when you left Government service, any decision you make with respect to your TSP account is subject to the following rights of spouses:

- If you are a participant covered by the Federal Employees' Retirement System (FERS), you and your current (or separated) spouse have a right to a joint life annuity with a 50% survivor benefit, level payments, and no cash refund. If you want to make another choice with respect to your account, e.g., transfer to an Individual Retirement Acccount (IRA), you and your current (or separated) spouse must waive that right in writing.
- If you are a participant covered by the Civil Service Retirement System (CSRS), the Board will notify your current (or separated) spouse of your withdrawal request. This notification does not give your spouse any right to the money in your TSP account.

If you were not eligible for immediate or deferred retirement benefits when you left Government service, you must transfer your vested TSP account balance into an IRA or other eligible retirement plan. Before the transfer is made, your current (or separated) spouse and any former spouse(s) will be notified of the transfer. (This applies to both FERS and CSRS employees). This notification does not give your spouse or former spouse(s) any right to the money in your TSP account.

If you are a FERS participant applying for a loan (you must be actively employed), your current (or separated) spouse must consent to your application.

If you are a CSRS participant applying for a loan (you must be actively employed), your current (or separated) spouse will be notified of your application.

If you do not know the whereabouts of your current (or separated) and/or former spouse(s) or if you are a FERS participant and exceptional circumstances make it inappropriate to comply with the consent requirement, you may apply for a waiver of the requirement by completing this form. However, waivers are only granted under limited conditions.

INSTRUCTIONS FOR SECTION I	All employees must complete this section. If you are an active employee applying for a loan, check "Yes" in Item 6. If you are not applying for a loan, check "No."
INSTRUCTIONS FOR SECTION II	**If you are a participant covered by FERS or CSRS,** and you are requesting a waiver because your current (or separated) or former spouse's **whereabouts are unknown,** you must attach three notarized affidavits (by you and two other persons, one of whom is not related to you) to this form. The affidavits must state (1) that your current (or separated) or former spouse(s) cannot be found; (2) give the full name(s) of the spouse and/or former spouse(s); (3) describe the efforts made to locate the individuals; and (4) state that you are requesting a waiver. (A declaration under penalty of perjury may be substituted for an affidavit (28 U.S.C., 1746)).

If you are a participant covered under FERS and written consent of your spouse is required, you may request a waiver if there are **exceptional circumstances** that make it impossible or inappropriate to get your current (or separated) spouse's signature. To request a waiver because of exceptional circumstances, you must attach an explanation of the exceptional circumstances and a copy of an order or determination of a court or other governmental body which supports the claim of exceptional circumstances.

The requirements for a waiver of spousal consent or notice are summarized in the chart below:

Summary of Spousal Notification and Consent Requirements

Activity	Retirement System	Eligible for Basic Annuity*	Requirement	Exception
Withdrawal	FERS	No	Notify spouse and former spouse	Whereabouts unknown
Withdrawal	CSRS	No	Notify spouse and former spouse	Whereabouts unknown
Withdrawal	FERS	Yes	Written consent of spouse	Whereabouts unknown or Exceptional circumstances
Withdrawal	CSRS	Yes	Notify spouse	Whereabouts unknown
Loan	FERS	N/A	Written consent of spouse	Whereabouts unknown or Exceptional circumstances
Loan	CSRS	N/A	Notify spouse	Whereabouts unknown

*Eligible for immediate or deferred basic retirement annuity (generally 5 or more years of creditable civilian service).

INSTRUCTIONS FOR SECTION III	You must sign and date this section certifying that the information you provided is true to the best of your knowledge.
INSTRUCTIONS FOR SECTION IV	Items 11 and 12 are completed by the NFC. The retirement system (FERS and CSRS) indicator is that reflected in the employee's TSP data record. The retirement eligibility is obtained from the TSP-18, Validation of Retirement Information, completed by the employee's former personnel office. Items 13 through 16 are completed by the Board.

FORM TSP-16 (Revised 8/88)

THRIFT SAVINGS PLAN
LOAN APPLICATION

TSP-20

Please read the instructions on the back.
Please type or print your responses.

I. INFORMATION ABOUT YOU

1. Name: _____
Last   First   Middle

2. Date of Birth: ____/____/____
Month Day Year

3. Social Security No.: _____-____-_____

4. Street Address: _____

_____

5. City: _____ **6.** State: _____ **7.** Zip: _____

8. Daytime phone (*area code and number*): (_____) _____-_____

9. Do you have a dual appointment? ☐ Yes ☐ No

10. Pay Schedule (*check box that indicates when you are paid*):
☐ Weekly
☐ Biweekly (*every two weeks, 26 times a year*)
☐ Semimonthly (*twice in each calendar month, 24 times a year*)
☐ Monthly (*once in each calendar month*)
☐ Other (*specify*)_____
_____

II. INFORMATION ABOUT THE LOAN

11. Amount of loan requested: (*You must have at least $1,000 of your own contributions and earnings in your account to be eligible for a loan; you may not borrow less than $1,000.*)

$ _____

12. If the amount you requested is more than the amount of your account available for a loan, do you wish to borrow the maximum available to you?
☐ Yes ☐ No

13. Purpose of loan (*check one only*):
☐ Educational expenses ☐ Purchase of primary
☐ Medical expenses   residence
To apply for a loan for financial hardship, you must use Form TSP-20-H. See the instructions on the back for details.

14. Amount of time to repay:
_____   and   _____
Year(s)   Months

III. INFORMATION ABOUT YOUR SPOUSE

15. Are you married (even if separated from your spouse)? ☐ Yes ☐ No

If yes, please give the name and address of your spouse:

16. Spouse's Name: _____
Last   First   Middle

17. Street Address: _____

18. City: _____ **19.** State: _____ **20.** Zip: _____

21. ☐ Check here if you do not know where your spouse is (or if special circumstances make it impossible to notify your spouse of your loan application or to obtain your spouse's consent for your loan).

22. ☐ Check here if Form TSP-16, Request for Waiver, is attached.

IV. CERTIFICATION AND SIGNATURE

I certify, under penalty of perjury, that the above information is correct and true to the best of my knowledge. Warning: Any intentional false statement in this application or willful misrepresentation concerning it is a violation of the law and is punishable by a fine of as much as $10,000 or imprisonment for as much as five years, or both.

23. Signature: _____ **24.** Date: _____

PRIVACY ACT NOTICE

We are authorized to request this information under Title 5, U.S. Code Chapter 84, Federal Employees' Retirement System, Subchapter III, Thrift Savings Plan. Executive Order 9397 authorizes us to ask for your Social Security number, which will be used to identify your account. We will use the information you give us to process and review your loan application. This information may be shared with other Federal agencies in order to administer your account or for statistical, auditing, or archiving purposes. It may also be shared with Federal, state, and local agencies to determine benefits under their programs, to obtain information necessary under this program, or to report income for tax purposes. In addition, we may share this information with the Parent Locator Service, Department of Health and Human Services, for the purpose of enforcing child support obligations against the TSP participant. We may share this information with law enforcement agencies when they are investigating a violation of civil or criminal law. We may give this information to financial institutions, private sector audit firms, annuity vendors, current spouses, and, to a limited extent, former spouses and beneficiaries. Finally, this information may also be disclosed to others on your written request. While the law does not require you to give any of the information we are asking for on this form, it may not be possible to process the actions you request by this form if you do not give us this information.

Form TSP-20 (Rev. 7/89)
PREVIOUS EDITION OBSOLETE

| **INSTRUCTIONS** | *To apply for a loan, you must have at least $1,000 of your own contributions and earnings in your account.* |

INSTRUCTIONS

To apply for a loan, you must have at least $1,000 of your own contributions and earnings in your account.

Before completing this application, read the booklet entitled, "Thrift Savings Plan Loan Program," which is available from your agency employing office. When you have completed the application, please send it to:

Thrift Savings Plan Service Office
National Finance Center
P.O. Box 61500
New Orleans, Louisiana 70161-1500

Do not send documentation for the amount of the loan with this form.

INFORMATION ABOUT YOU

1-7: Enter the requested information. *Please note that the address you provide on this form will be used only to return your loan agreement to you.* The loan check and all other correspondence regarding the loan will be sent to the address of record for your Thrift Savings Plan account. If the address on your last Participant Statement was incorrect, and you have not asked your agency to change it, please notify your agency personnel or payroll office immediately to ensure that the correct address is provided to the Thrift Savings Plan.

8: Daytime phone (area code and phone number). Enter your daytime phone number with area code. If you have an FTS number, write "FTS" in the area code field and the FTS phone number in the number field (e.g., (FTS) 555-1234).

9: Do you have a dual appointment? If you work at two different Federal Government jobs, this information may be considered in processing your loan.

10: Pay schedule. Your pay schedule is used to compute the amount of your loan payments. If you have a dual appointment, you should check the pay schedule of the payroll office that you want to handle your loan payments.

INFORMATION ABOUT THE LOAN

11: Amount of loan requested. You may not borrow more than the amount that you contributed to the Plan and the earnings on that amount. You may not borrow less than $1,000. To figure out the maximum amount you can borrow, you should use the Worksheet for Estimating Maximum New Loan Amount in the Thrift Savings Plan Loan Program booklet.

You should also be aware that you will be responsible for providing documentation for the amount you wish to borrow, so you should not request more than you will be able to justify.

12: Requested amount too large. If the amount you requested is more than the amount of your account available for a loan, you should indicate whether you want to apply for the amount that is available. If you do, and your Loan Application is otherwise in order, we will send you a Loan Agreement for the available amount. If you do not, we will notify you that you are not eligible for the loan you requested.

13: Purpose of loan. You may use this application to apply for a loan for only the three purposes listed. To apply for a loan for **financial hardship**, you must use Form TSP-20-H, Hardship Loan Application. To obtain Form TSP-20-H, write to the TSP Service Office at the address above, or call (504) 255-6050.

14: Amount of time to repay. For a loan for medical or educational expenses (or for financial hardship), you have between one and four years to repay. For a loan for the purchase of a primary residence, you have between one and fifteen years to repay. If, for example, you want two and one-half years to repay your loan, enter ___2___ and ___6___ .
Year(s)   Months

INFORMATION ABOUT YOUR SPOUSE

15: Are you married (even if separated from your spouse)? If you are married, even if separated from your spouse, check the "Yes" box and complete Items 16 through 22. For your loan to be processed, it is important that you supply the requested information about your spouse.

21-22: Notification or consent of spouse not possible. There is a requirement that your spouse be notified of your loan application if you are covered by the Civil Service Retirement System (CSRS), or equivalent retirement plan, or give consent to your loan if you are covered by the Federal Employees' Retirement System (FERS), or equivalent retirement plan. If your spouse's whereabouts are unknown to you or if you are covered by FERS and exceptional circumstances make it inappropriate to obtain your spouse's consent, we will send you Form TSP-16, Request for Waiver. You may also be able to obtain Form TSP-16 from your agency employing office. If you have already obtained Form TSP-16, you may complete it, attach it to this form, and check the box for Item 22.

CERTIFICATION AND SIGNATURE

23: Signature. Please read the certification and sign your name.

24: Date. Enter the date you signed the form.

THRIFT SAVINGS PLAN
INTERFUND TRANSFER REQUEST

TSP-30

Use this form *only* if you want to change the way the balance currently in your Thrift Savings Plan (TSP) account is invested in the three TSP Funds. (To change the way future contributions to your account are invested, you must submit a new Election Form (TSP-1) to your agency employing office.) You may make four interfund transfers in a calendar year. Before completing this form, please read the information on the back. **Type or print** all information. Return the completed form to:

> National Finance Center
> Thrift Savings Plan Service Office
> P.O. Box 60012
> New Orleans, LA 70161-0012

Forms received by the TSP Service Office by the 15th of the month will be effective as of the last day of that month. Forms received after the 15th will be effective as of the last day of the following month. **DO NOT submit this form to your agency. Your agency cannot process it.**

I.
INFORMATION
ABOUT YOU
	1. Name _____
	           (Last) *(First)* *(Middle)*
	
	2. Social Security No. _ _ _ – _ _ – _ _ _ _ **3.** Date of Birth _ _ / _ _ / _ _
	                                                      Month Day Year

II. **YOUR** **TRANSFER** **DECISION**	Show how you want your current account balance to be divided among the G, F, and C Funds as a result of the interfund transfer. Enter the percentage (in multiples of 5%) of your account balance that you want to be invested in each of the Funds. Do not use dollar amounts. The total of Items 4, 5, and 6 must equal 100%. The percentages that you choose will be applied to the total balance in your account (including, if you are a FERS employee, your Agency Automatic (1%) and Matching Contributions); they will not apply to future contributions or earnings. **4. G Fund** Government Securities Investment Fund _____.0% **5. F Fund** Fixed Income Index Investment Fund _____.0% **6. C Fund** Common Stock Index Investment Fund _____.0% **Total** 100.0%

III. **ACKNOWLEDGE-** **MENT OF RISK** *Also sign Section IV.*	If you invest in either the F or C Fund, you must sign Item 7; otherwise, your interfund transfer will not be processed. I have chosen to invest in the F and/or C Fund. I understand that I am making this investment at my own risk. I also understand that I am not protected by either the U.S. Government or the Federal Retirement Thrift Investment Board against investment loss in the F or C Fund, and that neither the U.S. Government nor the Federal Retirement Thrift Investment Board guarantees a return on my investment. **7.** _____ Participant's Signature

IV.
SIGNATURE
	You must sign Item 8 and date Item 9; otherwise, your interfund transfer will not be processed. Send the completed form, with your original signature, to the TSP Service Office at the address at the top of this form. Do not send a photocopy of the signed form.
	
	8. _____ - **9.** _____
	      Participant's Signature Date Signed
	
	10. (____) _____ ☐ FTS ☐ Commercial/Residential
	      Daytime Phone *(Area Code and Number)*

PRIVACY ACT **NOTICE**	We are authorized to request this information under Title 5, U.S. Code Chapter 84, Federal Employees' Retirement System, Subchapter III, Thrift Savings Plan. Executive Order 9397 authorizes us to use your Social Security number to identify your account. We will use the information you give us to process your interfund transfer request. This information may be shared with other Federal agencies in order to administer your account or for statistical, auditing, or archiving purposes. It may also be shared with Federal, state, and local agencies to determine benefits under their programs, to obtain information necessary under this program, or to report income for tax purposes. In addition, we may share this information with the Parent Locator Service, Department of Health and Human Services, for the purpose of enforcing child support obligations against the TSP participant. We may share this information with law enforcement agencies when they are investigating a violation of civil or criminal law. We may give this information to financial institutions, private sector audit firms, annuity vendors, current spouses and, to a limited extent, beneficiaries and former spouses. Finally, this information may also be disclosed to others on your written request. While the law does not require you to give any of the information we are asking for on this form, it may not be possible to process the actions you request by this form if you do not give us this information.

Form TSP-30   Revised 10/90
PREVIOUS EDITION OBSOLETE

Making an Interfund Transfer

An interfund transfer changes the way your TSP account is invested in the three TSP Funds. Each interfund transfer is a one-time transaction and affects your entire account balance as of the effective date of the transfer.

Who is eligible. All TSP participants can make interfund transfers, except those participants who have left Federal service and are receiving their account balances in a series of equal payments.

Number of transfers per year. You can make an interfund transfer up to four times in any calendar year, in any months that you choose. The annual limit is reached when four requests have been made effective during the calendar year.

How to request a transfer. Complete, sign, and date the front of this form. If you invest in the F or C Fund, be sure to read the acknowledgement of risk (Section III) carefully before you sign it. There is a risk of investment loss in both the F and C Funds.

Provide your daytime telephone number, so that the TSP Service Office can contact you if there is a question about your request. Make a copy for your records, and send the form with your original signature to the TSP Service Office at the address on the front of the form.

> **Note:** Your Social Security number and date of birth must match the information that is in your TSP account record or your interfund transfer cannot be processed. Also, the confirmation of your transfer will be mailed to the address for you that we have in our records. If these items are not correct on your most recent Participant Statement, contact your agency employing office immediately to have them corrected. If you have left Government service, contact the TSP Service Office.

Effective date of the transfer. If your Form TSP-30 is received by the TSP Service Office by the 15th of a month, it will be effective as of the last day of that month. (If the 15th day of the month falls on a weekend or Federal holiday, the deadline will be the next business day.) If your form is received after the deadline, the transfer will be made effective as of the last day of the following month.

Investment Considerations

How to find out your current account balance. To find out your current TSP account balance, call the TSP Inquiry Line at (504) 255-8777 from a Touch-Tone telephone. (You will need your Social Security number and your Personal Identification Number (PIN), which is printed on your Participant Statement.) The Inquiry Line will also tell you how your TSP account is currently distributed among the three Funds.

What to consider before making an interfund transfer. Your TSP account is invested for your retirement, and you should make your investment decisions with this long-term goal in mind. Before you make an interfund transfer, carefully review ail of the available information so that you understand the risks involved and the possible effects of your decision on your TSP account.

Information about the TSP Funds. Read the *Summary of the Thrift Savings Plan for Federal Employees*, which describes each of the Funds in detail and provides a 10-year history of investment returns on corresponding securities. The Summary is available from your agency employing office or, if you have left Government service, from the TSP Service Office.

In addition, your Participant Statement and the *TSP Highlights* that accompany it provide the most recent 10-year performance summary, as well as monthly detail on the TSP Funds and related securities and indexes.

Confirmation of the Transfer

How we will confirm your transfer. You will receive a Confirmation of Interfund Transfer (Form TSP-31) from the TSP Service Office by the end of the month following the transfer. You will also receive another Interfund Transfer Request form with your confirmation notice, to use for your next interfund transfer.

If you have questions about the transfer. If you have questions about your interfund transfer, or if you do not receive Form TSP-31, contact the TSP Service Office. Your agency is not involved in processing interfund transfers.

Cancelling or Changing a Transfer

How to cancel a transfer request. Notify the TSP Service Office in writing that you want to cancel your interfund transfer request. Your letter must be dated and signed by you and must include your Social Security number and date of birth. You should also provide your daytime telephone number. The TSP Service Office must receive your letter by the deadline for the month in which the transfer would have been effective. You will receive notice of the cancellation.

How to change a transfer request. Submit another Form TSP-30 to the TSP Service Office. If your second request is received by the deadline for the month in which your original request would have been effective, it will replace the previous Form TSP-30. If it is received after the deadline for that month, the original request will be processed as scheduled. Your second interfund transfer request will be effective as of the end of the following month. In that case, both transfers will count toward your annual limit of four transfers.

How to get another Interfund Transfer Request form. Interfund Transfer Request forms are available in agency employing offices. You can also request another Form TSP-30 by calling the TSP Inquiry Line (as described above) or by writing to the TSP Service Office at the address on the front of this form.

Federal Employees News Digest, Inc. PUBLICATION ORDER FORM

☐ **Yes!** Please help me make the most of my federal career and benefits! Send the following publications to me right away.

	Price	Qty	Total
Newsletter			
Federal Employees News Digest (1 yr.)	$49.00 x	____ =	_____
Books			
Federal Employees Almanac	$ 7.95 x	____ =	_____
Your Retirement (New 4th Edition)	$ 9.95 x	____ =	_____
Your Financial Guide	$17.95 x	____ =	_____
Your Job Rights	$16.95 x	____ =	_____
Your Thrift Savings Plan	$14.95 x	____ =	_____

Subtotal _____

Shipping & Handling _____
(Books only. Add $2.00 for first book and $1.00 for each additional book.)

TOTAL _____

Mail your order with payment to: **Federal Employees News Digest, Inc.**
P.O. Box 98123
Washington, DC 20090-8123

Please allow 4 weeks for delivery.

SHIP TO:

Name _____

Organization _____

Address _____

_____

City/State/Zip _____

METHOD OF PAYMENT:
☐ Check ☐ Purchase Order
☐ Visa ☐ MasterCard

For credit card orders, please provide the following:

Name on Card _____

Card number _____

Exp. date _____

Signature _____

FULL MONEY-BACK GUARANTEE
If you're not completely satisfied, return your purchase within 60 days and we'll refund your money.

 Call 1-800-989-3363 to place MasterCard or VISA orders.

C4ETSP

Federal Employees News Digest, Inc. PUBLICATION ORDER FORM

☐ **Yes!** Please help me make the most of my federal career and benefits! Send the following publications to me right away.

	Price	Qty	Total
Newsletter			
Federal Employees News Digest (1 yr.)	$49.00 x	____ =	_____
Books			
Federal Employees Almanac	$ 7.95 x	____ =	_____
Your Retirement (New 4th Edition)	$ 9.95 x	____ =	_____
Your Financial Guide	$17.95 x	____ =	_____
Your Job Rights	$16.95 x	____ =	_____
Your Thrift Savings Plan	$14.95 x	____ =	_____

Subtotal _____

Shipping & Handling _____
(Books only. Add $2.00 for first book and $1.00 for each additional book.)

TOTAL _____

Mail your order with payment to: **Federal Employees News Digest, Inc.**
P.O. Box 98123
Washington, DC 20090-8123

Please allow 4 weeks for delivery.

SHIP TO:

Name _____

Organization _____

Address _____

_____

City/State/Zip _____

METHOD OF PAYMENT:
☐ Check ☐ Purchase Order
☐ Visa ☐ MasterCard

For credit card orders, please provide the following:

Name on Card _____

Card number _____

Exp. date _____

Signature _____

FULL MONEY-BACK GUARANTEE
If you're not completely satisfied, return your purchase within 60 days and we'll refund your money.

 **Call 1-800-989-3363 to place MasterCard or VISA orders.**